SWEDEN 1 by Peter Cowie

Above: Bibi Andersson in *A Question of Rape*

 **screen** SERIES

SWEDEN 1

BY PETER COWIE

in collaboration with ARNE SVENSSON

A. ZWEMMER LIMITED, LONDON
A. S. BARNES & CO., NEW YORK

Acknowledgements

I OWE A CONSIDERABLE DEBT to the Swedish Institute for Cultural Relations both in London and Stockholm, for the generous aid and encouragement the' have given me. I am particularly grateful to Ove Svensson and Nils-Gustav Hildeman

Many other' people in Sweden have been exceptionally kind, among them Bibi An dersson, Astrid Björkholm, Agneta Ekmanner, Gunnel Hessel, Berit Haker, Ann-Mari Hedwall, Gun Hyltén-Cavallius, Chris Kuhn, Margareta Nordström; Jan Aghed, Yngv Bengtsson, Ingmar Bergman, David Bonnier, Jonas Cornell, Jörn Donner, Maurit Edström, Kenne Fant, Gunnar Fischer, Bengt Forslund, Christer Frunck, Kjell Grede Lenn Hjortzberg, Bo Johan Hultman, Göran Lindgren, K-H. Lindquist, Gordon Lö wenadler, Norman Potts, Vilgot Sjöman, Carl Henrik Svenstedt, Jan Troell, Rune Walde kranz, Bo Widerberg, and especially Torsten Jungstedt and Berndt Santesson.

Arne Svensson has worked with immense care and patience on the filmographie in this volume; the credit he deserves is considerable.

Photographs are reproduced by kind permission of the principal Swedish productio companies, and through the help of the Swedish Film Institute and the Swedish Institut for Cultural Relations.

Finally, this volume is dedicated, like *Sweden 2,* to my wife Elisabeth, whose to erance, practical help, and good humour have steered the project through its man strenuous stages.

COVER STILLS
Front: *Well, Well, Well* (courtesy of Svensk Filmindustri)
Back: Bibi Andersson in *The Black Palm Trees* (courtesy of Sandrews)

FIRST PUBLISHED 1970
Copyright © 1970 by Peter Cowie
Library of Congress Catalog Card No. 69-14905
SBN 302-02009-8 (U. K.)
SBN 498-07419-6 (U. S. A.)
Printed in the United States of America

Introduction

THE FILMOGRAPHIES that follow each director, actor, scriptwriter, etc., listed in the Guide, are *complete* unless there is an indication (e.g. "Main films") that a selection has been made. The basic details of the Swedish cinema have been thoroughly documented by Sven G. Winquist in a series of books published by the Swedish Film Institute ("Svenska stumfilmer 1896-1931 och deras regissörer," "Svenska ljudfilmer 1929-1966 och deras regissörer," and "Författare till svenska långfilmer samt svensk TV-teater") and the present book relies considerably on the data Winquist has assembled.

There are many other figures who could have been included but for the limitations of space; as it is, I have aimed at covering a broad spectrum of directors, actors, actresses, writers, producers, and the usually under-publicised (and undocumented) technicians. The Guide lists a player's parts insofar as they were retained in the final cut of the film (thus Rune Lindström is not included under *Fängelse/Prison,* and there is no reference to *Jazz Boy* in Gunnar Björnstrand's entry).

Short films have been included in director entries; not, in principle, under players' or technicians' names.

All films given a separate entry in this book are discussed at length in *Sweden 2,* the companion volume; for this reason only credits and plot synopses are supplied here. All titles are in English in the entries, but this is no guarantee that they have been released in English-speaking territories. The Swedish original of every feature film title mentioned can be found in the Index.

In no country except Sweden is a performer's career in the cinema so closely related to his career in the theatre. A glance at the biographies shows that the vast majority of players (and even some directors) have trained at the Royal Dramatic Theatre, Stockholm. For this reason, I have noted the principal phases of stage work in a personality's career.

For reasons of space, the date attributed to each film in the Guide is given by the last two digits only: thus 09 is an abbreviation for 1909, 69 for 1969, and so on. The dates of films are given under the entries for their directors or, if a director does not have a filmography to himself, after the title in the Index. The date given is that of the original Swedish release.

Titles of books are printed in inverted commas and without italic.

The following abbreviations have been used in the Guide:

assist.	*assistant*
co.	*collaborated on, or in collaboration with*
co-dir.	*co-directed*
doc.	*documentary*
co-prod.	*co-production*
B.	*birth place*

5

• 1 ABRAMSON, HANS (1930-   ).
B: Stockholm. Director. At first assistant
to Bergman and Kjellgren (both q.v.)
Has worked for theatre and TV. Among
his films there are two courageous but aca-
demic attempts to translate the novels of
Stig Dagerman (q.v.) into screen terms.
Worked on the script of Molander's *The
Unicorn* and has also scripted some of his
own films*. *The Brig "Three Lilies"* 61;
Dream of Happiness 63; *Just like Friends*
65; *The Serpent** 66; *Roseanna** 67;
Stimulantia (one episode) shot in 65 re-
leased in 67; *The Sinning Urge/Burnt
Child** 67; *Tintomara* 70.

• 2 ADOLPHSON, EDVIN (1893-
). B: Furingstad. Actor and director.
1912: stage *début*. One of the most familiar figures in Swedish film and theatre
since the Thirties—tall, handsome, soul-
ful. Films as actor: *Thomas Graal's First
Child* (as extra only), *The Eyes of Love,
The Surrounded House, Mrs. Andersson's
Charlie and His New Pranks, The Suitor
from the Lanes, Sten Stensson Stéen
from Eslöv, Where the Lighthouse Flashes,
Constable Paulus's Easter Bomb, The Flying Dutchman, The Tales of Ensign Steel,
To the Orient, She the Only One, Wedding
at Bränna, The Ghost Baron, Sealed Lips,
Women of Paris, Gustaf Wasa, Jansson's
Temptation, Triumph of the Heart, Say
It with Music* (co-dir. Jaenzon), *The
Two of Us, The General, Longing for
the Sea, Ship Ahoy!, Tango* (short), *Half-
way to Heaven, Love and Deficit, Dear*

*Relatives, The Atlantic Adventure, The
Song of the Scarlet Flower* (34), *On the
Sunny Side, Honeymoon Trip, Johan
Ulfstjerna, A Cold in the Head, John
Ericsson—the Victor at Hampton Roads,
Dollar, The Old Man Is Coming, Want-
ed, One Single Night, A Crime, With
You in My Arms, Life Goes On, Miss
Church Mouse, A Woman on Board,
Flames in the Dark, General von Döbeln,
Nothing Will Be Forgotten, She Thought
It Was Him, The Sixth Shot, A Day
Shall Dawn, The Royal Rabble, Marie
in the Windmill, Woman for Men,
Mandragora, Åsa-Hanna, Supper for Two,*

Opposite: Harriet Andersson and Hans Ernback in Abramson's THE SERPENT

People of Simlången Valley, A Swedish Tiger, Gentlemen of the Navy, The Wind Is My Lover, The Teacher's First Child, When Love Came to the Village, The Saucepan Journey, The Quartet that Split Up, Rolling Sea, One Summer of Happiness, One Fiancé at a Time, Dull Clang, The Road to Klockrike, Wing-beats in the Night, The Chief from Göinge, A Dreamer's Walk, Young Summer, Where the Summer Wind Blows, The Unicorn, Men in Darkness, Darling at Sea, Married Life (57), Paradise, A Little Place of One's Own, Stage Entrance, The Song of the Scarlet Flower (56), Synnöve Solbakken, A Square Peg in a Round Hole, The Phantom Carriage (58), Laila, May I Borrow Your Wife?, To One's Heart's Content, Wedding Day, Good Friends and Faithful Neighbours, Paw (in Denmark), Mother of Pearl, Do You Believe in Angels?, Prince Hat Below Ground, Parlour Games/The Game of Truth, Wedding—Swedish Style. Films as director (sometimes also acted* and co-scripted†): Say It with Music* (co-dir. Julius Jaenzon) 29; When Rose-buds Open† 30; Motley Leaves* (co-dir. Valdemar Dahlquist) 31; Modern Wives†* 32; What Do Men Know?† 33; Alfred Loved by the Girls†, The Count from Munkbro* (co-dir. Sigurd Wallén) 35; Clear the Decks for Action 37; Desire†* 46; No Way Back 47. Adolphson also scripted A Gentleman Maybe and co-scripted She Thought It Was Him (with Stolpe).

• 3 ALMROTH, GRETA (1888-   ). B: Stockholm. Actress. 1921-23: Berlin. Trained in the theatre. Spent five years in U.S.A. A "child of nature" in several bucolic films of the silent period. Flaxen hair and chubby cheeks added to this image. Films: A Secret Marriage, The Voice of Blood, Do Not Judge, Daughter of the High Mountain, Hearts that Meet, One out of Many, Expiated Guilt, His Wife's Past, Keep to Your Trade, The

Fight for the Rembrandt Painting, In This Way Which Is So Usual Nowadays, Sea Vultures, Old Age and Folly, The Lucky Brooch, Miller's Document, The Hermit's Wife, The Gold Spider, At the Eleventh Hour, The Million Inheritance, The Architect of One's Own Fortune, A Girl from the Marsh Croft, The Revenge, The Song of the Scarlet Flower/Across the Rapids (19), His Grace's Will (19), The Parson's Widow, The Executioner, The People of Simlången Valley, The Melody of the Sea, John Ericsson—the Victor at Hampton Roads, Good Friends and Faithful Neighbours, Heroes of the West Coast.

• 4 ANDERSSON, BIBI (1935-   ). B: Stockholm. Actress. 1954-56: trained at Royal Dramatic Theatre, Stockholm. Worked in Municipal Theatres of Malmö and Uppsala, and also at the RDT, Stockholm. 1952: film début in advertising spot made by Bergman. 1965: goes to Hollywood for part in Ralph Nelson's Duel at Diablo. Has also worked in Italy, Denmark, and Yugoslavia. Blonde, sincere actress, perhaps the finest of her generation, at her best in such Bergman films as *The Seventh Seal* and *Persona*. Married to Kjell Grede (q.v.). Films: *Stupid Bom, A Night at Glimminge Castle, Sir Arne's Treasure* (54), *Smiles of a Summer Night* (bit part), *Last Pair Out, Private Entrance, The Seventh Seal, A Summer Place Is Wanted, Wild Strawberries, So Close to Life/Brink of Life, The Face/ The Magician, The Love Game, The Devil's Eye, Wedding Day, Carnival, Pleasure Garden, The Mistress, Pan, Now about These Women, The Island, June Night, My Sister My Love, Persona, A Question of Rape, The Black Palm Trees, The Girls, A Passion, Think of a Number* (in Denmark).

• 5 ANDERSSON, HARRIET (1932-). B: Stockholm. Actress. Worked in revue and theatre before joining Malmö Municipal Theatre 1953-55. Several international awards. Her foreign appearances include *The Deadly Affair* and *Barbara*. Best known for *Summer with Monika*, but her study in schizophrenia in *Through a Glass Darkly* is probably beyond the range of any other Swedish actress. Films: *While the City Sleeps, Mrs. Andersson's Charlie, The Beef and the Banana, My Name Is Puck, House of Folly, Sabotage, U-Boat 39, Defiance, Summer with Monika, Sawdust and Tinsel, A Lesson in Love, Hoppsan!, Journey into Autumn, Smiles of a Summer Night, Last Pair Out, Children of the Night, Synnöve Solbakken, Woman in a Leopard-skin, Overlord of the Navy, Crime in Paradise, Through a Glass Darkly, Siska, Dream of Happiness, A Sunday in September, Now about These Women, To Love, Loving Couples, Just like Friends, The Vine Bridge, Adventure Starts Here, Stimulantia* (Donner episode), *The Serpent, Rooftree, People Meet, I Love You Love, The Girls.*

• 6 ANSIKTET/THE FACE/THE MAGICIAN. 1958. Script and Direction: Ingmar Bergman. Photography: Gunnar Fischer. Editing: Oscar Rosander. Music: Erik Nordgren. Art Direction: P. A. Lundgren. Players: Max von Sydow *(Albert Emanuel Vogler)*, Ingrid Thulin *(Manda, his wife)*, Åke Fridell *(Tubal, Vogler's manager)*, Naima Wifstrand *(Vogler's grandmother)*, Lars Ekborg *(Simson, the coachman)*, Gunnar Björnstrand *(Vergérus)*, Erland Josephson *(Consul Egerman)*, Gertrud Fridh *(Ottilia, his wife)*, Toivo Pawlo *(Starbeck, Chief of Police)*, Ulla Sjöblom *(Henrietta, his wife)*, Bengt Ekerot *(Johan Spegel)*, Sif Ruud *(Sofia Garp, the cook)*, Bibi Andersson *(Sara Lindqvist)*, Birgitta Pettersson *(Sanna)*, Oscar Ljung *(Antonsson)*, Axel Düberg *(Rustan)*. For Svensk Filmindustri. 101 mins.

PLOT: Sweden in 1846. Dr. Albert Emanuel Vogler, a mesmerist and magician, is travelling to Stockholm with his troupe, including his wife, Manda, disguised as a man. They are stopped at a customs post outside the city and brought

before three officials—the local Consul, the Chief of Police, and a Medical Officer named Vergérus. Vogler is accused of being a charlatan and is subjected to a harsh interrogation, even though he pretends to be dumb. The troupe stays overnight in the Consul's house and the next morning the officials order Vogler to give a private performance. The doctor in particular is fascinated by the presence of Vogler, and although he speaks sceptically about his powers, he is terrified by Vogler's tricks during an "autopsy" in the attic. Just as the officials believe that they have unmasked their opponent, however, a message comes from the Royal court, summoning Vogler before the King to present his magic turns. Vogler drives away with his colleagues in sunshine and triumph.

• 7 ARÉHN, NILS (1877-   ). B: •Sundsvall. Actor. 1900-06: trained at Royal Dramatic Theatre. After that appeared on many stages throughout Sweden. A major star of the silent period, especially in Sjöström's work. Films: *On the Fateful Roads of Life, Life's Conflicts, Do Not Judge, A Girl from the Marsh Croft, The Outlaw and His Wife, The Substitute, The People of Hemsö* (19), *His Grace's Will* (19), *Karin Daughter of Ingmar, Fishing Village,*

Carolina Rediviva, The Phantom Carriage/Thy Soul Shall Bear Witness, Thomas Graal's Ward, The Amateur Film, Pirates on Lake Mälar, 33.333, The Young Count Takes the Girl and the Prize, Kalle Utter, The Flying Dutchman, The Lady of the Camellias, Two Kings, The Ingmar Inheritance, The Girl in the Dress-coat (26), The Incendiary, Only a Dancing Girl, The Devil and the Man from Småland, The Magic Elk, Gustaf Wasa (Pts. I and II).

• 8 ATT ÄLSKA/TO LOVE. 1964. Script and Direction: Jörn Donner. Photography: Sven Nykvist. Editing: Lennart Wallén. Music: Bo Nilsson and Eje Thelin's Jazz Quintet. Art Direction: Jan Boleslaw. Players: Harriet Andersson (*Louise*), Zbigniew Cybulski (*Fredrik*), Isa Quensel (*Louise's mother*), Tomas Svanfeldt (*Jacob*), Jane Friedmann (*Nora*), Nils Eklund (*The Clergyman*), Jan-Erik Lindqvist (*The Speaker*).. 95 mins. For Sandrews.

PLOT: The sudden death of her husband leaves Louise a highly desirable widow in her early thirties, living alone with her mother and her younger son. At the funeral reception she meets Fredrik, a foreigner engaged as a travel agent in Stockholm. The two are attracted to each other, and soon Fredrik moves into the family apartment. Louise becomes gay and happy again. Fredrik, accepted by the son, Jacob, finds himself more and more involved with Louise. At last he proposes marriage. Louise is uncertain. But the relationship has been established even if the end seems already in sight.

Zbigniew Cybulski in TO LOVE

● 9 AXBERG, EDDIE (1947-).
Actor. Young and unspoilt leading player,
the perfect choice to personify Eyvind
Johnson's Olof in *Here Is Your Life*. Also
a sound engineer. Films: *The Brig "Three
Lilies," Winter Light, Thirty Times Your
Money, The Serpent, Here Is Your Life,
The Emigrants* and *Unto a Good Land*.

● 10 AXELMAN, TORBJÖRN (1932-
). B: Eskilstuna. Director. University
degree, former journalist. An exuberant
young talent, whose comedies resemble
Richard Lester's and whose zany sense of
humour is rather unappreciated in Sweden.
Co-scripted all his own films. Short: *Kana-
riehunden* 67. Features: *Well, Well, Well*
(also acted) 65; *Summer of the Lion/
Vibration* 67; *Hot Snow* 68.

*Above: Eddie Axberg. Below:
Torbjörn Axelman*

• 11 BARA EN MOR/ONLY A MOTHER. 1949. Script: Alf Sjöberg and Ivar Lo-Johansson, from the latter's novel. Direction: Alf Sjöberg. Photography: Martin Bodin. Music: Dag Wirén. Art Direction: Nils Svenwall. Players: Eva Dahlbeck (*Rya-Rya*), Ragnar Falck (*Henrik*), Ulf Palme (*Hammar*), Hugo Björne (*Eniel*), Åke Fridell (*Steward*), Max von Sydow (*Nils*), Mona Geijer-Falkner (*Emili*), Margaretha Krook (*Berta*), Mimi Pollak (*Erika Rost*). 99 mins. For Svensk Filmindustri.

PLOT: Rya-Rya plays out her miserable life among *statare,* gipsy-like folk who were forced to travel from estate to estate, working for their keep. Rya-Rya scandalises her community by bathing in the nude and, spurned by her *fiancé,* she yields in desperation to the advances of a peasant, Henrik, after a barn dance. So begins a life of rearing one child after another, and of coping with a more and more unreliable husband. A local steward lusts after her; she is forced to do menial work in order to feed the children. Eventually she collapses and dies.

• 12 BARNVAGNEN/THE PRAM/ THE BABY CARRIAGE. 1963. Script and Direction: Bo Widerberg. Photography: Jan Troell. Editing: Wic Kjellin. Music: Jan Johansson. Art Direction: C. Friberg. Players: Inger Taube (*Britt*), Thommy Berggren (*Björn*), Lars Passgård (*Robban*), Ulla Akselsson (*Britt's*

Inger Taube in THE PRAM

mother), Gunnar Öhlund (*Britt's father*), Bill Jönsson (*Britt's little brother*), Stig Torstensson (*The boy on the stairs*). 84 mins. For Europa Film.

PLOT: Britt Larsson is an eighteen-year-old girl who gets tired of her rather dull home and her mechanical work at a large Malmö industrial office. She takes up with a rock and roll singer, becomes pregnant, and moves to his flat. There she finds out that he is too immature to face the responsibilities of a husband. Britt meets a young intellectual, Björn. At first they get on well, but he is too influenced by his mother and the couple sense that they have no future together.

Britt has nobody to turn to, her parents being more interested in television programmes than in her. During her pregnancy she matures and chooses to remain alone rather than enter an unsatisfactory marriage. In the final shot Britt is seen in the street pushing her pram, a face in the crowd, a grown-up woman.

● 13 BAUMAN, SCHAMYL (1893-1966). B: Vimmerby. Director and scriptwriter. 1917: enters films. 1939: founds Sandrew-Bauman film with Anders Sandrew (q.v.). Made his name in the Thirties with a series of frothy, charming comedies. Films (sometimes also scripted or co-scripted*): *Love and Veteran Reserves* 31; *Saturday Evenings*, *Secret Agent Svensson* 33; *The Girls from the Old Town*, *The Women around Larsson* 34; *Larsson in His Second Marriage* 35; *Raggen—That's Me, The Family that Was a Merry-Go-Round* 36; *Old Gods Are Still Alive* (co. Gideon Wahlberg), *Witches' Night, Send No. 7 Home* (co. Wahlberg) 37; *Comrades in Uniform*, *Career* 38; *Wanted, The Two of Us, Life Begins Today*, *Her Little Majesty* 39; *Heroes in Yellow and Blue*, *Once More With Gösta Ekman, An Able Man, The Three of Us, Swing it Sir!* 40; *Miss Church Mouse, The Ghost Reporter, Teachers on a Summer Holiday* 41; *We*

Housemaids, People of Roslagen* 42; *In the Darkest Corner of Småland* 43; *Prince Gustaf* 44; *In the Beautiful Province of Roslagen, Girls of Småland* 45; *Salt Water Spray and Tough Old Boys, Hotell Kåkbrinken* 46; *Maj from Malö* 47; *Robinson of Roslagen* 48; *Playing Truant* 49; *My Sister and I, The Teacher's First Child* 50; *My Name Is Puck* 51; *One Fiancé at a Time, Class Mates* 52; *Dancing on Roses* 54; *Darling at Sea* (also edited) 55; *Mother Takes a Holiday* 57. Films as scriptwriter or co-scriptwriter: *The Ramshackles of Söder, Fridolf in the Lion's Cage, We from the Theatre*.

● 14 BECH, LILI (1885-1939). B: Denmark. Actress. At first acted in theatre in Copenhagen. Films for Nordisk Film, Copenhagen. Sjöström's (q.v.) second wife. Swedish films: *The Talisman, The Gardener, The Black Masks, The Vampire, The Child, Because of Her Love, The Stormy Petrel, Children of the Street, Daughter of the High Mountain, When Artists Love, One out of Many, Expiated Guilt, The Playmates, His Wife's Past, Ace of Thieves, The Dagger, The Mine-Pilot, The Governor's Daughters, Ships that Meet, She Was Victorious, The Wings, The Gold Spider, Thérèse*.

● 15 BERG, STINA (1869-1930). Actress. Stout, good-natured country woman in many silent films, especially Stiller's work. Films: *The Tyrannical Fiancé, On the Fateful Roads of Life, The Modern Suffragette, People of the Border, Half-breed, The Birthday Present, King Solomon's Judgment, The Way to the Man's Heart, The Chamberlain, Children of the Street, Expiated Guilt, The Playmates, Revenge Is Sweet, Keep to Your Trade, The Consequences of Jealousy, His Wedding Night, Her Royal Highness, The Lucky Brooch, Love and Journalism, The Million Inheritance, Sir Arne's Treasure* (19), *Erotikon, Mrs. Andersson's Charlie, Gunnar Hede's Saga, The Norrtull Gang,*

33.333, Constable Paulus's Easter Bomb, Her Little Majesty, Two Kings, Ebberöd's Bank, The Gyurkovics Girls, The Queen of Pellagonia, His English Wife, Sealed Lips, Sin, Jansson's Temptation, Say It with Music, People of Norrland, For Her Sake, Gentlemen in Uniform, Charlotte Löwensköld, Motley Leaves.

* 16 BERG-EJVIND OCH HANS HUSTRU/THE OUTLAW AND HIS WIFE. 1918. Script: Sam Ask and Victor Sjöström, based on the play by Johan Sigurjönsson. Direction: Victor Sjöström. Photography: J. Julius. Players: Victor Sjöström (*Berg-Ejvind*), Edith Erastoff (*Halla*), John Ekman, Nils Aréhn, Jenny Tschernichin-Larsson. 2,781 metres. For Svenska Bio.

PLOT: Iceland in the Nineteenth century. Berg-Ejvind, who is proscribed for stealing a sheep to feed his starving family, arrives at a farm and falls in love with the rich landowner, a widow named Halla. The local bailiff, who is a sly, thwarted figure, grows jealous of Berg-Ejvind and tries to arrest him. The outlaw flees to the mountains, and is joined there by Halla, who abandons her estates for the prospect of happiness with her lover. They have a child, and experience five years of contentment before they are betrayed and have to plunge higher and higher into the mountains. At last, old and tired, Halla and Berg-Ejvind commit suicide in the snow.

* 17 BERGGREN, THOMMY (1937-). B: Göteborg. Actor. Attended private theatre school in Göteborg. 1954: first stage engagement. 1961: first film role. 1963: joined Royal Dramatic Theatre, Stockholm, and has been directed by Bergman in productions of *Who's Afraid of Virginia Woolf?* and *Wozzeck*. Spontaneous and attractive young lead, familiar from his appearances in the films of Widerberg (q.v.). Films: *Mother of Pearl, The*

Pram, A Sunday in September, Raven's End, Love 65, Thirty Times Your Money, Elvira Madigan, The Black Palm Trees, Joe Hill (in U.S.A.)

* 18 BERGMAN, INGMAR (1918-). B: Uppsala. Director, scriptwriter, and playwright. 1940-42: assistant at the Stockholm Opera. Worked on scripts at Svensk Filmindustri 1940-44. Then stage director at, successively, Hälsingborg, Göteborg, Malmö, and Royal Dramatic Theatre, Stockholm. Two Academy Awards (*The Virgin Spring* and *Through a Glass Darkly*). The leading film director of the postwar period in Sweden. Has so far resisted all offers to work abroad. Also TV work. Scripted *Frenzy, Woman Without a Face, Eva, Divorced, Last Pair Out, Pleasure Garden* (co. Erland Josephson), and has written (or co-scripted) all his own films except*. Also wrote synopsis for *While the City Sleeps.* Features: *Crisis, It Rains on Our Love* 46; *A Ship Bound for India, Music in Darkness* 47; *Port of Call* 48; *Prison, Thirst/Three Strange Loves* 49; *To Joy, This Can't Happen*

15

Here/High Tension* 50; *Summer Interlude/Illicit Interlude* 51; *Waiting Women* 52; *Summer with Monika, Sawdust and Tinsel/The Naked Night* 53; *A Lesson in Love* 54; *Journey into Autumn/Dreams, Smiles of a Summer Night* 55; *The Seventh Seal, Wild Strawberries* 57; *So Close to Life/Brink of Life, The Face/The Magician* 58; *The Virgin Spring*, The Devil's Eye* 60; *Through a Glass Darkly* 61; *Winter Light, The Silence* 63; *Now about These Women* 64; *Persona* 66; *Stimulantia* (one episode) shot in 65 released in 67; *Hour of the Wolf, Shame* 68; *The Rite/ The Ritual* (for TV), *A Passion* 69.

● 19 BERGMAN, INGRID (1915-). B: Stockholm. Actress. 1933: trained at Royal Dramatic Theatre, Stockholm. 1938: to Germany and then to Hollywood. This international star came to prominence with *Intermezzo*, but has only appeared in one Swedish film during the past thirty years (*Stimulantia*). Swed-

● 20 BJÖRK, ANITA (1923-). B: Tällberg. Actress. Trained at Royal Dramatic Theatre, Stockholm. Since 1962: television drama. The perfect *Miss Julie* in Sjöberg's film, Anita Björk has given several elegant, passionate, and sometimes disdainful performances during her career. Also foreign films (Nunnally Johnson's *Night People*, for example). Films: *The Road to Heaven, Count the Happy Moments Only, A Hundred Accordions and One Girl, No Way Back, Woman without a Face, A Guest Came, On These Shoulders, The Realm of Men, The Quartet that Split Up, Miss Julie* (51),

Opposite: Anders Ek and Ingrid Thulin in Bergman's television play THE RITE

Memory of Love, Waiting Women/Secrets of Women, Song of the Scarlet Flower (56), *Married Life* (57), *Clouds over Hellesta, A Guest in One's Own Home, Lady in Black, The Phantom Carriage* (58), *Model in Red, The Die Is Cast, Good Friends and Faithful Neighbours, Woman in White, Loving Couples, The Slipper, Odd Lovers, The Ådalen Riots.*

● 21 BJÖRKMAN, STIG (1938-   ). B: Stockholm. Director. Björkman is editor of *Chaplin,* the principal Scandinavian film magazine, and is also qualified as an architect. 1962-64: film critic of *Svenska Dagbladet.* Made shorts before completing his first feature, which was partly financed by the Swedish Film Institute. Shorts: *Letizia* 64; *The True Story of Anna Susanna* 67; *No, The Band* 69. Feature: *I Love You Love* 68.

● 22 BJÖRNSTRAND, GUNNAR (1909-   ). B: Stockholm. Actor. 1933: trained at Royal Dramatic Theatre, Stockholm. Essentially a man of the theatre (having performed on virtually every important stage in Sweden), Björnstrand has also played in over a dozen Bergman films (the two men met in 1941), and sets a standard of courtly acting unsurpassed by any other Swedish player. Equally at ease in comedy and sombre drama. 1931: first screen appearance in the French version of *The False Millionaire.* Films: *Panic, Her Melody, Heroes in Yellow and Blue, An Able Man, Night in June, An Adventurer, General von Döbeln, Night in the Harbour, I Killed, My People Are Not Yours, New Order at Sjögårda, Live Dangerously, Frenzy/Torment, Sussie, You Who Are about to Enter, Kristin Takes Command, Bad Eggs, Peggy on a Spree, It Rains on Our Love/Man with an Umbrella, When the Door Was Closed, The Bride Came through the Ceiling, A Father Wanted, A Soldier's Duties, One Swallow Doesn't Make a Summer, Here We Come, Two Women, Music in Darkness/Night Is My Future, Each Goes His Own Way, A Swedish Tiger, Little Märta Returns, Private Bom, Playing Truant, The Girl from the Gallery, The Kiss on the Cruise, The White Cat, The Quartet that Split Up, My Sister and I, Pappa Bom, Fiancée*

for Hire, Bom the Customs-Officer, One Fiancé at a Time, Say It with Flowers, Waiting Women/Secrets of Women, Flying-Bomb, Up with the Green Lift, We Three Are Making Our Début, Sawdust and Tinsel/The Naked Night, Unmarried, Dance My Doll, A Lesson in Love, Merry Boys of the Navy, Victory in Darkness, Gabrielle Journey into Autumn/Dreams, Smiles of a Summer Night, The Pawnshop, It's Never Too Late, Seventh Heaven, The Rusk, The Seventh Seal, Wild Strawberries, Lights at Night, You Are My Adventure, A Summer Place Is Wanted, The Face, Miss April, Swinging at the Castle, Crime in Paradise, Good Heavens!, Pirates on Lake Mälar (59), The Devil's Eye, Through a Glass Darkly, Pleasure Garden, Winter Light, My Love Is a Rose, Dream of Happiness, The Dress, Loving Couples, Marriage Wrestler, My Sister My Love, Here Is Your Life, Persona, The Red Mantle/Hagbard and Signe (in Denmark), The Sadist, Stimulantia (Molander episode), The Slipper, Shame, The Girls, The Rite (for TV), Daddy Why Are You Angry?

• 23 BLADH, HILDING (1906-). B: Stockholm. Director of photography. At his best in the Forties and early Fifties. Films: A Crime (co. Löfstedt), An Able Man (co. Ekdahl), With You in My Arms (co. Löfstedt), Life Goes On (co. Löfstedt), A Poor Millionaire, Flames in the Dark, General von Döbeln, The Sixth Shot, Sonja, Narcosis, Like Most People, The Girl and the Devil, The Royal Rabble, Guttersnipes (co. Löfstedt), Three Cheers for Little Märta, Good Morning Bill (co. Nykvist and Strindberg), Once upon a Time (co. Thernelius and Wilén), In Death's Waiting Room, Love and Downhill Skiing, It Rains on Our Love/Man with an Umbrella (co. Strindberg), Supper for Two (co. Felix Forsman), No Way Back, Neglected by His Wife (co. Strindberg), The Evening of the Fair, Playing Truant,

Son of the Sea (co. Curt Jonsson), Fun with Boccaccio, My Sister and I, The Teacher's First Child, Jack of Hearts, When Bengt and Anders Swapped Wives, Motor Cavaliers, My Name Is Puck, The Revue at the Södran Theatre (co.), Helen of Troy, One Fiancé at a Time, Private 69 the Sergeant and I, Ursula—the Girl from the Forest Depths, In Major and Showers, Sawdust and Tinsel/The Naked Night (exteriors only), All the Joy of the Earth, Enchanted Walk, (co. Thermaenius), Young Man Seeks Company, Two Rascals (co. Strindberg), Murder My Little Friend, Journey into Autumn/Dreams, Girl in the Barracks, Hoppsan, Honestly and Cheatingly, Kulla-Gulla, Swing It Miss!, It's Never Too Late, The Manors around the Lake, Count on Trouble, Music on Board, Model in Red, Rider in Blue, When Darkness Falls, Swedish Floyd, Hällebäck Manor, Lady in White, One Zero Too Many, Wild West Story.

• 24 BORGSTRÖM, HILDA (1871-1953). B: Stockholm. Actress. 1920-38: Royal Dramatic Theatre, Stockholm, after ballet and stage training. An able and intelligent actress who played a series of poor, subdued wives during the silent period, and then appeared as a wise and understanding old lady in the Forties. Films: A Secret Marriage, A Summer Tale (probably unreleased), Lady Marion's Summer Flirtation, Ingeborg Holm, The Way to the Man's Heart, Do Not Judge, The Fireman, Carolina Rediviva, The Phantom Carriage/Thy Soul Shall Bear Witness (21), Anna-Clara and Her Brothers, The Girl from Paradise, The Lady of the Camellias, Married Life (26), The Poetry of Ådalen, The Land of Rye, People of Norrland, The People of Värmland (32), Grandmother's Revolution, What Do Men Know?, Simon from Backabo, Alfred Loved by the Girls, The Andersson Family, John Ericsson—the Victor at Hampton Roads, With the People for the Country, Wings around the

Lighthouse, A Woman's Face, Rejoice while You Are Young, The People of Högbo Farm, The Song of the Wilds, Like a Thief in the Night, Her Melody, The Fight Goes On, Fransson the Terrible, Göransson's Boy, The Downy Girl, Dangerous Roads, Flames in the Dark, Life on a Perch, Ride Tonight!, Women in Prison, That Girl Is a Discovery, A Girl for Me, Life Is There To Be Lived, I Killed, A Day Shall Dawn, Appassionata, Your Relatives Are Best, The Clock at Rönneberga, The Invisible Wall, I Am Fire and Air, The Girl and the Devil, Prince Gustaf, The Emperor of Portugal, The Royal Rabble, Mandragora, Good Morning Bill, Tired Teodor, Don't Try It with Me, Brita in the Wholesaler's House, Åsa-Hanna, Desire, Between Brothers, Eternal Links, The Song about Stockholm, The Key and the Ring, Music in Darkness/Night Is My Future, Each Goes His Own Way, Each Heart Has Its Story, Sin, Miss Sun-beam, The Banquet, Eva, The Girl from the Gallery.

gin Spring, Just Once More, The Serpent, Here Is Your Life, Hour of the Wolf, As the Naked Wind from the Sea.

● 25 BROST, GUDRUN (1910-   ). B: Malmö. Actress. Originally gym instructress. Since 1934: theatre work. Since 1954: attached to the Municipal Theatre, Malmö. Supporting actress now adept at playing maternal roles on screen. Films: *Poor Millionaires, Steel, Night in June, An Able Man, His Grace's Will, The Talk of the Town, In Paradise. . ., Teachers on a Summer Holiday, Suppose I Were to Marry the Clergyman, The Yellow Ward, The Road to Heaven, Anna Lans, And All These Women . . ., The Royal Rabble, A Woman for Men, Lazy Lena and Blue-Eyed Per, Sven Tusan, Girl with Hyacinths, When Lilacs Blossom, Sawdust and Tinsel, Young Man Seeks Company, Rasmus and the Tramp, The Seventh Seal, The Clergyman from Uddarbo, The Vir-*

● 26 BROSTRÖM, GUNNEL (1922-   ). B: Stockholm. Actress. 1941: trained at Royal Dramatic Theatre, Stockholm. 1943-51 and since 1960: engaged there. Extensive work for TV, including direction. An elegant, forthright actress whose sarcastic Mrs. Alman · in *Wild Strawberries* was a brilliant interpretation. Films: *Ride Tonight!, His Majesty's Rival, Your Relatives Are Best, Skipper Jansson, Mandragora, Peggy on a Spree, Bareback, The Bells of the Old Town, Crime in the Sun, Navvies, Unto the Gates of Hell, Swedish Horseman, U-boat 39, We Three Are Making Our Début, Storm over Tjurö, Salka Valka, Paradise, Married Life, Wild Strawberries, A Square Peg in a Round Hole, Rider in Blue, Prince Hat below Ground, Stimulantia* (Molander episode), *Rooftree, I Am Curious—Blue.*

Opposite: Gunnel Broström with Victor Sjöström in Bergman's WILD STRAWBERRIES

• 27 BRUNIUS, JOHN W. (1884-1937). B: Stockholm. Director. 1902: trained at Royal Dramatic Theatre, Stockholm, where he was later engaged as an actor. Also played at various other theatres. Manager of the Oscar Theatre, Stockholm. As an actor he preferred comic roles, often working in a bold, burlesque style. Films as director (sometimes also co-scriptwriter† or actor*): *Puss in Boots*†* 18; *Synnöve Solbakken*†, *Oh Tomorrow Night*† 19; *Thora van Deken*†, *The Gyurkovics* 20; *The Mill*†, *A Fortune Hunter*†, *A Wild Bird*† 21; *Hard Wills*†, *The Eyes of Love*† 22; *Johan Ulfstjerna* 23; *Maid among Maids* 24; *Charles XII* (Pts I and II) 25; *The Tales of Ensign Steel* (Pts I and II) 26; *Gustaf Wasa* (Pts I and II) 28; *The Two of Us, The Doctor's Secret* 30; *Red Day* (acting only), *Longing for the Sea** 31; *The Melody of the Sea* (co-dir. Prince Wilhelm), *False Greta* 34; *Happy Vestköping* (acting only).

• 28 CARLQUIST, MARGIT (1932-). B: Stockholm. Actress. 1949-51: trained at Royal Dramatic Theatre, Stockholm. Worked at Göteborg Municipal Theatre during the early Fifties. Occasional TV appearances. A subtle actress, whose feline sarcasm made her Charlotte in *Smiles of a Summer Night* (q.v.) a personality to be reckoned with. Films: *To Joy, Stronger than the Law, Meeting Life, She Came like a Wind, Dull Clang, The Road to Klockrike, Unmarried, Marianne, Taxi 13, In Smoke and Dancing, Where the Summer Wind Blows, Smiles of a Summer Night, The People of Hemsö* (55), *My Hot Desire, Stage Entrance, A Dreamer's Walk, The Manors around the Lake, No Tomorrow, Line Six, Female Spy 503* (in Denmark), *Do You Believe in Angels?, Lady in White, Hide and Seek, Prince Hat below Ground, Loving Couples, A Summer Adventure, Skrift i sne* (in Norway), *We Are All Dead Demons*.

• 29 CARLSSON, SICKAN (1915-). B: Stockholm. Actress. 1933: screen *début*. One of the few really adept comediennes in the Swedish cinema, and a mistress of farce. Films: *Dear Relatives, The Song to Her, Simon of Backabo, Love from Music, People of Småland, A Cold in the Head, Clear the Decks for Action, Oh What a Night, Thunder and Lightning, Only a Trumpeter, Nothing but the Truth, The Little WRAC of the Veteran Reserves, Oh What a Boy, Gentleman for Hire, The Little Shrew of the Veteran Reserves, Tonight or Never, The Girl in the Window Opposite, Hearts of Lieutenants, A Girl for Me, His Official Fiancée, The Green Lift, Girls of Småland, The Gay Party, Wedding Night, Father Wanted, Life at Forsbyholm, The Maid from Jungfrusund, Playing Truant, My Sister and I, The Teacher's First Child, My Name Is Puck, One Fiancé at a Time, Class Mates, Dancing on Roses, The Seventh Heaven, Darling at Sea, With the Halo Askew, You Are My Adventure, Miss Chic, Good Heavens!, Pleasure Garden*.

• 30 CEDERLUND, GÖSTA (1888-
). B: Stockholm. Actor. Studied thea-
tre in several countries. 1908-26: stage
work in Stockholm and Göteborg. 1926-
29: manager of the Municipal Theatre,
Hälsingborg. Has also directed for screen
and stage. Long and distinguished career.
Films: *A Girl from the Marsh Croft*
(17), *The People of Hemsö* (19), *A
Dangerous Proposal, Thora van Deken,
The Mill, Youth of Today, The Mar-
riage Game, Are We Married?, Our Boy,
My Mother-in-law—the Dancer, The
Girls of Uppåkra, Conflict, Sara Learns
Manners, A Rich Man's Son, Comrades
in Uniform, Milly Maria and I, With
The People for the Country, Sigge Nilsson
and I, Career, The Nature Healer, Mr.
Housekeeper, The Two of Us, Rejoice
while You Are Young, Her Little Majesty,
Oh What a Boy, Towards New Times,
The Melody from the Old Town, Be-
tween Us Barons, They Staked Their
Lives, Heroes in Yellow and Blue, My
Little Brother and I, Like a Thief in the
Night, A Crime, An Able Man, Oh What
a Lawyer, Her Melody, The Three of*

• 31 CORNELL, JONAS (1938-   ).
B: Stockholm. Director, married to Agneta
Ekmanner (q.v.). Also novelist. New-
comer from the Film School, where he
made one short entitled *Hej!*, shown on
Sveriges TV. Cornell's wry sense of humour and precise style made *Hugs and
Kisses* a hit in several countries. From
1967: also stage director. Founder and
editor of *Dialog*, an important theatre
magazine. Scripted all his own films and

Jonas Cornell with his wife Agneta Ekmanner

I Love You Love (co. Björkman). Features: *Hugs and Kisses* 67; *Like Night and Day* 69; *The Pig Hunt* 70.

● 32 DAGERMAN, STIG (1923-1954). B. Älvkarleby. Novelist. After studying art and literature Dagerman became a journalist, mainly for a unionist newspaper. Sometime married to Anita Björk (q.v.). His idea formed the basis of Mattsson's *The Doll*. In retrospect his work can be seen as the summary of an era and the young postwar Swedish intelligentsia. His novels and stories are marked by *angst* and are hardly good material for films, although producer Tore Sjöberg (q.v.) has a certain predilection (deplored by his critics) for Dagerman's work. His

suicide deprived Swedish literature of one of its major talents. Films from his work: *To Kill a Child* (short), *A Night at Glimminge Castle* (from *Bröllopsbesvär*), *Games at Night* (short), *Wedding—Swedish Style* (from *Bröllopsbesvär*), *The Serpent, The Sinning Urge/Burnt Child.*

● 33 DAHLBECK, EVA (1920-   ). B: Stockholm. Actress. 1944: trained at Royal Dramatic Theatre, Stockholm. Stately and accomplished heroine of Bergman comedies. Also scriptwriter (*Woman of Darkness*). Known to foreign audiences for her appearance in George Seaton's *The Counterfeit Traitor* (1961). Films: *Ride Tonight!, Count the Happy Moments Only, The Serious Game, Black Roses,*

Between Us Thieves, Brita in the Wholesaler's House, Love and Downhill Skiing, Nightly Encounter, The Key and the Ring, Two Women, People of Simlången Valley, Lars Hård, Each Goes His Own Way, Eva, The Girl from the Mountain Village, Woman in White, Only a Mother, Jack of Hearts, The Saucepan Journey, Fiancée for Hire, Rolling Sea, Helen of Troy, U-boat 39, Defiance, Waiting Women/Secrets of Women, Sabotage, The Shadow, Barabbas, House of Women, The Chief from Göinge, A Lesson in Love, Night Journey, Journey into Autumn/Dreams, Smiles of a Summer Night, Paradise, Last Pair Out, Tarps Elin, Encounters at Dusk, A Summer Place Is Wanted, So Close to Life/ Brink of Life, Decimals of Love, Three Wishes, Ticket to Paradise, Now about These Women, Loving Couples, The Cats, Morianna, Les Créatures (co-prod. with France), *The Red Mantle/Hagbard and Signe* (co-prod. in Denmark), *People Meet* (co-prod. in Denmark).

• 34 DANIELSSON, TAGE (1928-). B: Linköping. Director. 1954: uni-versity degree. 1959-62: head of the entertainment section of Swedish Radio. Revues, books, various TV and radio pieces. One of the foremost Swedish entertainers, with a bizarre and very personal sense of humour. Often working with Hans Alfredson, who has co-scripted* and co-directed† some of his screen work. Films: *Swedish Portraits** (also acted) 64; *To Go Ashore** (also acted) 65; *Stimulantia* (one episode)*† shot in 65 released in 67; *Skrållan, Ruskprick and Knorrhane* (acted only), *The Box** (filmed revue, also acted), *Out of an Old Man's Head** (feature cartoon) 68.

• 35 DEGERMARK, PIA (1949-). B: Stockholm. Actress. Educated in private school in Sigtuna, this delicate blonde star has made only a few film appearances since her *début*, at sixteen, in *Elvira Madigan*. Won Golden Palm for Best Actress at Cannes, 1967, and shortly afterwards contracted by Columbia. Features: *Elvira Madigan, The Looking Glass War* (in England), *Brief Season* (in Italy).

25

● 36 DEN STARKASTE/THE STRONGEST. 1929. Script and Direction: Alf Sjöberg and Axel Lindblom. Photography: Axel Lindblom and Åke Dahlqvist. Art Direction: Vilhelm Bryde. Players: Bengt Djurberg (*Gustaf*), Gunn Holmqvist (*Ingeborg*), Anders Henrikson (*Ole*), Hjalmar Peters (*Skipper Larsen*), Maria Röhr (*Ingeborg's grandmother*), Sivert Braekemo, Gösta Gustafsson, Kåre Pedersen. 2,394 metres (95 mins.). For Svensk Filmindustri.

PLOT: In Tromsö harbour in Norway, boats are being prepared for the hunting season in the Arctic. Gustaf, an ordinary seaman, meets the beautiful Ingeborg on the road. He helps her and her grandmother and is employed as a farm hand by Ingeborg's father, Skipper Larsen. Gustaf and Ingeborg fall in love. But then Ole, Skipper Larsen's best shot and harpooner, comes home and Gustaf is asked to leave.

In the spring Gustaf goes north to the Arctic ocean. He is lost in the fog, and left for dead by an enemy on a drifting ice floe. Ole arrives on the scene and is generous enough to save his rival. Gustaf recovers and gets a reputation as a crack shot, but then is falsely accused of having stolen his gun from Ole. When a bear is about to kill Ole, Gustaf saves his life and, rehabilitated, he returns home to his reward—Ingeborg and Skipper Larsen's blessings.

● 37 DET SJUNDE INSEGLET/THE SEVENTH SEAL. 1957. Script and Direction: Ingmar Bergman. Photography: Gunnar Fischer. Editing: Lennart Wallén. Music: Erik Nordgren. Art Direction: P. A. Lundgren. Players: Max von Sydow (*Antonius Blok*), Gunnar Björnstrand (*Jöns, his Squire*), Nils Poppe (*Jof*), Bibi Andersson (*Mia*), Bengt Ekerot (*Death*), Åke Fridell (*Plog*), Inga Gill (*Lisa, his wife*), Erik Strandmark (*Skat*), Bertil Anderberg (*Raval*), Gunnel Lindblom (*The Girl*), Maud Hansson (*The witch*), Inga Landgré (*Blok's wife*), Anders Ek (*The Monk*), Gunnar Olsson (*Painter in church*), Lars Lind (*Young Monk*),

Bibi Andersson and Nils Poppe in the final scene of THE SEVENTH SEAL

Bengt-Åke Benktsson (*Merchant*), Gudrun Brost (*Woman at inn*), Ulf Johansson (*Soldier*), Ove Svensson (*Corpse on hillside*). 95 mins. For Svensk Filmindustri.

PLOT: The film begins with a Knight, Antonius Blok, and his Squire, Jöns, returning from the Crusades to a plague-stricken Sweden. As they journey towards his castle, the Knight struggles to forestall Death in a game of chess. He meets a trio of wandering players, Jof, Mia, and Skat, and takes them through the forest to avoid the plague. Subsequently he diverts Death's attention so that Jof and Mia can escape with their baby child while he and his company are trapped in the castle and are forced to join the Dance of Death.

● 38 DET STORA ÄVENTYRET/ THE GREAT ADVENTURE. 1953. Script, Direction, Photography, Editing: Arne Sucksdorff. Assistants: Sigvard Kihlgren and Åke Bäcklund. Music: Lars-Erik Larsson. Commentator: Gunnar Sjöberg. Players: Anders Nohrborg (*Anders*), Kjell Sucksdorff (*Kjell*), Holger Stockman (*Kvast-Emil*), Sigvard Kihlgren (*Bonden*), Arne Sucksdorff (*Father*). 73 mins. For Arne Sucksdorff/Sandrews.

PLOT: Anders and Kjell are the sons of a farmer in central Sweden. Each new season brings a changing landscape. The wild animals fight for survival in the woods near the farm. One winter, the two boys capture an otter, and keep her in a cage in the farm buildings. They tame her, feeding her secretly. They call her Utti, and take her with them when they go for walks. Spring arrives, and Kjell and Anders allow Utti to swim in the lake. But they make the mistake of turning their heads away for a moment, and suddenly the otter has vanished. When the farm labourers celebrate the arrival of summer, the two boys are gloomy because they have lost their pet. Then they see the cranes flying north

Above: Bibi Andersson in THE SEVENTH SEAL

27

again after the winter migration, and they realise that the "great adventure" of life is only just beginning. . .

• 39 DJÄVULENS ÖGA/THE DEVIL'S EYE. 1960. Script and Direction: Ingmar Bergman. Photography: Gunnar Fischer. Editing: Oscar Rosander. Music: Domenico Scarlatti. Art Direction: P. A. Lundgren. Players: Jarl Kulle (*Don Juan*), Bibi Andersson (*Britt-Marie*), Nils Poppe (*The Pastor*), Sture Lagerwall (*Pablo*), Stig Järrel (*Satan*), Gertrud Fridh (*The Pastor's Wife*), Torsten Winge (*Old Devil*), Axel Düberg (*Britt-Marie's fiancé*), Gunnar Björnstrand (*The Actor*), Allan Edwall (*The Ear Devil*), Georg Funkquist (*Count Armand de Rochefoucauld*), Gunnar Sjöberg (*Marquis Giuseppe de Maccopazza*), Kristina Adolphson, Ragnar Arvedson, Börje Lund, Lenn Hjortzberg. 90 mins. For Svensk Filmindustri.

PLOT: The story is taken from an Irish proverb—"A woman's chastity is a sty in the Devil's eye"—invented by Bergman himself. Satan, angered by a sore eye, sends Don Juan up from Hell to seduce Britt-Marie, a pastor's daughter who is the cause of the trouble because she is still a virgin. Pablo, Don Juan's assistant, concerns himself with the seduction of the pastor's wife, while Don Juan tries to woo Britt-Marie. But he is defeated when she tells him that she feels only pity for him and not desire. Realising that he is falling in love with this attractive girl, Don Juan abandons his mission and returns with Pablo, who has been rather more successful. On her wedding night, Britt-Marie tells her husband that she has never even been kissed by another man. It is a lie, for she embraced Don Juan. This lie is enough to cure Satan's sty.

• 40 DONNER, JÖRN (1933-   ). B: Helsinki. Finnish director, reporter, writer, and critic. 1952-60: journalist and film critic in Finland. 1957: Co-founder of the Finnish Film Archive. Has completed a dozen books, among them *Report from Berlin* and a study of Ingmar Bergman. Was film critic for *Dagens Nyheter*

Opposite: Jörn Donner on location. Above: Harriet Andersson in Donner's ADVENTURE STARTS HERE

in the early Sixties. Now works in Finland. Scripts all his own features. Shorts: *Aamua kaupungissa, Näiaä päivinä* 55; *Vettä* 56; *Porkkala* 57 (last four in Finland; *Vittnesbörd om henne* 61. Features: *A Sunday in September* 63; *To Love* 64; *Adventure Starts Here* 65; *Stimulantia* (one episode) shot in 65 released in 67; *Rooftree* (also edited) 67; *Black on White* 68; *Sixtynine* 69 (last two in Finland).

• 41 DÜBERG, AXEL (1927-   ). Actor. Reliable supporting player in several Bergman pictures, and especially convincing as the thin herdsman in *The Virgin Spring*. Films: *Journey into Autumn/ Dreams, The Face/The Magician, The Virgin Spring, The Devil's Eye, Carnival, The Wonderful Adventures of Nils, Hide and Seek, A Sunday in September, Adam and Eve, Now about These Women, Just Like Friends, Woman of Darkness, The Princess, The Father.*

• 42 DYMLING, CARL ANDERS (1898-1961). The enlightened Head of

Svensk Filmindustri (q.v.) for some twenty years (1942-1961), during which time he revived the Swedish film world, discovered Ingmar Bergman (q.v.), and encouraged Arne Sucksdorff (q.v.). From 1936-42 he had proved to be an outstanding Head of Swedish Radio. He was also a translator and director of several radio plays. Although he rarely took any credit, he can be considered the "producer" of nearly all SF's films between 1942 and 1961.

● 43 EDGREN, GUSTAF (1895-1954). B: Östra Fågelvik. Director. At first journalist. One of the little known (outside Sweden) figures of the Thirties, who remained some thirty years in the film industry. Scripted or co-scripted all his films except*. *The Young Lady of Björneborg* 22; *People of Närke* 23; *The King of Trollebo* 24; *40 Skipper's Street, Mr. Karlsson Mate and His Sweethearts* 25; *She He and Andersson* 26; *The Ghost Baron* 27; *Black Rudolf* 28; *False Svensson* 29; *The Crown's Cavaliers* 30; *The Red Day*, Tired Teodor, Ship Ahoy!* 31; *People of Värmland* 32; *Karl-Fredrik Reigns, Simon from Backabo** 34; *Walpurgis Night* 35; *Johan Ulfstjerna* 36; *A Cold in the Head, John Ericsson—the Victor at Hampton Roads* 37; *Mr. Karlsson Mate and His Sweethearts* (re-make) 38; *A Big Hug* 40; *Katrina, Little Napoleon* 43; *Dolly Takes Her Chance* 44; *His Majesty Will Have to Wait* 45; *Kristin Takes Command, If Dew Falls Rain Follows* 46; *A Girl from the Marsh Croft* 47; *A Swedish Tiger* 48; *Gentlemen of the Navy, A Swedish Horseman* 49; *Helen of Troy* 51.

● 44 EDWALL, ALLAN (1924-   ). B: Rödön. Actor. 1949-52: trained at Royal Dramatic Theatre, Stockholm. Has performed in many theatres and on TV. Writer of radio plays. Spoke commentary for *My Home Is Copacabana* (q.v.). One of the most versatile actors in Sweden—

watchful and laconic, and outstanding as the old log floater in *Here Is Your Life* (q.v.). Films: *God and the Gipsyman, Journey to You, Wild Birds, The Flame, No Tomorrow, The Phantom Carriage* (58), *The Virgin Spring, To One's Heart's Content, The Devil's Eye, On a Bench in a Park, The Die Is Cast, Wedding Day, The Summer Night Is Sweet, The Brig "Three Lilies," Pan, Winter Light, Now about These Women, 4 x 4,* (Troell episode), *The Ball Room, Here Is Your Life, The Sadist, The Murderer —an Ordinary Person, The Bookseller Who Stopped Bathing, Eriksson* (also dir. and scripted 69), *The Emigrants* and *Unto a Good Land, We Are All Dead Demons.*

● 45 EK, ANDERS (1916-   ). B: Göteborg. Actor. 1938-41: Trained at Royal Dramatic Theatre, Stockholm. Various theatres. Since 1960: Municipal Theatre, Stockholm. A fine supporting screen actor whose anguished features have been best used by Ekman (in *Girl with Hyacinths*—q.v.) and Bergman (in *Sawdust* and *Tinsel/The Naked Night*, q.v., when Ek portrayed the clown, Frost). Films: *Ride Tonight!, The Awakening of Youth, We Need Each Other, God Pulls Johansson's Hair, Stop! Think of Something Else, The Girl and the Devil, Black Roses, Girl with Hyacinths, The Road to Klockrike, Sawdust and Tinsel/The Naked Night, The Seventh Seal, I Am Curious—Yellow, The Rite* (for TV).

● 46 EKBERG, ANITA (1931-   ). B: Malmö. Actress. At first model. Won "Miss Sweden" title in 1951, and went to Hollywood the same year. 1958: to Italy. International blonde star who never made a Swedish film but who has worked with such directors as Fellini (*La Dolce Vita*), King Vidor (*War and Peace*), and William Wellman (*Blood Alley*).

● 47 EKBORG, LARS (1926-1969). B: Uppsala. Actor. 1948-51: trained at Royal Dramatic Theatre, Stockholm. More familiar from stage, radio, and TV appearances than from his screen work. Ekborg's boyish, rather disgruntled face made him an easy prey for Harriet Andersson in *Summer with Monika* (q.v.). Films: *Backyard, Mrs. Andersson's Charlie, Poker, When Lilacs Blossom, U-Boat 39, Meeting Life, Wing-beats in the Night, Summer with Monika, The "Lunchbreak" Café, Yellow Squadron, In*

Anders Ek with Gun Wållgren in Faustman's THE GIRL AND THE DEVIL

Lars Ekborg with Harriet Andersson in Bergman's SUMMER WITH MONIKA

Smoke and Dancing, Dangerous Freedom, Blocked Rails, The Dance Hall, Violence, Private Entrance, Little Fridolf and I, Stage Entrance, The Flame, A Guest in One's Own Home, Never in Your Life, Lights at Night, Little Fridolf Becomes a Grandfather, No Tomorrow, The Face/ The Magician, Fridolf Is Rebellious, The Love Game, A Thief in the Bedroom, Three Wishes, Ticket to Paradise, Siska, Wedding—Swedish Style, Swedish Portraits, To Go Ashore, Stimulantia (Sjöman episode), *The Murderer—an Ordinary Person, Duet for Cannibals.*

• 48 EKELUND, KARIN (1913-). B: Ystad. Actress. 1930-33: trained

at Royal Dramatic Theatre, Stockholm. 1934-44: stage work. 1963-64: producer and director for radio. A gay young comedienne of the Thirties who surprised everyone with her deeply moving performance as the playboy's wife in *A Crime* (q.v.). She played other successful roles opposite Edvin Adolphson (q.v.) before leaving the cinema—far before her time. Films: *Marriageable Daughters, People of Hälsingland, The Girls from the Old Town, Synnöve Solbakken, Flirtation in the Archipelago, Girls in a Factory, Are We Married?, Our Boy, The Family that Was a Merry-Go-Round, Old Gods Are Still Alive, People of Bergslagen, Storm over the Skerries, Wings around the Lighthouse,*

The Merry Boys of the Coast Artillery, You Free Old Country, A Crime, With You in My Arms, Only a Woman, A Schoolmistress on the Spree, A Woman on Board, Dangerous Roads, The Big Crash, As You Like Me, The Sixth Shot, The Snow Storm, Narcosis, Between Us Thieves, Supper for Two, Love Chastised.

Cruise, Skipper in Stormy Weather, Rolling Sea, She Came like a Wind, Summer with Monika, Sir Arne's Treasure (54), *Murder My Little Friend, Men in Darkness, Children of the Night, Clouds over Hellesta, Laila, Crime in Paradise, The Job, The Doll, Tjorven and Skrållen, The Myth, Tjorven and Mysak, Skrållan Ruskprick and Knorrhane, Shame.*

● 49   EKEROT, BENGT (1920-   ). B: Stockholm. Actor and occasional director. 1938-41: trained at Royal Dramatic Theatre, Stockholm. Various theatres. Since 1960: Municipal Theatre of Stockholm. Memorable as the personification of Death in *The Seventh Seal*. Films as director only: *The Gay Party, Bareback* 46; *Stage Entrance* (also acted) 56. Films as actor: *They Staked Their Lives, Hanna in Society, The Talk of the Town, Scanian Guerilla, Flames in the Dark, The Knockout Clergyman, Night in the Harbour, The Awakening of Youth, Sonja, Gentleman with a Briefcase, The Royal Rabble, Three Sons Went to the Air Force, The Rose of Thistle Island, Three Cheers for Little Märta* (also assist. dir.), *Crime and Punishment, 13 Chairs, Brita in the Wholesaler's House, In Death's Waiting Room* (also assist. dir.), *Dynamite, The Seventh Seal, The Jazz Boy, The Face/ The Magician, On a Bench in a Park, The Myth, Here Is Your Life, Life's Just Great, Ola and Julia, Who Saw Him Die?, The Corridor.*

● 50   EKLUND, BENGT (1925-   ). B: Stockholm. Actor. 1944-47: trained at Royal Dramatic Theatre, Stockholm. Sturdy and forthright leading man of the late Forties and early Fifties. Has also performed in numerous theatres. Films: *The Balloon, When Meadows Bloom, Harald Handfaste, The Duties of a Soldier, Navvies, Loffe as a Vagabond, Music in Darkness, Life Begins Now, Port of Call, Thirst, Backyard, The Kiss on the*

● 51   EKMAN, GÖSTA (1890-1938). B: Stockholm. Actor. 1908: stage *début*. 1913-25: engaged by the Swedish Theatre in Stockholm. 1926-30: co-Head of the Öscar Theatre. 1931-35: owner of the Vasa Theatre. Many Shakespearian roles. A legendary actor with an enormous range, covering farce as well as tragedy. Combined splendid technique with intense feeling. His style seems to have been best suited to the theatre. Films: *Only a Dream, The Temptations of Stockholm, The Sisters, The Gardener* (banned), *The Unknown Woman, Life's Conflicts, Puss in Boots, The Bomb, Thora van Deken, The Gyurkovics, Family Traditions, A*

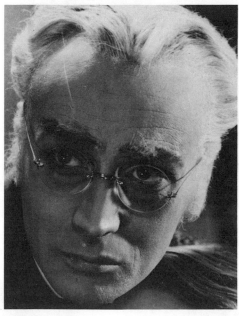

33

*Fortune Hunter, Love's Crucible, The
Eyes of Love, The Courier of Charles XII,
The Young Count Takes the Girl and
the Prize, Charles XII* (Pts I and II),
Faust (in Germany, dir. F. W. Murnau),
The Clown (in Denmark), *His English
Wife, A Perfect Gentleman* (also co-dir.),
Gustaf Wasa (Pts I and II), *For Her
Sake, Motley Leaves, A Poet Maybe, Dear
Relatives, Two Men and a Widow,
Swedenhielms, The King Is Coming, Johan
Ulfstjerna, Intermezzo, Witches' Night,
Father and Son* (uncompleted but shown
in 1940 as *Once More with Gösta Ek-
man*).

● 52 EKMAN, HASSE (1915-   ).
B: Stockholm. Actor and director. Son
of Gösta Ekman (q.v.). 1935: trip to
Hollywood. 1940-45 and 1948-52: at
Terra Film. 1946-47: at Europa Film.
Also scriptwriter, especially for his own
films. Acted in several of his pictures*. A
suave and elegant actor in such films as
Sawdust and Tinsel/The Naked Night,

Ekman has also directed a number of acute-
ly observed dramas. At his best during
the Forties. At one time married to Eva
Henning (q.v.). Now lives abroad. Films
as director: *With You in My Arms* 40;
First Division* 41; *Flames in the Dark*,
Luck Arrives* 42; *Changing Trains/Un-
expected Meeting*, The Sixth Shot* 43;
A Day Shall Dawn, His Excellency, Like
Most People* 44; *The Royal Rabble*,
Wandering with the Moon*, Three Cheers
for Little Märta** 45; *In Death's Waiting
Room*, Nightly Encounter*, When the
Door Was Closed** 46; *One Swallow
Doesn't Make a Summer** 47; *Each Goes
His Own Way*, Little Märta Returns*,
The Banquet** 48; *The Girl from the
Gallery** 49; *Girl with Hyacinths/The
Suicide, Jack of Hearts*, The White Cat*
50; *The Fire Bird* 52; *We Three Are
Making Our Début* 53; *Gabrielle* 54;
Private Entrance, The Seventh Heaven*
(also scored and song lyrics), *Ratataa**
56; *With the Halo Askew*, A Summer
Place Is Wanted* 57; *The Great Ama-
teur*, The Jazz Boy** (also song lyrics)
58; *Miss Chic*, Good Heavens!** 59; *The
Decimals of Love*, On a Bench in a Park**
60; *The Job* 61; *My Love Is a Rose* 63;
The Marriage Wrestler 64. Films as ac-
tor: *Housemaids, A Night at Smygeholm,
Dear Relatives, Intermezzo, John Erics-
son—the Victor at Hampton Roads, Thun-
der and Lightning, With the People for
the Country, Fellow Cadets, Night in
June, An Able Man, Life Goes On,
Teachers On a Summer Holiday, A Mat-
ter of Life and Death, I Am Fire and Air,
Stop! Think of Something Else, Prison/
The Devil's Wanton, Thirst / Three
Strange Loves, Unmarried, Sawdust and
Tinsel/The Naked Night, In Smoke and
Dancing, Yellow Squadron.* Films as
scriptwriter: *Thunder and Lightning,
Heroes in Yellow and Blue, An Able Man*
(co.), *Swing It Sir!* (co.), *Miss Church
Mouse* (co.), *Ghost Reporter, Teachers
on a Summer Holiday, Men-of-War* (co.),
A Matter of Life and Death, Love and

Downhill Skiing (co.), The Kiss on the Cruise (co.), Journey to You, Unmarried (co.), You Are My Adventure (co. Stig Olin), Swinging at the Castle (co. Olin).

• 53 EKMAN, JOHN (1880-1949). B: Stockholm. Actor. Studied as a painter but turned to the stage, where he covered most of the classical repertoire. Engaged by the Municipal Theatre of Göteborg from 1936 to 1949. Many appearances in silent films. *The Death-Ride under the Big Top, The Black Masks, A Secret Marriage, Lady Marion's Summer Flirtation, The Voice of Blood, Love Stronger than Hate, The Brothers, People of the Border, Half-Breed, The Miracle, Do Not Judge, Children of the Street, Daughter of the High Mountain, Hearts that Meet, The Strike, His Wife's Past, The Ace of Thieves, The Fight for the Rembrandt Painting, His Father's Crime, Judas Money, Madame de Thèbes, The Avenger, The Governor's Daughters, Sea Vultures, Old Age and Folly, The Lucky Brooch, The Hermit's Wife, At the Eleventh Hour, Who Fired?, The Jungle Queen's Jewels, Slave to Yourself, The Living Mummy, The Outlaw and His Wife, The Song of the Scarlet Flower (19), The Executioner, Family Traditions, The Phantom Carriage/Thy Soul Shall Bear Witness (21), For High Ends, The Suitor from the Roads, Johan Ulfstjerna, The Norrtull Gang, The Young Count Takes the Girl and the Prize, Kalle Utter, A Merchant House in the Archipelago, The Ingmar Inheritance, The Girls at Solvik, What Woman Wants, Sin (28), Black Rudolf, The Secret of the Paradise Hotel, The Atlantic Adventure, Synnöve Solbakken (34), The Song of the Scarlet Flower (34), Outlawed, 33.333, Bombi Bitt and I, Baldevin's Wedding, His Grace's Will (40), The Gentleman Gangster, The Fight Goes On, Lasse-Maja, Scanian Guerilla, General von Döbeln, Count the Happy Moments Only, The Rose of Thistle Island, Black Roses,*

The Serious Game, Don't Try It with Me, The Evening of the Fair, Lars Hård, Janne Vängman's New Adventures, Tall Lasse from Delsbo, To Joy.

• 54 EKMANNER, AGNETA (1938-   ). B: Stockholm. Actress. Studied at Stockholm and Lund Universities, and later attended Malmö theatre school. Tall, pert, and chic (a former model), Miss Ekmanner is the wife of Jonas Cornell (q.v.) and has played in two of his features as well as in his short *Hej!* Features: *Love 65, Hugs and Kisses, I Love You Love, The Corridor, Like Night and Day, Duet for Cannibals.*

Pia Degermark and Thommy Berggren in ELVIRA MADIGAN

• 55 ELVIRA MADIGAN. 1967. Script, Direction and Editing: Bo Widerberg. Photography (Eastmancolor): Jörgen Persson. Music: Mozart's Piano Concerto no. 1 and extracts from Vivaldi's Violin Concerti. Art Direction: none. Players: Pia Degermark (*Elvira*), Thommy Berggren (*Count Sixten Sparre*), Lennart Malmer (*Kristoffer*), Nina Widerberg (*Little girl*), Cleo Jensen (*Cook*). 95 mins. For Europa Film.

PLOT: Elvira Madigan is a young tightrope dancer passionately in love with a Swedish army officer, Count Sixten Sparre. Together they flee to Denmark. For one short summer they have a marvellous affair. Then, as money runs out,

the atmosphere changes. Sixten is discovered and tacitly reproached by a friend for having deserted his wife and two children. Small quarrels do not help matters. Elvira and Sixten try to live off the woods, eating berries and mushrooms. Finally, rather than return to society and to emotional defeat, they decide to commit suicide together.

• 56 EN DJUNGELSAGA / THE FLUTE AND THE ARROW. 1957. Script and Direction: Arne Sucksdorff. Photography (AgaScope, color): Arne Sucksdorff. Editing: Arne Sucksdorff.

Technical assistants: M. M. Sharma, Hans Olsson, Astrid Bergman-Sucksdorff, Arvind Shah. Music: Ravi Shankar. Commentary: William Sansom. Speaker (Swedish): Gunnar Sjöberg. (English): Arthur Howard. 90 mins. For Sandrews.

PLOT: The film is set in a remote village of India, where the Muria tribe of Indians have a settlement. The Murians' traditions and culture pre-date the invasions of northern India by Aryan, Mongolian, and Dravidian tribes. Their primitive religious beliefs stem from the basic elements of nature around them; there is a God of earth and sky, guardian spirits invested in flowers and evoked in song, and evil demons embodied in jungle creatures like the leopard. The ravages of one of these leopards provide the fictional theme of *The Flute and the Arrow,* and the film describes the villagers' fight to defeat the animal and the sacrifice of one man's life to appease the Gods and drive away the leopard.

● 57 EN LEKTION I KÄRLEK/A LESSON IN LOVE. 1954. Script and Direction: Ingmar Bergman. Photography: Martin Bodin. Editing: Oscar Rosander. Music: Dag Wirén. Art Direction: P. A. Lundgren. Players: Eva Dahlbeck (*Marianne Erneman*), Gunnar Björnstrand (*David Erneman*), Yvonne Lombard (*Susanne*), Harriet Andersson (*Nix, the Ernemans' daughter*), Åke Grönberg (*Carl-Adam*), Olof Winnerstrand (*Professor Henrik Erneman*), Renée Björling (*Svea, his wife*), Birgitte Reimer (*Lise*), John Elfström (*Sam*), Dagmar Ebbesen (*Nurse*), Helge Hagerman (*Travelling Salesman*), Sigge Fürst (*Clergyman*), Gösta Prüzelius (*Train Conductor*), Carl Ström, Arne Lindblad, Torsten Lilliecrona, Yvonne Brosset. 95 mins. For Svensk Filmindustri.

PLOT: David Erneman is a gynaecologist who, having been married for sixteen years, yields to the charms of Susanne, a female patient, and has an affair that disrupts his marriage. His wife Marianne flounces off to Copenhagen to sleep with her former *fiancé* Carl-Adam, who is a sculptor. David eventually gives up his liaison with Susanne, and recaptures his wife despite the opposition of Carl-Adam in a Copenhagen night club.

● 58 EN SÖNDAG I SEPTEMBER/ A SUNDAY IN SEPTEMBER. 1963. Script and Direction: Jörn Donner. Photography: Tony Forsberg. Editing: Wic Kjellin. Music: Bo Nilsson. Art Direction: Eric Aes. Players: Harriet Andersson (*Birgitta*), Thommy Berggren (*Stig*), Barbro Kollberg (*Mother*), Harry Ahlin (*Father*), Axel Düberg (*Brother*), Jan-Erik Lindqvist (*Ing. Karlsson*), Ellika Mann (*Mrs. Karlsson*), Roland Söderberg (*Clergyman*), Nils Kihlberg (*Dr. Hjälm*). 113 mins. For Europa Film.

PLOT: After a documentary prologue —street interviews about the possibilities of love today—Donner tells the story of a marriage in four movements: falling in love, wedding day, rupture, and divorce. Stig and Birgitta are two ordinary young people who meet and fall in love. On the wedding day Birgitta is already pregnant. In the third episode the feeling of estrangement grows more acute, epitomised in the desolate after-dinner scene. Stig finds a meaning in his work, but the nervous Birgitta is unable to settle down. Both of them are egotists, and their marriage ends with a matter-of-fact divorce, handled as dispassionately as a business transaction.

● 59 ERASTOFF, EDITH (1887-1945). B: Helsinki. Actress. Came to Sweden in 1914. Married Sjöström (q.v.) and went with him to Hollywood. With her natural freshness, she specialised in arrogant and temperamental peasant women in films like *The Outlaw and His Wife.* Films: *People of the Border, A Hero in spite of Himself, The First Prize, The Avenger, Old Age and Folly, Mrs. B's*

Harriet Andersson and Thommy Berggren in A SUNDAY IN SEPTEMBER

Lapse, Terje Vigen, The Architect of One's Own Fortune, The Secret of the Inn, Chanson Triste, The Outlaw and His Wife, The Song of the Scarlet Flower (19), *For High Ends, Johan Ulfstjerna.*

• 60 ERNBACK, HANS (1942-   ). Young actor relying on his charm and vitality in a succession of more or less sexy films. *The Serpent, I Need a Woman, Roseanna, The Sinning Urge/Burnt Child, Waltz of Sex, The Swedish Fanny Hill.*

• 61 EROTIKON. 1920. Script: Mauritz Stiller and Gustaf Molander, from a play by Franz Herzeg. Direction: Mauritz Stiller. Photography: Henrik Jaenzon. Art Direction: Axel Esbensen. Players: Lars Hanson (*Preben Wells, sculptor*), Anders de Wahl (*Professor Leo Charpentier*), Tora Teje (*Irene, his wife*), Karin Molander (*Marthe, his niece*), Carina Ari

(*Schaname*), Stina Berg (*The maid*), Gucken Cederborg (*The cook*), Torsten Hammarén (*Professor Sedonius*), Vilhelm Bryde (*Baron Felix*), Bell Hedqvist (*Baron Felix's friend*), John Lindlöf (*Preben's friend*), Vilhelm Berntsson (*Servant*), Elin Lagergren (*Irene's mother*), Greta Lindgren (*Model*), Martin Oscar (*The Shah*), Carl Wallin (*Fur dealer*). 5,800 ft. For Svensk Filmindustri.

PLOT: Professor Charpentier, an entomologist, devotes more time to his science than to his charming young wife Irene. His niece Marthe starts flirting with him to take over Irene's place. Marthe pretends to share the professor's interests and cooks his favourite dishes, and he likes her. Meanwhile Irene is flirting with Baron Felix, a well-known *roué,* but secretly she loves Preben, a sculptor. Preben thinks that Irene is Felix's mistress and tries to manoeuvre the professor into a duel with Felix. But at Felix's home Preben discovers his fatal mistake. Irene has been faithful to her husband, but now she divorces him to marry Preben. The professor marries Marthe, who will probably develop more expensive and sophisticated habits after the wedding.

● 62 ETT BROTT/A CRIME. 1940. Script: Carlo Keil-Möller, Bengt Idestam-Almquist, and Anders Henrikson, from the play by Sigfrid Siwertz. Direction: Anders Henrikson. Photography: Hilding Bladh and Evert Löfstedt. Editing: Rolf Husberg. Music: Bo Rosendahl and Gunnar Malmgren. Art Direction: Arthur Spjuth. Players: Edvin Adolphson (*Rutger von Degerfeldt*), Karin Ekelund (*Maud,* his wife), Anders Henrikson (*Hans von Degerfeldt*), Ziri Gun Eriksson (*Maria von Degerfeldt*), Carl Barcklind (*Andreas von Degerfeldt*), Hilda Borgström (*Miss Alma Furuvik*), Gösta Cederlund (*Lilja, Police Inspector*), Håkan Westergren (*Risberg, a journalist*), Ulla Sorbon (*Lisa Waldemars*), Einar Axelson (*Dr. Bernhard Gilljams*), Åke Claesson (*Dr. Forenius*), Gösta Bodin (*Mr. Dunér, the concierge*), Dagmar Ebbesen (*Mrs. Sofia Dunér, his wife*), Karin Alexandersson (*Kristin*), Ivar Kåge (*Rosenschöld*), Sten Hedlund (*A Police Sergeant*), with Gösta Hillberg, Oscar Åberg, Astrid Bodin, Åke Brodin, Valter Lindström, Tord Benheim, and Helge Karlsson. 93 mins. For Terra Film (Lorens Marmstedt).

Lars Hanson and Tora Teje (both at right) in EROTIKON

PLOT: The old magistrate, Andreas von Degerfeldt, is a tyrant in his family. He is ashamed of his brother Hugo, and forbids his sons to mix with him. One night Rutger disobeys these orders, and the next day it is read in the newspapers that Hugo has been murdered. There is a long and exhaustive police inquiry. Rutger is soon arrested. He is suspected of having supplied Hugo with drugs, and when confronted by his father in the police station he confesses to the crime. He is sent to prison. Hans, his brother, takes Rutger's wife, Maud, away to Italy for a holiday. But directly on her return she visits the prison and, while the warder is not looking, manages to slip a suicide pill to her husband. She swallows one herself at the same moment.

● 63 EUROPA FILM. Founded in 1930 by Gustav Scheutz (1900-1967), a glass manufacturer. He began with his own Svensk-Engelska Film Company. When sound was introduced into Swedish studios, he decided to enter production. His first film was *Love and Veteran Reserves,* shot in Finland. This was a big success. Subsequently Scheutz built up Europa with the aid of the films of Edvard Persson and Fridolf Rhudin (both q.v.). 1936: Europa studios established. 1965: *La Guerre est Finie,* the first Franco-Swedish co-production, is shot in the Europa studios. The company now owns some seventy to eighty cinemas throughout Sweden. Scheutz produced at least 150 films during his career.

● 64 FALCK, ÅKE (1925-   ). B: Göteborg. Director. 1946-55: worked in Swedish Radio. Also TV and theatre director. Vivid pictures of pastoral life, but Falck tends to sacrifice his sequences in order to achieve a few striking compositions. Films: *The Die Is Cast* (acted only), *Fire Bird* (acted only), *Adam and Eve* 63; *Wedding—Swedish Style* 64; *The Princess* 66; *Waltz of Sex* (also co-scripted) 68.

● 65 FANT, GEORGE (1916-   ). B: Stockholm. Actor. Theatre *début* in 1937. Engaged by Svensk Filmindustri 1937-42. Head of Norrbotten Theatre in Luleå since 1967. A "lady-killer" in films of the Thirties and early Forties, but only rare appearances in recent years. Films: *It Pays to Advertise, Johan Ulfstjerna, The Adventure, He She and the Money, Intermezzo, A Cold in the Head, Clear the Decks for Action, John Ericsson—the Victor at Hampton Roads, A Rich Man's Son, Milly Maria and I, With the People for the Country, Mr. Karlsson Mate and His Sweethearts, The Old Man Is Coming, Variety Is the Spice of Life, The Little WRAC of the Veteran Reserves, Fellow Cadets, Steel, Gentleman for Hire, Bright Prospects, The Little Shrew of the Veteran Reserves, The Downy Girl, Scanian Guerilla, Youth in Chains, A Spring in Arms, Life in the Country, Katrina, Train 56, Three Sons Went to the Air Force, The Rose of Thistle Island, Blood and Fire, Brita in the Wholesaler's House, The Bells of the Old Town, Harald Handfaste, Maria, Lars Hård, Foreign Harbour, Where the Winds Lead, House Number 17, The Time of Desire, Night Journey, Married Life* (57), *The Manors around the Lake, Mother Takes a Holiday, The Phantom Carriage* (58), *Good Friends and Faithful Neighbours, When Darkness Falls, Do You Believe in Angels?, Murder Weapon for Sale, Just like Friends.*

● 66 FANT, KENNE (1923-   ). B: Strängnäs. Actor, director and producer. Now Head of Svensk Filmindustri, Kenne Fant trained at the Royal Dramatic Theatre, Stockholm, from 1945 to 1949, and worked as a director at Nordisk Tonefilm from 1952 to 1962. Appointed Head of Production at SF in 1962, and overall chief from 1963. An attractive actor and

competent director. Films as director only: *Shortage* (short) 51; *The Shadow* (also scripted), *Wing-beats in the Night* (also acted) 53; *Young Summer* 54; *Love Chastised* 55; *Tarps Elin* 57; *The Clergyman from Uddarbo* 58; *The Love Game* 59; *Wedding Day* 60; *The Wonderful Adventures of Nils* (also prod.) 62. Films as actor only: *Women in a Waiting Room, Youth in Danger, The Most Beautiful Thing on Earth, Life in the Depths of the Forest, People of Simlången Valley, Each Heart Has Its Story, The Poetry of Ådalen, The Woman Who Disappeared, Prison/The Devil's Wanton, Swedish Horseman, Poker, Kalle Karlsson from Jularbo, When Lilacs Blossom, Dance My Doll, The Girl from Backafall, All the Joy of Earth.*

● 67 FAUSTMAN, ERIK "HAMPE" (1919-1961). B: Stockholm. Actor and director. 1937: trained at Royal Dramatic Theatre, Stockholm. The most "committed" of the middle generation in Swedish cinema. Many of his films showed his interest in Soviet Russia. Married to Gun Wållgren (q.v.). Films as director (two of which he co-scripted*): *Night in the Harbour, Sonja** 43; *We Need Each Other* (also acted), *The Girl and the Devil* 43; *Crime and Punishment* (also acted) 45; *When Meadows Bloom* (also acted) 46; *Harald Handfaste, A Soldier's Duties* 47; *Lars Hård* (also acted) *Foreign Harbour* 48·; *Vagabond Blacksmiths** (also acted) 49; *The Intimate Restaurant* 50; *Woman behind Everything* (two episodes, shot 50-51, released 56); *The Talking Wire, About Bikes, Gold in Green Forests* (shorts) 51; *U-boat 39, She Came like a Wind* 52; *House of Women* 53; *The "Lunch-break" Café, God and the Gipsyman* 54; *Night Journey, No One Is Crazier than I Am* 55. Films as actor only: *They Staked Their Lives, A Woman on Board, Ride Tonight!, Women in Prison, Katrina, A Spring in Arms, There Burned a Flame, Darling I Surrender, His Excellency, My People Are Not Yours, When the Door Was Closed, Never in Your Life.*

● 68 FISCHER, GUNNAR (1910-). B: Ljungby. Director of photography. 1935: joins Svensk Filmindustri as assistant to Julius Jaenzon (q.v.). 1939: collab. on photography of *Whalers*. An international name due to his work for Bergman*, Fischer is also an accomplished illustrator of children's books. Main films: *It Is My Music, Night in the Harbour* (also co-scripted), *Two People, Bluejackets* (45), *Aunt Green Aunt Brown and Aunt Lilac, Don't Give Up, A Soldier's Duties, Private Bom, Port of Call**, *Thirst/Three Strange Loves**, *To Joy**, *This Can't Happen Here**, *The Beef and the Banana, Summer Interlude/Illicit Interlude**, *Waiting Women/Secrets of Women**, *We Three Are Making Our Début, Hidden in the Fog, Summer with Monika**, *Gabrielle, Victory in Darkness, Smiles of a Summer Night**, *The Pawn Shop, Private Entrance, The Tough Game, Encounters at Dusk, The Seventh Seal**,

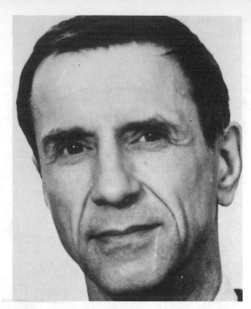

Wild Strawberries*, Playing on the Rainbow, You Are My Adventure, The Face/ The Magician*, Swinging at the Castle, The Devil's Eye*, The Boy in the Tree, Two Living One Dead, Pleasure Garden, One among Many (in Denmark), *Siska, Pan, My Love Is a Rose, 491, Just like Friends, June Night, Well Well Well, Stimulantia* (Donner, Arnbom, and Molander episodes), *Ola & Julia, I Need a Woman, The Black Palm Trees, Made in Sweden, Miss and Mrs. Sweden.*

● 69 FLICKA OCH HYACINTER/ GIRL WITH HYACINTHS/THE SUICIDE. 1950. Script and Direction: Hasse Ekman. Photography: Göran Strindberg. Editing: Lennart Wallén. Music: Erland von Koch. Art Direction: Bibi Lindström. Players: Eva Henning (*Dagmar Brink*), Ulf Palme (*Anders Holmsen*), Birgit Tengroth (*Britt Holmsen*), Anders Ek (*Elias Körner*), Gudrun Brost (*Körner's girl friend*), Marianne Löfgren (*Gullan Wiklund*), Keve Hjelm (*Captain Brink*), Karl-Arne Holmsten (*Willy Borge*), Anne-Marie Brunius (*Redhead*),

Björn Berglund (*Police Commissioner Lövgren*), Gösta Cederlund (*Von Lieven*). 89 mins. For Terra Film.

PLOT: A lonely young girl, Dagmar Brink, commits suicide in her room. A writer and his wife, living in the flat next door, find that the dead girl has left all her belongings to them. The writer, Anders Holmsen, is puzzled by the tragedy and sets about investigating Dagmar's past life. Her divorced husband tells him of a lover called Alex. Her father says that he would have nothing to do with her. Elias Körner, a drunken painter with whom Dagmar lived for a while, is also questioned by Anders, as is an actress with whom she shared a flat. The solution to the mystery rests with Willy Borge, a recording star who tried in vain to seduce Dagmar. It appears that the dead girl was a Lesbian and that a chance meeting with her former lover, Alex (a woman), had so depressed her that she committed suicide.

● 70 FORSLUND, BENGT (1932-). B: Grödinge. Producer and script-

42

Above: Åke Fridell in Troell's
HERE IS YOUR LIFE

writer. At first school teacher. Founder of the leading Swedish film magazine, *Chaplin,* then joined Svensk Filmindustri (1960), launching there a trio of art cinemas. Started production in 1964 and has discovered many new directors. Forslund has also helped to script some of the films* he has produced. Main shorts: *Oh, You Are like a Rose, The Piano Lesson, When People Meet.* Features: *4 x 4*, Well, Well, Well*, The Myth, Here Is Your Life*, Life's Just Great*, Who Saw Him Die?*, Ola & Julia*, The Corridor*, Made in Sweden, A Dream of Freedom*, The Emigrants* and *Unto a Good Land*.*

● 71 FRIDELL, ÅKE (1919-   ). B: Gävle. Actor. After two years at Witzansky's Theatre School he joined Bergman (q.v.) at Hälsingborg Municipal Theatre. Much stage work since. An always amusing and polished actor who usually plays mischievous or seemingly malicious roles in Bergman's films. *The Clock at Rönneberga, We Need Each Other, It Rains on Our Love/Man with an Umbrella, When Meadows Bloom, A Soldier's Duties, A Ship Bound for India, I Am with You, Lars Hård, Robinson of Roslagen, Foreign Harbour, The Street, Vagabond Blacksmiths, Prison/The Devil's Wanton, The Woman Who Disappeared, Spring at Sjösala, Only a Mother, House Number 17, Stora Hopare Lane and Heaven, Jack of Hearts, When Love Came to the Village, Backyard, Miss Julie, A Ghost on Holiday, House of Folly, Stronger than the Law, When Lilacs Blossom, The Rose of the Regiment, Summer with Monika, Ursula—the Girl from the Forest Depths, Barabbas, Sawdust and Tinsel/The Naked Night, Rasmus and the Tramp, Smiles of a Summer Night, Children of the Night, The Seventh Seal, The Rusk, Wild Strawberries, A Square Peg in a Round Hole, The Face/The Magician, A Lion in Town, To One's Heart's Content, Decimals of Love,*

43

Mother of Pearl, Just Once More, Murder Weapon for Sale, Swedish Portraits, The Dream Boy, The Big Bang, The Sadist, Here Is Your Life, Odd Lovers.

- 72 FRIDH, GERTRUD (1921-). B. Göteborg. Actress. 1941-44: trained at Municipal Theatre, Göteborg. 1945: film *début*. A classical actress of considerable power (*Hedda Gabler* in Bergman's stage production, for instance), Miss Fridh has an uncanny flair for suggesting a submerged eroticism and vulnerability beneath her usually aloof and sarcastic poise. Films: *Trotting Hope and Charity, A Ship Bound for India, Backyard, Jack of Hearts, The White Cat, Yellow Squadron, Wild Birds, Private Entrance, Wild Strawberries, The Face/ The Magician, The Devil's Eye, Siska, Dream of Happiness, Now about These Women, Hour of the Wolf.*

- 73 FRÄMMANDE HAMN/FOREIGN HARBOUR. 1948. Script: Herbert Grevenius, from the play "Unknown Swedish Soldier," by Josef Kjellgren. Direction: Erik "Hampe" Faustman. Photography: Carl Edlund. Editing: Lennart Wallén. Music: Carl-Olof Anderberg. Art Direction: P. A. Lundgren. Players: Georg Fant (*Håkan, a sailor*), Adolf Jahr (*The Captain*), Illona Wieselmann (*Mimi, a Jewish refugee*), Stig Järrel (*A Gun-runner*), Åke Fridell (*Steward*), Fritiof Billquist (*First Mate*), Gösta Holmström (*Second Mate*), Carl Ström (*First Engineer*), Stig Johansson (*Jerker*), Anders Börje (*Christian*), Jan Molander (*Shipping Agent*), Josua Bengtsson (*Mastman*), Anders Andelius (*Norwegian Boy*), Georg Skarstedt (*Strandmark*), Henake Schubak (*Toivo*), Birger Lensander (*The cook*), Nils Hallberg (*The stoker*), Sten Larsson (*Unknown man*), Alexander von Baumgarten (*Dirty Dick*), Emanuel Warhaftig (*Police Officer*), Janina (*Innocent Girl*). 85 mins. For Sandrews (Rune Waldekranz).

PLOT: Gdynia, Poland, in 1938. The captain of a Swedish cargo ship is ordered to take on board munitions disguised as preserves. When he protests, he is threatened with dismissal. Unwilling to risk his livelihood for the moral satisfaction of his men, the captain gives in. But when the members of the crew discover that they are about to sail for Seville with guns for Franco's army, they mutiny. The captain tries to recruit a fresh crew so that the departure of the vessel will not be delayed. Then, stirred by the communal loyalty of his old mates, he decides to resign from the ship altogether, fully aware that his career is ruined. Finally, the crew wins the day. The noxious cargo is unloaded and the ship draws out of the harbour, bound for Stockholm with a consignment of coal.

- 74 FRÖKEN JULIE/MISS JULIE. 1951. Script and Direction: Alf Sjöberg, from the play by August Strindberg. Photography: Göran Strindberg. Editing: Lennart Wallén. Music: Dag Wirén. Art

Anita Björk and Ulf Palme in MISS JULIE (with Märta Dorff)

Direction: Bibi Lindström. Players: Anita Björk (*Miss Julie*), Ulf Palme (*Jean*), Märta Dorff (*Kristin*), Anders Henrikson (*The Count*), Lissi Alandh (*The Countess*), Inger Norberg (*Julie as a child*), Jan Jagerman (*Jean as a child*), Åke Fridell (*Robert*), Inger Gill (*Viola*), Åke Claesson (*Doctor*), Kurt-Olof Sundström (*The Fiancé*), Max von Sydow (*Groom*), Margaretha Krook. 90 mins. For Sandrew Bauman.

PLOT: It is Midsummer's Eve. Miss Julie, daughter of a wealthy Count, is bored. She sees the folk of the manor dancing to celebrate the occasion, and she decides to join them. There she forces Jean, the Count's groom, to dance with her, much to his embarrassment and her amusement. Miss Julie is a very capricious girl. She humiliates her *fiancé,* and she then proceeds to seduce Jean, despite his protestations about their difference of social class. She tells Jean of her upbringing, of her cruel and domineering mother, and he feels sorry for her. They plan to run away together to Switzerland. But then the Count returns from his trip, and rings for his groom. Miss Julie, realising that she can never regain her former propriety or dignity, cuts her throat with a razor.

● 75 FUNKQUIST, GEORG (1900-). B: Uppsala. Actor. 1921-23: trained at Royal Dramatic Theatre, Stockholm. Much film and stage work.

Often used as a speaker by Swedish radio and by Sucksdorff (q.v.) for some of his nature films. Unforgettable as the bitter uncle Erland in *Summer Interlude*. Films: *The Amateur Film, Charles XII* (Pts I and II), *We Must Have Love, Poor Millionaires, Happy Vestköping, Mother Marries, Kalle på Spången, Her Melody, Romance, To Chastise a Husband, Home from Babylon, Poor Ferdinand, Luck Arrives, Changing Trains, The Big Crash, Women in Prison, Little Napoleon, Anna Lans, Kajan Goes to Sea, Appassionata, We Need Each Other, The Turnstile, Nothing but Old Nobility, Crime and Punishment, You Who Are about to Enter, Woman without a Face, May I Sir?, Unto the Gates of Hell, Miss Sunbeam, That Woman Drives Me Crazy, The Wind Is My Lover, Summer Interlude, In Smoke and Dancing, The Stranger from the Sky, Ratataa, Woman in a Leopardskin, Jazz Boy, Swinging at the Castle, The Devil's Eye, Åsa-Nisse on Mallorca, Dream of Happiness, Now about These Women, Sailors and Sextants.*

● 76 FÜRST, SIGGE (1905-   ). B: Stockholm. Actor. 1925-30: worked as a policeman. Then screen and stage appearances. Revues. Very popular as a radio entertainer in the late Forties and early Fifties. Reliable supporting actor, mostly in light-weight films. *Tired Teodor, The House of Silence, The Melody of the Sea, False Greta, Karl Fredrik Reigns, Marauders, She or No One, Privates 65 66 and I, A Cold in the Head, Adolf Armstrong, Happy Vestköping, A Rich Man's Son, Comrades in Uniform, Career, The Merry Boys of the Coast Artillery, Mr. Housekeeper, Her Little Majesty, Brave Boys in Uniform, Heroes in Yellow and Blue, Kiss Her, The Merry-Go-Round in Full Swing, Gentleman for Hire, Our Boys in Uniform, Göransson's Boy, A Schoolmistress on the Spree, Unlucky Fellow no. 13* (also dir. 42), *The Knockout Clergyman, Ghosts! Ghosts!, Night in the Harbour, My Husband Is Getting Married Today, The Actor, His Excellency, Professor Poppe's Crazy Eccentricities, The New Affairs of Pettersson and Bendel, Wandering with the Moon, The Rose of Thistle Island, Jarl the Widower, Mandragora, The Girls of Småland, Money, A Hundred Accordions and One Girl, Love and Downhill Skiing, Nightly Encounter, The Balloon, Hotell Kåkbrinken, Here We Come, Kronblom, Aunt Green Aunt Brown and Aunt Lilac, Blomqvist the Master Detective, Don't Give Up, The Evening of the Fair, The Count from the Lane, The Girl from the Gallery, Woman in White, The Devil and the Man from Småland, Pippi Long-Stocking, Love Will Conquer, Knockout at the "Breakfast Club," When Love Came to the Village, The Saucepan Journey, When Bengt and Anders Swapped Wives, Motor Cavaliers, Helen of Troy, Summer with Monika, The King of Dalarna, In Major and Showers, The Master Detective and Rasmus, The Journey to You, Never with My Jemmy, Storm over Tjurö, A Lesson in Love, Salka Valka, Men in Darkness,*

Darling at Sea, Smiles of a Summer Night, A Little Place of One's Own, Private Entrance, The Seventh Heaven, Ratataa, Sinners in the Cinema Paradise, Girl in a Dress-coat, Little Fridolf and I, Little Fridolf Becomes a Grandfather, Encounters at Dusk, The Master Detective Leads a Dangerous Life, A Summer Place Is Wanted, The Overlord of the Navy, The Jazz Boy, Miss Chic, Hand Me a Count, Only a Waiter, Good Heavens!, A Lion in Town, The Die Is Cast, Decimals of Love, On a Bench in a Park, When Darkness Falls, Do You Believe in Angels?, Mother of Pearl, The Brig "Three Lilies," Ticket to Paradise, The Raggare Gang, Dream of Happiness, The Marriage Wrestler, Just like Friends, The Ball Room, **Odd Lovers, Shame, A Passion.**

• 77 FÄNGELSE/PRISON/THE DEVIL'S WANTON. 1949. Script and Direction: Ingmar Bergman. Photography: Göran Strindberg. Editing: Lennart Wallén. Music: Erland von Koch. Art Direction: P. A. Lundgren. Players: Doris Svedlund (*Birgitta-Carolina*), Birger Malmsten (*Tomas*), Eva Henning (*Sofi*), Hasse Ekman (*Martin*), Stig Olin (*Peter*), Irma Christenson (*Linnéa*), Anders Henrikson (*The Old Professor*), Marianne Löfgren (*Mrs. Bohlin*), Carl-Henrik ("Kenne") Fant (*Arne*), Inger Juel (*Greta*), Curt Masreliez (*Alf*), Åke Fridell, Bibi Lindqvist, Arne Ragneborn. 80 mins. For Terra Film (Lorens Marmstedt).

PLOT: At a film studio outside Stock-

Below: Sigge Fürst in Bergman's SHAME

Ingmar Bergman (centre, smiling at rear) with the cast of NOW ABOUT THESE WOMEN

holm, Martin, a director, is visited by his former mathematics teacher, who has been suffering from a mental illness. The old professor has an idea for a new film: a film about hell and the devil, based on the premise that hell is here on earth and the devil has unlimited power over human lives. Martin ridicules the idea, but he mentions it to a friend, Tomas, a journalist who writes film scripts. Tomas is married to Sofi. He believes the film could be a success because he has met the ideal heroine, Birgitta-Carolina, whom he has interviewed about night life in Stockholm. Birgitta-Carolina lives with her protector, Peter, and his sister, who do not hesitate to kill the child she gives birth to. Exasperated, Birgitta-Carolina runs away, encounters

Tomas, who is downcast himself after imagining he has murdered his wife, and the two of them live briefly in a rooming house attic. But Birgitta-Carolina cannot bear to drag Tomas down with her. They part, and shortly afterwards she commits suicide in a cellar. Tomas returns to Sofi. Back in the studio, the director hears the news. What use is there in asking about the meaning of life? There is nobody to ask, in any event. . . .

● 78 FÖR ATT INTE TALA OM ALLA DESSA KVINNOR/NOW ABOUT THESE WOMEN. 1964. Script: Ingmar Bergman and Erland Josephson under the pseudonym Buntel Ericsson. Direction: Ingmar Bergman.

Photography (Eastmancolor): Sven Nykvist. Editing: Ulla Ryghe. Music: Erik Nordgren. Art Direction: P. A. Lundgren. Players: Jarl Kulle (*Cornelius*), Georg Funkquist (*Tristan*), Eva Dahlbeck (*Adelaide*), Karin Kavli (*Madame Tussaud*), Harriet Andersson (*Isolde*), Gertrud Fridh (*Traviata*), Bibi Andersson (*Bumble-Bee*), Barbro Hiort af Ornäs (*Beatrice*), Mona Malm (*Cecilia*), Allan Edwall (*Jillker*), Gösta Prüzelius (*Swedish Radio Announcer*), Jan-Olof Strandberg (*German Radio Announcer*), Göran Graffman (*French Radio Announcer*), Jan Blomberg (*British Radio Announcer*), Ulf Johanson, Axel Düberg, Lars-Erik Liedholm (*Men in Black Suits*), Lars-Owe Carlberg (*The Driver*), Carl Billquist (*A Young Man*), Doris Funcke, Yvonne Igell (*Housemaids*). 80 mins. For Svensk Filmindustri.

PLOT: Cornelius, a rather precious music critic, visits the summer residence of Felix, the distinguished 'cellist, in order to write his biography, and finds himself surrounded by a bevy of women, each of whom is obviously the mistress of the great musician. He is refused permission to see Felix, and grows more and more exasperated and compromised. Eventually, he threatens not to write the biography. But when Felix makes his appearance (though he never faces his critic) at a concert, he dies before he can strike a note. Cornelius is just reading his draft of the biography to Jillker, Tristan and the ladies, when a down-at-heels young 'cellist arrives at the mansion. A room is immediately prepared for him, and Cornelius reaches for his notebook. . . .

● 79 GAMLIN, YNGVE (1926-). B: Strömsund. Director. Studied art in Copenhagen and Paris. Comes from northwest Sweden, where his recent films have been set. Gamlin has worked in TV, radio, and theatre, and is a set and costume designer. Also a sculptor and painter. His ebullient personality is only occasionally perceptible in a rather portentous style. Many shorts. Acted in: *Ratataa* (also designed), *The Great Amateur* (also designed), *Miss Chic, Beautiful Susan and the Old Men, Summer and Sinners, Ticket to Paradise*. Films as designer only: *With the Halo Askew, The Square, Jet* (last two also acted), *Maximum*. Films as director: *In Smoke and Dancing* (co. Bengt Blomgren) 54; *You Must Be Crazy Darling!* 64; *The Hunt* 65; *The Bathers* 68; *The Souvenir Hunters* 70.

● 80 GARBO, GRETA (1905-). B: Stockholm. Actress. 1922-24: trained at Royal Dramatic Theatre, Stockholm. 1920: *début* on screen in *Fortune Hunter*. 1921: advertising films for PUB store. From 1924: works abroad. The most celebrated Swedish actress in the history of the cinema. Swedish films: *Peter the Tramp, The Saga of Gösta Berling*.

● 81 GENTELE, GÖRAN (1917-). B: Stockholm. Director. 1941-44: trained at Royal Dramatic Theatre, Stockholm. From 1963: Head of Stockholm

Opposite: Greta Garbo in Stiller's THE SAGA OF GÖSTA BERLING. Above: Anita Björk in MARRIED LIFE

Opera. Films (all scripted by Gentele except*): *Crime in the Sun* 47; *Unto the Gates of Hell** 48; *Living at "The Hope"* 51; *People of Värmland* 57; *Miss April* 58; *A Thief in the Bedroom* 59; *Three Wishes* 60; *One Fine Day* 63; *Miss and Mrs. Sweden* 70. Gentele also acted in *Three Sons Went to the Air Force*.

• 82 GIFTAS / MARRIED LIFE. 1957. Script: Katherine and Tage Aurell, from the stories by August Strindberg. Direction: Anders Henrikson. Photography: Karl-Erik Alberts. Editing: Wic Kjellin. Music: Herbert Sandberg. Art Direction: Arne Åkermark. Players: (ETT DOCKHEM) George Fant (*Captain Pall*), Mai Zetterling (*Gurli, his wife*), Gunnel Broström (*Ottilia*), Hjördis Pettersson (*Gurli's mother*), Torsten Lilliecrona (*The Naval surgeon*), Einar Axelsson (*The commissary*), Charlotte Lindell (*Lilian*), Artillio Bergholtz (*Jonathan*), Carin Lundeqvist (*A servant girl*), Svea Bruce (*Lovisa*), Marianne Lindberg (*First maid*), Gittan Larsson (*Second maid*), Wilma Malmlöf (*Boarding-house landlady*), Mats Bjärne (*An officer*), Åke Svensson (*Postman*), Axel Högel (*Boatswain*), Hans Stråat (*Second in command*), Hans Sundberg (*The helmsman*). (GIFTAS) Anita Björk (*General's daughter*), Anders Henrikson (*Albert*), Elsa Carlsson (*Aunt Emilia*),

Edvin Adolphson (*The General*), Gerda Lundequist (*Her Royal Highness*), Holger Löwenadler (*The lecturer*), Ragnar Arvedson (*Lt-colonel*), Gösta Cederlund (*The colonel*), Gull Natorp (*Colonel's wife*), Linnéa Hallberg (*Malin*), Inger Juel (*Professor's wife*), Astrid Bodin (*Lova*), Ingemar Pallin (*Lt. A*), Herman Ahlsell, Leif Hedenberg (*Officers*), Curt Löwgren (*Postman*), Carl-Gunnar Wingård (*Fat lecturer*), Renée Björling (*Elderly lady*), Olle Ekblad (*Steward*), Ellika Mann (*A girl*), Märta Dorff, Signe Wirff, Nancy Dalunde (*Three aunts*), Edvin Fredriksson (*Teacher*), Håkan Westergren (*Drawing-master*), Olle Hilding (*Farm hand*), Emy Storm (*Lady's maid*). 132 mins. For Europa Film.

PLOT: (ETT DOCKHEM / A DOLL'S HOUSE) Captain Pall lives happily with his attractive wife Gurli. During a long voyage he finds that the letters from Gurli are changing. They are becoming more impersonal and religious, and he discovers that she is influenced by Ottilia, a blue stocking. When he arrives home, Gurli's bedroom is closed to him, and she talks about spiritual values. In desperation Pall turns to Gurli's mother for advice. He also starts flirting with Ottilia under the pretence of teaching her astronomy and mathematics. The plan succeeds perfectly. Gurli gets jealous and her friendship with Ottilia cools off. Pall's former marital bliss is restored.

(GIFTAS/MARRIED LIFE) Helene, a General's daughter, loses her mother early and grows up in masculine, isolated, and snooty surroundings. She begins to detest sex when she happens to see two horses mating, and she decides never to marry. When the General dies she finds herself ruined, and her friends turn away from her. She takes a more critical attitude to society and becomes a blue stocking, but finds that she is ignored as long as she is unmarried. Without loving him she marries a lecturer from Uppsala. When he wants to sleep with her she at first refuses, but later develops into a cunning erotic blackmailer. Her husband understands it, but he loves her, and he needs her. Together they survive in their vicious circle.

● 83 GREDE, KJELL (1936-   ). B: Stockholm. Director. Also journalist, writer, teacher, and spare-time painter. Married to Bibi Andersson (q.v.). Made one short (*The Chimney Sweep*, 1966) before *Hugo and Josefin*, a children's film that earned him awards and international recognition. Also scripted *Carnival*. Films: *Hugo and Josefin* 67; *Gay Harry* 69.

● 84 GREVENIUS, HERBERT (1901-   ). B: Stockholm. Scriptwriter. Author of plays for stage and radio. At first journalist and critic. Head of the Radio Theatre 1950-57. Since 1966: engaged by the Royal Dramatic Theatre, Stockholm. Notable for his frequent collaboration with Ingmar Bergman (q.v.). Films: *The Clock at Rönneberga* (co.), *Like Most People* (co., responsible for dialogue), *It Rains on Our Love/Man with*

an *Umbrella* (co. Bergman), *A Soldier's Duties, Foreign Harbour, Thirst/Three Strange Loves, This Can't Happen Here* (co.), *Summer Interlude/Illicit Interlude* (co. Bergman), *Divorced* (co. Bergman), *U-boat 39, She Came like a Wind, We Three Are Making Our Début* (co. Olof Molander), *The "Lunchbreak" Café, A Little Place of One's Own, The Girl in a Dress-Coat* (56).

● 85 GRÖNBERG, ÅKE (1914-1969). B: Stockholm. Actor. Stout and expressive lead in *Sawdust and Tinsel/The Naked Night.* Supporting roles elsewhere. Films: *Towards New Times, The Melody from the Old Town, We from Sunny Glade, Brave Boys in Uniform, The Merry-Go-Round in Full Swing, Everybody at His Station, Our Boys in Uniform, Boys from the South of Stockholm, Our Gang, A Sailor in a Dress-coat, Tomorrow's Melody, The Yellow Ward, A Singing Girl, People of Roslagen, Take Care of Ulla, Nothing Will Be Forgotten, Woman Takes Command, Lack of Evidence, The Halta Lotta Tavern, Captivated by a Voice, Anna Lans, Young Blood, Sonja, Count the Happy Moments Only, Watch Out for Spies!, Marie in the Windmill, Girls in the Harbour, In the Beautiful Province of Roslagen, The Girls from Småland, The Six Karlssons, Brita in the Wholesaler's House, Between Brothers, A Woman on Board, Handsome Augusta, The Song about Stockholm, Woman without a Face, Navvies, The Night Watchman's Wife, Each Goes His Own Way, Life Begins Now, Dangerous Spring, The Intimate Restaurant, The Kiss on the Cruise, The Beef and the Banana, Ingenious Johansson, Skipper in Stormy Weather, Blondie the Beef and the Banana, She Came like a Wind, Summer with Monika, People on Manoeuvres, Barabbas, We Three Are Making Our Début, Sawdust and Tinsel/The Naked Night, Merry Boys of the Navy, Seven Black Brassières, Never with My Jemmy, Storm* over *Tjurö, A Lesson in Love, Sir Arne's Treasure* (54), *Simon the Sinner, Dolls and Balls, Beat It, Dangerous Freedom, The Merry-Go-Round in the Mountains, Paradise, Rasmus and the Tramp, The Matrimonial Advertisement, The Tough Game, Encounters at Dusk, Klarar Bananen Biffen?, Line Six, Pirates on Lake Mälar, Private 91 Karlsson Is Demobbed or So He Thinks* (also dir. 60), *Adam and Eve, My Love Is a Rose, 491, Loving Couples, Sailors and Sextants, A Summer Adventure.*

● 86 .GYCKLARNAS AFTON/SAW-DUST AND TINSEL/THE NAKED NIGHT. 1954. Script and Direction: Ingmar Bergman. Photography: Sven Nykvist (interiors), Hilding Bladh (exteriors). Editing: Carl-Olov Skeppstedt. Music: Karl-Birger Blomdahl. Art Direction: Bibi Lindström. Players: Åke Grönberg (*Albert Johansson*), Harriet Andersson (*Anne*), Hasse Ekman (*Frans*), Anders Ek (*Teodor Frost*), Gudrun Brost (*Frost's wife*), Annika Tretow

Hasse Ekman and Harriet Andersson in SAWDUST AND TINSEL

(*Agda, Albert's wife*), Gunnar Björn-strand (*Sjuberg*), Erik Strandmark (*Jens*), Kiki (*The Dwarf*), Åke Fridell (*The Officer*). 90 mins. For Sandrews (Rune Waldekranz).

PLOT: Albert Johansson is the corpulent owner of a travelling circus. His mistress is Anne, a voluptuous equestrienne in the Alberti troupe. The circus stops for a one-night stand at a town in southern Skåne. While Albert visits his wife and has his plea for a revival of their marriage rejected, Anne is callously seduced by Frans, a young actor in the town. During the gala performance given by the circus that evening, Frans taunts Albert about his liaison with Anne. There is a bloody fight in the ring. Albert is severely beaten.

He tries to shoot himself in his caravan, but the revolver does not fire properly, and, lacking the nerve to try a second time, Albert shoots the circus bear in its cage instead. As the troupe moves off at dawn, Albert is seen trudging along with Anne behind the caravans, with the whining of the circus music in the background.

● 87 GYLLENSPETZ, ANN-MARIE (1932-   ). B: Göteborg. Actress. At first mostly theatre work. Modest, observant blonde. Films: *No Man's Woman, Yellow Squadron, Simon the Sinner, The Pawn Shop, The Tough Game, The Shining Light from Lund, Song of the Scarlet Flower* (56), *As You Make Your Bed, Encounters at Dusk, The Clergyman*

54

from Uddarbo, So Close to Life/Brink of Life, Travel to Sun and Spring, Laila, We on Väddö, A Lion in Town, Love 65, Who Saw Him Die?, The Pig Hunt.

● 88 GÖSTA BERLINGS SAGA/ THE SAGA OF GÖSTA BERLING/ ATONEMENT OF GÖSTA BERLING 1924. Script: Mauritz Stiller and Ragnar Hyltén-Cavallius, from the novel by Selma Lagerlöf. Direction: Mauritz Stiller. Photography: Julius Jaenzon. Art Direction: Ragnar Brattén and Vilhelm Bryde. Players: Lars Hanson (*Gösta Berling*), Gerda Lundeqvist (*The Wife of Major Samszelius*), Hilda Forslund (*Her mother*), Otto Elg-Lundberg (*Major Samszelius*), Sixten Malmerfeldt (*Melchior Sinclair*), Karin Swanström (*Gustava, his wife*), Jenny Hasselquist (*Marianne, their daughter*), Ellen Cederström (*Countess Märta Dohna*), Mona Mårtensson (*Countess Ebba Dohna*), Torsten Hammarén (*Count Henry, her son*), Greta Garbo (*Elisabeth, his wife*), Sven Scholander (*Sintram*), Svend Kornbaeck (*Captain Kristian Bergh*), Hugo Rönnblad (*Beerencreutz*), Knut Lambert (*Rutger von Örneclou*), Oscar Bergström (*Julius*), Gaston Portefaix (*Major Anders Fuchs*), Albert Stahl (*Uncle Eberhard*), Anton de Verdier (*Cousin Kristoffer*), Axel Jacobsson (*Lilliencrona*), Jan de Mayere (*Löwenborg*), Edmund Hodendorf (*Kevenheuler*). 4,534 metres. For Svensk Filmindustri.

PLOT: Gösta Berling is a defrocked minister who is tutor to a young girl, Ebba Dohna. Ebba's mother thinks that Gösta is a good man in spite of his behaviour. Gösta leaves the Dohna family and becomes a "cavalier" at Ekeby Manor. He is one of the irresponsible gentlemen who have been given a refuge there by a Major's wife. When Gösta is on the brink of committing suicide, he is saved by the Major's wife. After a quarrel with the Major, she is driven away and the cavaliers assume control of Ekeby.

Gösta falls in love with the beautiful Marianne Sinclair and takes her to Ekeby, but her beauty is ruined by an attack of smallpox. Angry people set fire to Ekeby, and Gösta rescues Marianne, but now she wants to return to her home. Gösta meets Elisabeth Dohna and she reforms him. Finally, the Major's wife gives the couple her blessings as well as Ekeby Manor, and Gösta sets about rebuilding the house.

● 89 HALLDOFF, JAN (1939-   ). B: Stockholm. Director. Began as press photographer on *491, The Dress, To Love,* and *My Sister My Love* (co.). Also TV work. An energetic young director with an acute and sympathetic understanding of the pop movement and the younger generation. Acted in *Well, Well, Well* and *Me and You.* Co-scripted all his own films. Shorts: *Leffe and I, Rest Period 64; Nilsson 66.* Features: *The Myth 65; Life's Just Great, Ola & Julia 67; The Corridor 68; A Dream of Freedom 69.*

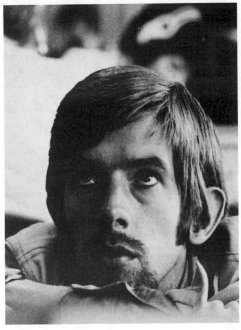

romance and sadness marking all her roles. Films: *The Ballet Primadonna, Sumurun* (in Germany, dir. Ernst Lubitsch), *Johan, The Exiles, Love's Crucible, Fire on Board, The Suitor from the Roads, The Saga of Gösta Berling, The Ingmar Inheritance, To the Orient, My Wife Has a Fiancé, Children of the Storm, Say It with Music, The Dangerous Game.*

• 92 HASSO, SIGNE (1915-   ). B: Stockholm. Actress. 1932-34: trained at Royal Dramatic Theatre, Stockholm. From 1934: acting in various theatres. 1940-50: Hollywood. 1957: Broadway. Hard and cool actress best known for her Hollywood roles (*The House on Ninety-Second Street, A Scandal in Paris* etc.). Films in Sweden: *House of Silence* (under maiden name of Signe Larsson), *Witches' Night, Career, Money from the Sky, The Two of Us, Emilie Högquist, Song of the Wild, Steel, A Big Hug, The Three of Us, Bright Prospects, This Can't Happen Here, Taxi 13, Gentle Thief of Love* (co-prod. with U.S.A.).

• 93 HELL, ERIK (1911-   ). B: Kalliokoski (Finland). Actor. 1939-42: trained at Royal Dramatic Theatre, Stockholm. Since 1966: engaged there. Has appeared at various other theatres in Sweden. Consistent supporting player in many familiar films, although his most forceful role was surely the scout in *The Bread of Love*. Films: *Ride Tonight!, The Road to Heaven, The Royal Hunt, The Clock at Rönneberga, The Invisible Wall, Between Us Thieves, Money, The Balloon, When Meadows Bloom, Bareback, The Most Beautiful Thing on Earth, A Ship Bound for India, On These Shoulders, Port of Call, The Realm of Man, Stora Hopare Lane and Heaven, One Summer of Happiness, U-boat 39, A Dull Clang, Because of My Hot Youth, Barabbas, The Bread of Love, The Chief from Göinge, Enchanted Walk, Storm over Tjurö, The Witch* (co-prod. with France), *Rider in*

• 90 HANSON, LARS (1886-1965). B: Göteborg. Actor. 1906: trained at Royal Dramatic Theatre, Stockholm. 1915: film *début*. Tall, handsome leading man of the silent era, who went to Hollywood to star with Lillian Gish in *The Scarlet Letter* and *The Wind* (both directed by Victor Sjöström, q.v.). Married to Karin Molander (q.v.). Films: *The Dagger, The Gold Spider, The Wings, Thérèse, A Girl from the Marsh Croft, The Ballet Primadonna, Synnöve Solbakken* (19), *Song of the Scarlet Flower* (19), *A Dangerous Proposal, Erotikon, Fishing Village, The Exiles, The Saga of Gösta Berling, The Ingmar Inheritance, To the Orient, Sin, Walpurgis Night, On the Sunny Side, Conflict, Wings around the Lighthouse, First Division, Ride Tonight!, There Burned a Flame, His Excellency, Unto the Gates of Hell.*

• 91 HASSELQVIST, JENNY (1894-   ). B: Stockholm. Actress. Primarily a ballet dancer, she also appeared in some important silent films. She was considered a genuine Swedish type, with a trace of

and *Night Journey.*

Blue, *The Summer Night Is Sweet, Mother of Pearl, The Wonderful Adventures of Nils, Yes He Has Been with Me, 491, Dear John, Morianna, I—A Woman, The Island, The Murderer—an Ordinary Person, The Slipper, The Vicious Circle, Waltz of Sex, Odd Lovers, The Rite* (for TV), *Carmilla, A Passion.*

● 94 HELLBOM, OLLE (1925-   ). B: Stockholm. Director. 1948-50: Head of advertising films division at Nordisk Tonefilm. Shorts include the excellent 1952 documentary on Axel Petersson's wood sculpture, *Döderhultare,* and *Dalmålningar* (1958). Also TV work. Now best known for his children's feature films, mostly produced by Olle Nordemar. Films: *The Master Detective Leads a Dangerous Life* 57; *Blackjackets* (also scripted) 59; *All We Children from Bullerbyn* 60; *Only Fun at Bullerbyn* 61; *Tjorven Boatswain and Moses* 64; *Tjorven and Skrållen* 65; *Tjorven and Mysak* 66; *Skrållan Ruskprick and Knorrhane* 67. Hellbom also scripted: *When Love Came to the Village* (co.), *Marianna,*

● 95 HELLSTRÖM, GUNNAR (1928-   ). B: Alnö. Actor and director. Joined the well-known Terserus drama school and then trained at Royal Dramatic Theatre, Stockholm. 1954: *début* as film director. 1961: to Hollywood. Writes the scripts of all his own films except *Chans.* Efficient director, ardent player. Films as actor: *While the City Sleeps, U-boat 39, She Came like a Wind, Barabbas, Chief from Göinge, Marianne, Karin Månsdotter, The Judge, The Job, Carnival, Nightmare.* Films as director: *Simon the Sinner* (also acted) 55; *Children of the Night* (also acted) 56; *Synnöve Solbakken* (also acted) 57; *Just Once More* (*Chans*) 62.

● 96 HEMSÖBORNA/THE PEOPLE OF HEMSÖ. 1955. Script: Rune Lindström, from the novel by August Strindberg. Direction: Arne Mattsson. Photography (Eastmancolor): Max Wilén. Editing: Lennart Lindgren. Music:

Sven Sköld. Art Direction: Bibi Lind-ström. Players: Erik Strandmark (*Carls-son*), Hjördis Pettersson (*Mrs. Flod*), Nils Hallberg (*Gusten*), John Norman (*Rundquist*), Curt Löwgren (*Norman*), Birgitta Pettersson (*Lotten*), Ulla Sjö-blom (*Clara*), Margit Carlquist (*Ida*), Douglas Håge (*Pastor Nordström*), Georg Rydeberg (*The Professor*). For Nordisk Tonefilm.

PLOT: Carlsson, a farmer from Värm-land, comes to the island of Hemsö to look after Mrs. Flod's land. Mrs. Flod has recently been left a widow, and her son Gusten, and the farm-hands, Rund-quist and Norman, show little interest in the estate. They dislike Carlsson, and sus-pect that he is eager to lay his hands on the mother's hidden savings. They also dislike his efficient farming methods, which are mostly at their expense. In spite of Gusten's intervention, and of a brief flir-tation with a maid, Ida, Carlsson manages to persuade Mrs. Flod to marry him. There is a lavish wedding reception, at which the local priest falls dead drunk under the table. Winter comes. Mrs. Flod alters her will in favour of her new hus-band. But she begins to suspect that Carls-son is carrying on with Clara, another maid. She contracts a severe cold, and on her deathbed she realises what a rascal Carlsson really is. She asks Gusten to burn her will. Her coffin is dragged over the ice to the church, but a terrible snow-storm is raging, and when the ice sud-denly cracks, Carlsson is dragged beneath it after the coffin itself, while the others run for their lives.

● 97 HENNING, EVA (1920-   ). B: New York. Actress. 1938-40: trained at Royal Dramatic Theatre, Stockholm. Since 1958: working in Norway. The personification of bitter romance in the late Forties, especially in *Prison* and *Thirst*. At one time married to Hasse Ek-man (q.v.). Films: *Gentleman for Hire, We Are All Errand Boys, Boys from the*

South of Stockholm, Bright Prospects, Only a Woman, Scanian Guerilla, It Is My Music, General von Döbeln, Elvira Madigan (43), The Awakening of Youth, Stop! Think of Something Else, The Royal Rabble, Wandering with the Moon, The Rose of Thistle Island, One Swallow Doesn't Make a Summer, The Banquet, Prison/The Devil's Wanton, Thirst/ Three Strange Loves, The Girl from the Gallery, Girl with Hyacinths, The White Cat, The Fire Bird, Hidden in the Fog, Unmarried, Gabrielle, The Decimals of Love, The Black Palm Trees.

● 98 HENRIKSON, ANDERS (1896-1965). B: Stockholm. Actor and director. At first studied music. 1915-16: trained at Royal Dramatic Theatre, Stockholm. Directed several stage plays and operas as well as films. Henrikson's *A Crime* (q.v.) was the signal for a renaissance in Swedish cinema during the Forties. He was also a powerful actor, impressing as the Count in *Miss Julie* (q.v.) and as the self-cen-tred husband in his own version of Strind-berg's *Married Life* (q.v.). Films as director (sometimes co-scripted† and act-ed* also): *The Girl from the Department Store* (co. Torsten Lundqvist) 33; *Your Relatives Are Worst, It Pays to Advertise*, *He She and the Money*, *Privates 65 66 and I 36; Oh What a Night** 37; *The Great Love*†*, *Only a Trumpeter**, *Thunder and Lightning* 38; *Whalers* 39; *A Crime*†*, *The Björck Family, Everybody* *at His Station*†* 40; *Only a Woman*†*, *Life Goes On*†* 41; *Dangerous Roads**, *The Ingegerd Bremssen Case**, *Youth in Chains** 42; *Mr. Collin's Adventures*†* 43; *Train 56**, *I Am Fire and Air** 44; *Nothing but Old Nobility*†*, *Blood and Fire**, *Tired Teodor** 45; *Åsa-Hanna** 46; *The Most Beautiful Thing on Earth**, *The Key and the Ring** 47; *The Girl*

Birgitta Pettersson and (in background) Ulla Sjöblom in THE PEOPLE OF HEMSÖ

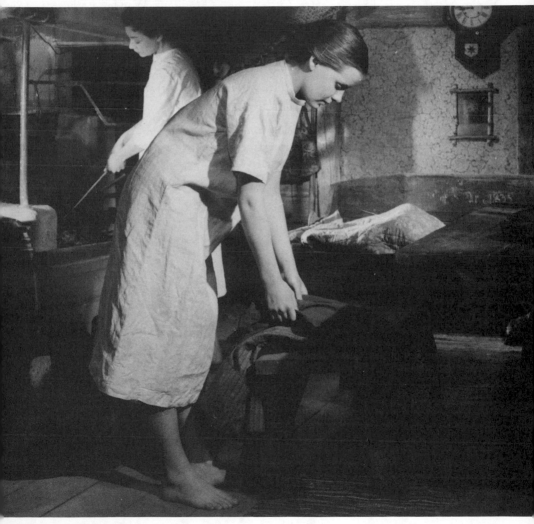

59

from the Mountain Village 48; Married Life* 57. Films as actor only: Sir Arne's Treasure (19, as extra only), The Strongest, The Song of the Scarlet Flower (34), Alfred Loved by the Girls, Walpurgis Night, 33.333, Intermezzo, Conflict, A Cold in the Head, John Ericsson—the Victor at Hampton Roads, Let's Have Success, With the People for the Country, Mr. Karlsson Mate and His Sweethearts, A Woman's Face, Rejoice while You Are Young, At the Lady's Service, Her Little Majesty, They Staked Their Lives, Home from Babylon, The Road to Heaven, I Killed, Prison/The Devil's Wanton, Miss Julie (51), Defiance, Love, The Journey to You, The Road to Klockrike, Barabbas, Sir Arne's Treasure (54), The Girl in a Dress-coat (56), The Clergyman from Uddarbo, The Boy in the Tree, Morianna.

● 99 HERR ARNES PENGAR/SIR ARNE'S TREASURE. 1919. Script: Gustaf Molander and Mauritz Stiller from the novel by Selma Lagerlöf. Direction: Mauritz Stiller. Photography: Julius Jaenzon. Art Direction: Harry Dahlström. Players: Hjalmar Selander (Sir Arne), Concordia Selander (His wife), Richard Lund (Sir Archie), Mary Johnson (Elsalill), Wanda Rothgardt (Sir Arne's daughter), Axel Nilsson (Torarin), Stina Berg (Hostess), Erik Stocklassa (Sir Reginald), Bror Berger (Sir Filip), Gustaf Aronson (The Captain), Dagmar Ebbesen (Torarin's mother), Gösta Gustafsson (Clergyman). 2,219 metres. For Svenska Bio.

Richard Lund with Mary Johnson in SIR ARNE'S TREASURE

PLOT: In the Sixteenth century rebellious Scottish mercenaries are driven out of Sweden. Their leaders are imprisoned, but three of them escape and try to reach the port of Marstrand, where they hope to find a ship for Scotland. On their flight they come to a rich farm, Solberga, which they burn down after stealing Sir Arne's treasure and killing the people in the house. But one has escaped—the young Elsalill who has seen the soldiers murder her little sister.

The sea is frozen and the soldiers are waiting at Marstrand. Elsalill is brought there and falls in love with the handsome Sir Archie, never suspecting that he is her sister's murderer. But suddenly she realises who he is. Sir Archie tries to flee to the vessel and uses Elsalill as a shield. She is killed on a spear, and the women of Marstrand bear her corpse from the vessel in a long procession over the ice.

- 100 HETS/FRENZY/TORMENT. 1944. Script: Ingmar Bergman. Direction: Alf Sjöberg. Photography: Martin Bodin. Editing: Oscar Rosander. Music: Hilding Rosenberg. Art Direction: Arne Åkermark. Players: Stig Järrel (*Caligula*), Alf Kjellin (*Jan-Erik Widgren*), Mai Zetterling (*Bertha Olsson*), Olof Winnerstrand (*The Principal*), Gösta Cederlund (*Pippi*), Stig Olin (*Sandman*), Jan Molander (*Pettersson*), Olav Riego (*Mr. Widgren*), Märta Arbin (*His wife*), Hugo Björne (*The Physician*), Gunnar Björnstrand (*A Teacher*), Curt Edgard, Anders Nyström, Birger Malmsten. 101 mins. For Svensk Filmindustri.

PLOT: Jan-Erik is a pupil at high school in Stockholm. He is viciously humiliated in class by one of his teachers, who is nicknamed "Caligula." One day, after lessons, he meets Bertha in a tobacconist's, and later finds her wandering round the city in a drunken depression. She leads him home to her room and persuades him to spend the night there, telling him how she fears that a strange,

sinister man is constantly following her. Jan-Erik falls desperately in love with Bertha, and they continue to meet in spite of his parents' opposition and the imminence of his matriculation exams. One evening Jan-Erik arrives to find Bertha dead in her room. Caligula is hiding pathetically in the hallway. He is obviously responsible for the tragedy, but an autopsy suggests that Bertha died of a weak heart. Caligula is released, and sees to it that Jan-Erik is prevented from sitting his exams. Jan-Erik watches the matriculation ceremony, and then sets about earning a living. The school Principal visits him and offers him any help he may need.

- 101 HIMLASPELET/THE ROAD TO HEAVEN. 1942. Script: Alf Sjöberg and Rune Lindström, from the play by the latter. Direction: Alf Sjöberg. Photography: Gösta Roosling. Editing: Oscar Rosander. Music: Lillebror Söderlundh. Art Direction: Arne Åkermark. Players: Rune Lindström (*Mats Ersson*), Eivor Landström (*Marit Knutsdotter*), Gudrun Brost (*Solomon's wench*), Anders Henrikson (*Good Father*), Arnold Sjöstrand (*Rood Painter*), Holger Löwenadler (*Solomon*), Emil Fjellström (*Gammel-Jerk*), Björn Berglund (*Josef*), Inga-Lilly Forsström (*Maria*), Anita Björk (*Anna*). 106 mins. For Wivefilm.

PLOT: Mats is a young, rather naïve farmer from the province of Dalarna. He is in love with Marit, a girl who is pure in heart. But soon their idyll is threatened. Marit's purity and happiness arouse the jealousy of her neighbours, and rumours are spread that she is a witch. She dies just before she is to be burnt at the stake, and Mats, outraged, sets out on the road to heaven to demand justice on her behalf. It is a long journey, and many things happen to Mats. But ultimately he fails. He becomes an evildoer, because God has allowed an innocent girl to be sacrificed. He dies as a rich and lonely man who has

Above: Rune Lindström in THE ROAD TO HEAVEN (with Arnold Sjöstrand).
Below right: Keve Hjelm

lost his soul, only to be reprieved by the Good Father and to awake in the fields beside his long-lost *fiancée*.

● 102 HJELM, KEVE (1922-   ). B: Gnesta. Actor. Has worked as star and director at the major municipal theatres of Sweden, and on screen generally plays the cautious, watchful middle-aged man with emotional problems. Films: *When Meadows Bloom, A Soldier's Duties, A Girl from the Marsh Croft* (47), *Navvies, On These Shoulders, The Street, The Woman Who Disappeared, Girl with Hyacinths, Helen of Troy, The Merry Boys of the Navy, A Dreamer's Walk, Children of the Night* (56), *We on Väddö, Hide and Seek, Murder Weapon for*

Sale, Raven's End, Love 65, Night Games, Roseanna, The Sinning Urge/Burnt Child, Life's Just Great, Waltz of Sex, The Swedish Fanny Hill, Teddy Bear, Like Night and Day, The Pig Hunt.

● 103 HON DANSADE EN SOMMAR/ONE SUMMER OF HAPPINESS. 1951. Script: Wolodja Semitjov, from the novel by Per Olof Ekström. Direction: Arne Mattsson. Photography: Göran Strindberg. Editing: Lennart Wallén. Music: Sven Sköld. Art Direction: Bibi Lindström. Players: Folke Sundquist (*Göran*), Ulla Jacobsson (*Kerstin*), Edvin Adolphson (*Anders Persson*), Irma Christenson (*Sigrid*), Gösta Gustavsson (*Berndt Larsson*), Berta Hall (*Anna*),

John Elfström (*The Clergyman*), Erik Hell (*Torsten*), Nils Hallberg (*Nisse*), Sten Maltsson (*Olle*), Arne Källerud (*Viberg*), Gunvor Pontén (*Sylvia*), Hedvig Lindby (*The grandmother*), Axel Högel (*The grandfather*), Sten Lindgren (*Stendal*). 93 mins. For Nordisk Tonefilm.

PLOT: When Göran has graduated from college, he goes for a rest on his uncle Anders Persson's farm. There he meets Kerstin, a neighbour's daughter. The young people of the village are at odds with the local clergyman, who attacks their way of life. Although the vicar is supported by Kerstin's aunt and uncle, he is defied by Anders Persson, who allows the youngsters to meet regularly in

Folke Sundquist and Ulla Jacobsson in ONE SUMMER OF HAPPINESS

Eddie Axberg (at right, with Stig Törnblom) in HERE IS YOUR LIFE

one of his barns. Göran and Kerstin fall wildly in love, and when his uncle is hurt in an accident, Göran assumes responsibility for the farm. But Kerstin's aunt discovers the young lovers in the attic one night during a storm. Kerstin is sent away, but Göran finds out where she is staying, and they become lovers. Despite the opposition of his parents, Göran returns to the farm and one evening after putting on a show for the local folk, they go home together on Göran's motorcycle. There is a crash, and Kerstin dies. The vicar inveighs against him at the funeral, and Göran rushes away from the service, trying to console himself with his memories.

• 104 HÄR HAR DU DITT LIV/ HERE IS YOUR LIFE. 1966. Script: Bengt Forslund and Jan Troell from

"The Story of Olof" by Eyvind Johnson. Direction, Photography and Editing: Jan Troell. Music: Erik Nordgren. Art Direction: Rolf Boman. Players: Eddie Axberg (*Olof*), Gudrun Brost (*Foster mother*), Ulla Akselson (*Mother*), Holger Löwenadler (*Kristiansson*), Allan Edwall (*August*), Anna Maria Blind (*His wife*), Max von Sydow (*Smålands-Pelle*), Ulf Palme (*Larsson*), Jan-Erik Lindqvist (*Johansson*), Gunnar Björnstrand (*Lundgren*), Signe Stade (*Maria*), Stig Törnblom (*Fredrik*), Åke Fridell (*Nicke Larsson*), Ulla Sjöblom (*Olivia*), Friedrich Ochsner (*The Smith*), Catharina Edfeldt (*Maja*), Ulla Blomstrand (*Efrisina*), Per Oscarsson (*Niklas*), Bengt Ekerot (*Byberg*). 167 mins. For Svensk Filmindustri.

PLOT: It is 1914 in Norrbotten, in northern Sweden. Olof is fourteen and leaves his foster mother in order to learn a trade. He gets his first job as a log floater. Later in the autumn he is taken on at a brickworks and in the winter he moves to a sawmill. In the spring of 1916 he is given a post as a bill sticker and sweet seller at a cinema in Boden. Lundgren is in charge of the cinema, and soon he promotes Olof to be projectionist. As such he goes on tour round Norrland during the summer from one fair to another, screening films for local audiences. Back at Boden, he quarrels with Lundgren after selling some socialist pamphlets, and he is fired. For a short time he lives with Olivia, "Queen of the Rifle Range," whom he met while touring the fairs. But he reads more and more, and comes into closer contact with the labour movement. After being out of work for a period, he finds a job on the railways. He forms a union with one of his workmates, Niklas, but a strike they arrange is a failure, and, disillusioned, Olof sets off again, this time heading south.

● 105 INGEBORG HOLM/GIVE US THIS DAY. 1913. Script and Direction: Victor Sjöström, from the play by Nils Krook. Photography: Henrik Jaenzon. Players: Hilda Borgström (*Ingeborg Holm*), Eric Lindholm, Georg Grönroos, William Larsson, Aron Lindgren, Richard Lund. 2,006 metres. For Svenska Bio.

PLOT: Ingeborg Holm is happily married and has three children with her husband, a hard-working grocer. Suddenly he falls ill and dies of tuberculosis. Mrs. Holm tries to run the little shop, but she is too inexperienced and goes bankrupt. Due to illness and poverty she has to turn to the workhouse. As she is not allowed to bring her children there, they are "sold" by auction.

When Mrs. Holm hears that one of her daughters is ill, she runs away from the workhouse to visit her. The girl dies and Mrs. Holm is brought back to the workhouse, but the shock has affected her mentally. She carries a rag-doll or a piece of wood in her arms, believing them to be children. Her case is considered hopeless, but some years later her son, now a sailor, returns and brings her back to sanity.

● 106 INTERMEZZO. 1936. Script: Gustaf Molander and Gösta Stevens. Direction: Gustaf Molander. Photography: Åke Dahlquist. Music: Heinz Provost (song). Players: Gösta Ekman (*Professor Holger Brandt*), Ingrid Bergman (*Anita Hoffmann*), Inga Tidblad (*Holger's wife*), Hasse Ekman (*His son*), Erik Berglund. For Svensk Filmindustri.

Gösta Ekman and Ingrid Bergman in INTERMEZZO

PLOT: The "Kungsholm" is approaching Vinga lighthouse off Göteborg. On board is Professor Holger Brandt, a Swedish violinist of world renown, who is returning home after a two-year tour. He is about forty-five, tall and slender, impulsive and cultured. In Stockholm he is reunited with his wife and two children. The home atmosphere strikes him as excessively bourgeois, and he tries to persuade his wife to accompany him on a tour, but she has to think of the children. Professor Brandt falls in love with Anita Hoffmann, his daughter's music teacher. He admires her youth and talent. She tries to go away but he has already confessed to his wife, so they are both free—and lonely. Professor Brandt continues to travel, but finally he comes back to his home and his family. Anita has left him and embarked on an independent artistic career.

● 107 IRIS OCH LÖJTNANTS-HJÄRTA/IRIS AND THE LIEUTEN-ANT/IRIS. 1946. Script: Alf Sjöberg and Olle Hedberg, from the latter's novel. Direction: Alf Sjöberg. Photography: Gösta Roosling. Music: Lars-Erik Larsson. Art Direction: Arne Åkermark. Players: Mai Zetterling (*Iris*), Alf Kjellin (*Robert*), Holger Löwenadler (*Baltzar*), Margareta Fahlén (*Greta*), Åke Claesson (*Oscar*), Ingrid Borthen (*Mary*), Einar Axelsson (*Frans*), Stig Järrel (*Harald*). 86 mins. For Svensk Filmindustri.

PLOT: The young lieutenant, Robert Motander, exasperates his family and his domineering father in particular, by falling in love with a maid, Iris. Dynastic and financial ambitions dictate that he should marry a wealthy heiress of the Wolfram line. Then he is killed unexpectedly in a road accident. Iris is shattered. She is pregnant, and Robert's elder brother, Baltzar, behaves kindly and offers to find her a more respectable position, although obviously he is anxious for the family to

be rid of embarrassment. But Iris returns to her post as maid to the elderly Baroness von Asp, proud in her resolution to bring up her child alone.

● 108 ISAKSSON, ULLA (1916-). B: Stockholm. Scriptwriter, better known as a novelist and short story writer. She collaborated on the script of *Siska* with Vilgot Sjöman. Films based on her work, some also scripted* by her: *House of Women, So Close to Life/Brink of Life** (from a story in her collection *The Aunt of Death*, published in 1954), *The Virgin Spring**, *The Dress**.

● 109 ISEDAL, TOR (1924-). B: Norrköping. Actor. Various stage appearances. A regular on TV since 1959. 1964-66: Municipal Theatre, Stockholm. Since Bergman brought him to prominence with *The Virgin Spring* (q.v.), as one of the rapists, he has often been typecast as a heavy. His acting style has immense authority. Films: *She Came like a Wind, Barabbas, Girl without a Name, The Virgin Spring, The Job, Lady in White, The Doll, One Zero Too Many, Siska, Hide and Seek, You Must Be Crazy Darling!, Wedding—Swedish Style, Morianna, The Serpent, I Need a Woman, Roseanna, What a Beautiful Day, Odd Lovers.*

● 110 JACOBSSON, ULLA (1929-). B: Göteborg. Actress. Like nearly every Swedish star, Miss Jacobsson was trained in the theatre, but in recent years she has appeared in several foreign films, in West Germany, France, and Britain (*Zulu, The Heroes of Telemark* etc.). Her success was founded on *One Summer of Happiness,* where she played opposite Folke Sundquist (q.v.). Films: *Rolling Sea, One Summer of Happiness, All the Joy of Earth, Karin Månsdotter, Sir*

films of Sjöström and Stiller (both q.v.) would never have been so famous. Films in Sweden (probably incomplete): *Regina von Emmeritz and Gustavus Adolphus, The Wedding at Ulfåsa, The Iron-Carrier, The Opium Den* (also dir. 11), *Condemned by Society* (also dir. 12), *Uncle John's Arrival in Stockholm* (also dir. 12), *The Vagabond's Galoshes* (co-dir. Magnusson 12), *Laban Petterqvist Training for the Olympic Games, The Green Necklace, The Adventures of Two Swedish Emigrants in America* (also dir. 12), *Agaton and Fina* (also dir. 12), *The Gardener, Breakers* or *Stolen Happiness, Mother and Daughter, The Black Masks, In the Spring of Life, The Vampire, The Marriage Bureau, Smiles and Tears, When Love Kills, When the Alarm Bell Rings, The Child, Lady Marion's Summer Flirtation, The Model, The Voice of Blood, On the Fateful Roads of Life, Life's Conflicts, The Clergyman, Love Stronger than Hate, The Brothers, People of the Border* (co.), *The Miracle, The Chamberlain, Stormy Petrel, The Shot, The Red Tower, Daughter of the High Mountain, The*

Arne's Treasure (54), *Smiles of a Summer Night, The Song of the Scarlet Flower* (56), *The Phantom Carriage* (58), *There Came Two Men* (in Spain), *Nightmare, Teddy Bear.*

● 111 JAENZON, JULIUS (1885-1961). B: Göteborg. The finest lighting cameraman of his generation, with over a hundred credits. 1910: joined Svenska Bio. Also worked under pseudonym of J. Julius. His brother Henrik Jaenzon photographed several famous films of the silent period too. JJ was a pioneer in location photography and a sympathetic instructor at the Svensk Filmindustri studios for decades. Without his resplendent camerawork, the

Strike, When Artists Love, His Wife's Past, Ace of Thieves, The First Prize, Judas Money, Madame de Thèbes, The Dagger, The Governor's Daughters, Sea Vultures, The Wings, Thérèse, The Ballet Primadonna, Kiss of Death, Terje Vigen, Alexander the Great, The Outlaw and His Wife, The Sons of Ingmar (Pts I and II), *The Song of the Scarlet Flower* (co. ?), *Sir Arne's Treasure, The Downy Girl* (co-dir. Ivan Hedqvist 19), *The Executioner* (?), *The Phantom Carriage/ Thy Soul Shall Bear Witness, Love's Crucible, Gunnar Hede's Saga, Fire on Board* (co.), *The Merry-Go-Round, The Saga of Gösta Berling, Life in the Country, Two Kings, The Ingmar Inheritance, To the Orient, She the Only One, His English Wife, Sealed Lips, Women of Paris, Sin, Say It with Music* (also co-dir. Edvin Adolphson), *Triumph of the Heart, For Her Sake, Ulla My Ulla* (also dir. 30), *Markurells i Wadköping, Mother-in-Law Is Coming, Love and Deficit* (co. Brodén), *Sten Stensson Stéen from Eslöv on New Adventures, Marriageable Daughters, Two Men and a Widow, What Do Men Know?, Royal Johansson, The Song of the Scarlet Flower* (34), *Breakers, People of Småland, The Marriage Game* (co. Åke Dahlqvist), *Conscientious Adolf, The Honeymoon Trip, Johan Ulfstjerna, The Adventure, Clear the Decks for Action* (co. Bodin), *Sara Learns Manners, Walking along the Main Road, A Rich Man's Son, Whalers* (co. Fischer and others), *A Big Hug, The Little Shrew of the Veteran Reserves, Göransson's Boy, Life on a Perch, Hearts of Lieutenants, Nothing Will Be Forgotten, Katrina, His Majesty's Rival, His Official Fiancée, Jolanta—the Elusive Sow, The Exploits of Private 91 Karlsson, Life at Forsbyholm.*

● 112 JAG ÄR NYFIKEN—GUL/ I AM CURIOUS—YELLOW. 1967. Script and Direction: Vilgot Sjöman. Photography: Peter Wester. Editing: Wic

Kjellin. Music: Bengt Ernryd. Art Direction: none. Players: Lena Nyman (*Lena*), Peter Lindgren (*Rune, Lena's father*), Börje Ahlstedt (*Börje*), Vilgot Sjöman (*The Director*), Chris Wahlström (*Rune's friend*), Magnus Nilsson (*Magnus*), Ulla Lyttkens (*Ulla*), Anders Ek (*The Instructor*), Öllegård Wellton (*Interpreter*), Sven Wollter (*The Captain*), Yevgeni Yevtushenko, Martin Luther King, Olof Palme (*Themselves*). 121 mins. For Sandrews (Göran Lindgren).

PLOT: Vilgot Sjöman is shooting a film featuring Lena Nyman. To gather material, she goes round Stockholm interviewing people at random about socialism, violence and non-violence, religion etc. She lives with her father, and has turned her room into an archive for social studies. She meets a young man named Börje and begins an affair with him. But when she learns that he already has a mistress, she goes into retreat to meditate and practise yoga. Börje follows her, and she realises that she is still sexually attracted to him. There is a series of quarrels both with Börje and her father, and eventually Lena decides to abandon all her political activities. Sjöman has been jealous of her affair, and in the end Lena goes south with Börje.

● 113 JAHR, ADOLF (1893-1964). B: Sundsvall. Actor. Began his career as an opera singer but turned to film and theatre work. Engaged by the Royal Dramatic Theatre, Stockholm, a few years before his death. Often hero of popular comedies about country folk in Sweden, but also an honest character actor (e.g. as the drunken Captain in *Foreign Harbour*). Films: *The Old Manor, Millionaire for a Day, Quick as Lightning* (also dir. and script, 27), *What Woman Wants, On the Cruise with the "Lightning," The*

Hatter's Ball, Mother-in-law Is Coming, Sten Stensson Stéen from Eslöv on New Adventures, A Night at Smygeholm, Pettersson and Bendel, False Greta, My Aunt's Millions, A Wedding Night at Stjärnehov, A Gentleman Maybe, Conscientious Adolf, Are We Married?, Poor Millionaires, The Ghost of Bragehus, Adolf Armstrong, A Sailor Goes Ashore, Adolf Makes It (also co-dir. 38), *Only a Trumpeter, On the Cruise with the "Albertina," Adolf as a Fireman, Between Us Barons, An Able Man, Swing It Sir!, The Downy Girl* (41), *Sailor in a Dresscoat, The People of Hemsö* (44), *Gutter-snipes, The Virago of the Österman Brothers, The Wedding at Solö, Evenings at Djurgården, Ebberöds bank* (also dir. and script 47), *The Poetry of Ådalen, The Evening of the Fair, Lars Hård, Robinson of Roslagen, Foreign Harbour, The Exploits of Janne Vängman, Janne Vängman on New Adventures, While the City Sleeps, Young and in Love, The Quartet that Split Up, Skipper in Stormy Weather, Janne Vängman Is Busy, The King of Dalecarlia, Dance My Doll, God and the Gipsyman, Storm over Tjurö, Österman's Will, Janne Vängman and the Big Comet, The Matrimonial Announcement, The People from the Depths of the Forest, Johan at Snippen, Johan at Snippen Wins the Game, The People of Värmland, Only a Waiter, Beautiful Susan and the Old Men, When Darkness Falls.*

● 114 JOHAN. 1921. Script: Mauritz Stiller and Arthur Nordéen, from the novel by Juhani Aho. Direction: Mauritz Stiller. Photography: Henrik Jaenzon. Art Direction: Axel Esbensen. Players: Urho Somersalmi (*Vallavan*), Jenny Hasselqvist (*Marit*), Mathias Taube (*Johan*), Lilly Berg (*His servant*), Hildegard Harring (*His mother*). 1,900 metres. For Svenska Bio.
PLOT: Johan lives on a remote farm

where his hard mother treats him like a labourer. He feels affection for Marit, an orphan who has been brought up on the farm. When Johan fractures his leg, Marit brings him home. Johan's mother notices that they are falling in love and tries to get rid of Marit, but finally Johan takes command and marries Marit. Johan is a kind husband, but too reticent. A talkative stranger, Vallavan, arrives one day to court Marit, and finally she runs away with him down the river in order to escape Johan's quarrelsome mother. When Johan catches up with them, he attacks Vallavan. But Marit confesses that she followed the stranger of her own accord. Johan is depressed, but he is ready to forgive, and the couple row homewards to make a fresh start.

● 115 JOHNSON, MARY (1896-). B: Eskilstuna. Actress. At first worked in the theatre. Entered films through the Hasselblad studios at Göteborg, often starring in the films of Georg af Klercker (q.v.). Appeared in several German films in the Twenties, and was married to Rudolf Klein-Rogge. Her mild personality and gentle style of acting made her an ideal Elsalill in *Sir Arne's Treasure*. Films: *Love Will Conquer, Children of the Night* (16), *"Gift of Health" Ltd., Bengt's New Love, The Mystery of the Night of the 25th, Between Life and Death, The Clergyman from the Suburbs, Reveille, Dangers of a Big City, The Nobel Prize Winner, The Daughter of the Lighthouse Keeper, Puss in Boots, Sir Arne's Treasure* (19), *Robinson in the Archipelago, Family Traditions, A Fortune Hunter, Gunnar Hede's Saga, Johan Ulfstjerna.*

● 116 JOSEPHSON, ERLAND (19?-). Actor and scriptwriter. A close friend of Bergman (q.v.), and Head Director at Royal Dramatic Theatre Stockholm, since 1966. Usually plays rather pompous, insensitive husbands. Films: *To*

Joy, *Pleasure Garden* (also co-scripted with Bergman), *So Close to Life/Brink of Life, The Devil's Eye, Now about These Women* (co-scripted with Bergman only), *Hour of the Wolf, The Girls, A Passion.*

● JULIUS, J. *see* JAENZON, JULIUS.

● 117 JUNGFRUKÄLLAN/THE VIRGIN SPRING. 1960. Script: Ulla Isaksson, from a Fourteenth century legend. Direction: Ingmar Bergman. Photography: Sven Nykvist. Editing: Oscar Rosander. Music: Erik Nordgren. Art Direction: P. A. Lundgren. Players: Max von Sydow (*Töre*), Birgitta Valberg (*Märeta, his wife*), Gunnel Lindblom

At left: Erland Josephson. Below: Max von Sydow and Tor Isedal in THE VIRGIN SPRING

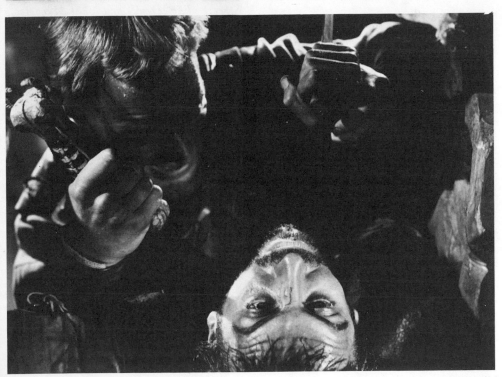

(*Ingeri*), Birgitta Pettersson (*Karin*), Axel Düberg (*The Thin Herdsman*), Tor Isedal (*The Mute Herdsman*), Allan Edwall (*The Beggar*), Ove Porath (*Boy*), Axel Slangus (*Old Man at Ford*), Gudrun Brost (*Frida*), Oscar Ljung (*Simon*), Tor Borong, Leif Forstenberg (*Farm labourers*). 85 mins. For Svensk Filmindustri.

PLOT: Karin, a proud young girl, is sent by her parents to ride to church with the Virgin's candles. In the forest she is waylaid, raped and killed by three herdsmen. The murderers ask unwittingly for shelter at the girl's home, and when her father, Töre, realises what has happened, he slaughters the trio as the sun rises next morning. He and his wife find their daughter's corpse in a glade. Töre vows to build a church to her memory, and a spring wells up beneath the dead girl's head.

● 118 JÄRREL, STIG (1910-   ). B: Malmberget. Actor. 1929-31: trained at Royal Dramatic Theatre, Stockholm. Has worked extensively in stage productions and on radio and TV. Järrel's study of the sadistic schoolmaster in *Frenzy/ Torment* remains his finest effort. His acting carries with it a relaxed cynicism, a faintly sinister and controlled love of luxury. A noted comedian in the Swedish theatre. Films: *Larsson in His Second Marriage, Walpurgis Night, Conscientious Adolf, Raggen—that's Me, Are We Married?, Happy Vestköping, A Girl Comes to Town, Send no. 7 Home, We from the Theatre, Mr. Housekeeper, The Two of Us, Her Melody, Like a Thief in the Night, An Able Man, The Three of Us, Hanna in Society, With You in My Arms, Romance, Newly Married, Wife and Comrade, To Chastise a Husband, First Division, Miss Wildcat, A Poor Millionaire, Life Goes On, Sailor in a Dress-coat, Flames in the Dark, Luck Arrives, We Met the Storm, As You Like Me, There Burned a Flame, My Husband Is Getting Married Today, Gentleman with a Briefcase, Mr. Collin's Adventures, The Royal Hunt, His Excellency, Live Dangerously, His Official Fiancée, Frenzy/Torment, The Invisible Wall, I Am Fire and Air, Like Most People, The Girl and the Devil, And All These Women, The Royal Rabble, Wandering with the Moon, Three Cheers for Little Märta, Good Morning Bill, 13 Chairs, Between Us Thieves, When the Door Was Closed, In Death's Waiting Room, Peggy on a Spree, It's My Model, Bad Eggs, Iris and the Lieutenant, Evil Eyes* (also dir. 47), *The Bride Came through the Ceiling, May I, Sir?, The Sixth Commandment* (also dir. 47), *Maria, The Most Beautiful Thing on Earth, Don't Give Up, Love Sunshine and Song, Each Goes His Own Way, Foreign Harbour, Little Märta Returns, Sin* (48), *Pippi Long-stocking, Spring at Sjösala, That Woman Drives Me Crazy, The Street, The Devil and the Man from Småland, Fun with Boccaccio, Store Hopare Lane and Heaven, When Love Came to the Village, Backyard, The White Cat, A Gentleman Maybe, Ghost on Holiday, Poker, Motor Cavaliers, A Fiancée for Hire, Helen of Troy, Defiance, Dream Holiday, Kalle Karlsson from Jularbo, Up with the Green Lift* (also co-scripted), *Say It with Flowers, One Fiancé at a Time, The Road to Klockrike, Possessed by Speed, The Journey to You, Seven Black Brassières, In Smoke and Dancing, The Girl with a Melody, Girl without a Name, The "Lunchbreak" Café, Karin Månsdotter, Simon the Sinner, Merry Boys of the Fleet, The Merry Shoemaker, Paradise, A Little Place of One's Own, The Right to Love, The Seventh Heaven, Children of the Night* (56), *Little Fridolf and I, Rasmus Pontus and Fool, Ratataa, Sinners in the Cinema Paradise, Never in Your Life, With the Halo Askew, The Hermit Johannes, Nothin' but Blondes, Mother Takes a Holiday, The Hermit in Stormy Weather, Miss Chic, Good Heavens!, The Devil's*

Eye, The Decimals of Love, Three Wishes, The Summer Night Is Sweet, Pleasure Garden, Ticket to Paradise, Parlour Games, The Slipper.

● 119   KARIN MÅNSDOTTER. 1954. Script: Alf Sjöberg, based on the central episode of the play *Erik XIV* by August Strindberg. Direction: Alf Sjöberg. Photography (prologue in Gevacolor): Sven Nykvist. Editing: Eric Nordemar. Music: Lillebror Söderlundh. Art Direction: Bibi Lindström and (for prologue) Ulla Friberger. Players: Ulla Jacobsson (*Karin*), Jarl Kulle (*Erik XIV*), Ulf Palme (*Göran Persson*), Per Oscarsson (*Anders*), Bengt Blomgren (*Max*), Kurt Olof Sundström (*Johan*), Birgitta Valberg (*Änkedrottningen*), Åke Claesson (*Svante Sture*), Måns Westfelt (*Nils Sture*), Curt Pettersson (*Erik Sture*), and Margaretha Krook. 106 mins. For Sandrews.

PLOT: Prince Erik of Sweden notices Karin, the daughter of a common soldier, and is attracted by her. Karin, being a woman of the people, is exploited by Göran Persson, who wants to reduce the influence of the nobles. She gives birth to two of Erik's children, but he wants to marry Queen Elizabeth I of England. When this proves impossible, he comes more and more under the influence of Persson and Karin. Finally Karin is crowned Queen of Sweden; but Erik is overthrown, Persson is beheaded, and Erik's brother Johan crowned.

Erik and his family are taken to Åbo in Finland and from there to Gripsholm Castle. Erik's temper grows increasingly violent. Finally King Johan separates Erik and Karin, and she starts to hate him; but they are reconciled before he is murdered. Karin decides to devote her life to her daughter.

● 120   KJELLGREN, LARS-ERIC (1919-   ). B: Arvika. Director. 1943: worked at Svensk Filmindustri in script department. Became an ideal director for

the comedian Nils Poppe (q.v.) in the late Forties, and is now an important figure in Swedish TV. Films: *Don't Give Up* 47; *Private Bom* 48; *The Count from the Lane* 49; *Pappa Bom, While the City Sleeps* (also co-scripted) 50; *Bom the Customs-Officer* 51; *Say It with Flowers, Flying Bomb, Blondie the Beef and the Banana* 52; *Hidden in the Fog, No Man's Woman* 53; *Violence* (also co-scripted) 55; *The Tough Game* 56; *Lights at Night* (also scripted) 57; *Travel to Sun and Spring, Playing on the Rainbow* 58; *Crime in Paradise* 59. Kjellgren also co-scripted *Night in the Harbour,* and was assistant director on *Sextuplets, The Knockout Clergyman, The Word.*

● 121   KJELLIN, ALF (1920-   ). B: Lund. Actor and director. Studied theatre, but apart from the occasional stage appearance has given most of his career to films. During the late Thirties and early Forties he visited Hollywood and worked for Selznick, and in 1949 he starred in Minnelli's *Madame Bovary.* During the Sixties he has worked almost

exclusively in the U.S.A.—for Hitchcock on a series of TV films, and for such directors as Kramer (*Ship of Fools*) and John Sturges (*Ice Station Zebra*). He was the tall, handsome young idol of the Swedish film world in the Forties, sometimes teamed with Mai Zetterling*. Films as director: *The Girl in the Rain* (also co-scripted and acted), *Seventeen Years Old* (also co-scripted), *Encounters at Dusk* 57; *Swinging at the Castle* 59; *Only a Waiter* 60; *Pleasure Garden* 61; *Siska* 62. Films as actor: *John Ericsson—the Victor at Hampton Roads, Good Friends and Faithful Neighbours, With the People for the Country, Whalers* (dubbing only), *The Old Man Is Coming, Rejoice While You Are Young, Fellow Cadets, Night in June, Steel, His Grace's Will* (40), *Bright Prospects, The Fight Goes On, Night in the Harbour, I Killed*, Gentleman with a Briefcase, Appassionata, Frenzy/Torment*, The Invisible Wall, Prince Gustaf*, Wandering with the Moon, If Dew Falls Rain Follows*, Iris and the Lieutenant*, It's My Model, A Girl from the Marsh Croft* (47), *Woman without a Face, The Wind Is My Lover, This Can't Happen Here, The White Cat, Summer Interlude/Illicit Interlude, Divorced, Rolling Sea, The Chief from Göinge, No Man's Woman, Girl without a Name, Blocked Rails, Private Entrance, My Hot Desire, The Stranger from the Sky, A Guest in One's Own Home, A Summer Place Is Wanted, Playing on the Rainbow*, Panic in Paradise* (in Denmark), *Two Living and One Dead, Carnival, My Love Is a Rose*.

• 122 KLERCKER, GEORG AF (1877-1951). B: Kristianstad. Director, scriptwriter, and actor. 1907: stage *début*. 1909-11: drama studies in Germany and Finland. 1911: engaged at Royal Dramatic Theatre, Stockholm. 1912: Head of Svenska Bio studios in Lidingö. 1915-18: Head of Hasselblad studios in Göteborg. A former lieutenant of the Svea Life

Guards in Stockholm, Klercker was a major talent of the silent period, his style and use of locations every bit as imaginative as Sjöström's and Stiller's. 1919: became hotel proprietor. 1926: to Malmö. 1931-32: to Paris, where he collaborated on Swedish versions of American productions. He scripted*, co-scripted**, or acted† in some of his films. *Two Brothers, The Death Ride under the Big Top* 12; *The Power of Music†, Arms in Your Hands*†, The Scandal*†, The Knife Grinder, Ringvall on Adventures*, For Your Country*† 13; The Rose of Thistle Island*, In Uniform 15; Tied to One's Memories†, The First Prize*†, Charlie's New Underwear, The Ministerial President*, Mother-in-law on the Spree*, Love Will Conquer*†, Perseverance Does It*, Children of the Night*, Charlie as a Millionaire*, The Prisoner at Karlsten Fort**, "Gift of Health" Ltd., Bengt's New Love, The Way Downhill* 16; The Mystery of the Night of the 25th**, Between Life and Death*, In the Chains of Darkness**, The Clergyman from the Suburbs, Lieutenant Madcap*, The Criminal Court*

Judge, For Home and Hearth, There Are
No Gods on Earth*, Reveille* 17; *Nightly
Music*, The Nobel Prize Winner, The
Daughter of the Lighthouse Keeper*** 18;
The Girls at Solvik 26. Films as actor only:
*In the Spring of Life, When Love Kills,
The Virago of the Österman Brothers, The
Secret of the Paradise Hotel, South of the
Main Road.*

● 123 KOCH, ERLAND VON (1910-
). B: Stockholm. Composer. 1943-
45: worked for Swedish Radio. Since
1953: teaching at the Music Academy in
Stockholm. Has composed symphonies,
string quartets, ballets, film and TV music.
His scores for early Bergman films* have
the same suggestive quality as Jaubert's
do for Carné's work in the Thirties. Films:
Crisis, It Rains on Our Love/Man with
an Umbrella*, When Meadows Bloom,
Dynamite, A Ship Bound for India*, The
People of Simlången Valley, Music in
Darkness/Night Is My Future*, Lapp
Blood, Lars Hård, On These Shoulders,
Port of Call*, Prison/The Devil's Wan-
ton*, Son of the Sea, The Realm of Man,
Sampo the Little Lapp, Girl with Hya-
cinths, The White Cat, Rolling Sea,
Wing-beats in the Night, The Chief of
Göinge, God and the Gipsyman, Victory
in Darkness, The Girl in the Rain, The
Song of the Scarlet Flower* (56), *Tarps
Elin.*

● 124 KORRIDOREN/THE COR-
RIDOR. 1968. Script: Bengt Bratt, Bengt
Forslund, Jan Halldoff. Direction: Jan
Halldoff. Photography (Eastmancolor):
Inge Roos. Music: Verdi (extract). Play-
ers: Per Ragnar (*Dr. Jan Eriksson*),
Agneta Ekmanner (*Kerstin, his wife*),
Ann Norstedt (*Maria, his sister*), Åke
Lindström (*His father*), Inga Landgré
(*His mother*), Professor Gunnar Björck
(*Himself*), Leif Lilieroth (*Dr. Forslund*),
Lars Amble (*Stig*), Bengt Ekerot (*Cancer
patient*), Arne Källerud, Stig Törnblom

Per Ragnar in THE CORRIDOR

75

(Other patients). 95 mins. For Svensk Filmindustri (Bengt Forslund).

PLOT: The film opens with an autopsy, during which the young doctor Jan Eriksson sees another intern undergoing an attack of nausea. In his hospital work Jan suffers from a constant, nagging sense of inadequacy. Patients try to engage him in conversation, but he must hurry on, offering only empty, consolatory phrases. On his way home one day he accidentally hits a cat with his car, but he cannot bring himself to kill the crippled creature. At home with his wife he always seems tired and distracted.

Jan visits his parents, but he faces new problems ·here too. His young sister is pregnant and wants an abortion. His father is furious, but supports her, thinking of his reputation as a clergyman. Jan tries to dissuade her. Back at the hospital he hears that a depressed woman he should have talked to has committed suicide. Later he is at a loss to tell a patient that he is dying of cancer. Finally, Jan comes to the conclusion that he must leave hospital work and devote himself to research instead.

● 125 KROOK, MARGARETHA (1925-). B: Stockholm. Actress. 1951: trained at Royal Dramatic Theatre, Stockholm. Since 1963: frequent appearances in TV dramas. Best known for her work as an interpreter of tragic roles on the stage,

Margaretha Krook in Kulle's THE BOOKSELLER WHO GAVE UP BATHING

76

Jarl Kulle in Bergman's SMILES OF A SUMMER NIGHT

Miss Krook has appeared in few films. But she is always impressive (as the Doctor in *Persona*, for example). Films: *Only a Mother, Miss Julie, Barabbas, Storm over Tjurö, Karin Månsdotter* (prologue), *Salka Valka, So Close to Life, Trust Me Darling, Adam and Eve, Swedish Portraits, Wedding—Swedish Style, I, The Sadist, Persona, I Need a Woman, The Bookseller Who Gave Up Bathing.*

● 126 KULLE, JARL (1927-   ). B: Ängelholm. Actor. 1946-49: trained at Royal Dramatic Theatre, Stockholm. Has appeared in many plays and musical entertainments (*My Fair Lady, How to Succeed in Business without Really Trying* etc.). Kulle is among the most popular of postwar Swedish stars in his own country. He is most familiar in comedies, but in *Karin Månsdotter* and *My Sister My Love* (both q.v.), he proved himself capable of a great dramatic performance. Films: *Youth in Danger, The Quartet that Split Up, Living at the "Hope," Defiance, Private 69 the Sergeant and I, Waiting Women/Secrets of Women, Love, Barabbas, Karin Månsdotter, Smiles of a Summer Night, Song of the Scarlet Flower* (56), *Last Pair Out, A Dreamer's Walk, No Tomorrow, Miss April, A Thief in the Bedroom, To One's Heart's Content, The Devil's Eye, Do You Believe in Angels?, Trust Me Darling, The Dear Family* (in Denmark), *Pan, The Girl and the Press Photographer* (in Denmark), *Wedding—Swedish Style, Now about These Women, You Must Be Crazy Darling, Dear John, My Sister My Love, The Bookseller Who Gave Up Bathing* (also dir. and script, 69), *Miss and Mrs. Sweden.*

● 127 KVARTERET KORPEN/RAVEN'S END. 1963. Script and Direction: Bo Widerberg. Photography: Jan Lindeström. Editing: Wic Kjellin. Music: Trumpet Concerto in D by Torelli. Art Direction: Einar Nettelbladt. Players:

Thommy Berggren in RAVEN'S END

Thommy Berggren (*Anders*), Keve Hjelm (*His father*), Emy Storm (*His mother*), Ingvar Hirdwall (*Sixten*), Christina Frambäck (*Elsie*), Agneta Prytz (*A Neighbour*), Nina Widerberg (*Nina*). 100 mins. For Europa Film (Gunnar Oldin).

PLOT: The film is set in Malmö in 1936. Anders is a young factory worker with aspirations as a novelist. His father, a failed underwear salesman, steeps himself in alcohol in an effort to sustain his dreams of better conditions. His mother is despondent and does scrubbing and washing to bolster the family income. They are three months behind with the rent. There is news of the Spanish Civil War and of Hitler's rise to power. Anders writes assiduously, and is encouraged by an invitation from a Stockholm publisher.

But he returns home disconsolate. His novel has been rejected. He becomes involved with a local girl, and she is quickly pregnant. Spurred by the prospect of a horrible marriage, Anders at last plucks up sufficient courage to leave Raven's End.

● 128 KVINNA UTAN ANSIKTE/ WOMAN WITHOUT A FACE. 1947. Script: Ingmar Bergman. Direction: Gustaf Molander. Photography: Åke Dahlquist. Editing: Oscar Rosander. Music: Erik Nordgren. Art Direction: Arne Åkermark. Players: Alf Kjellin (*Martin Grandé*), Gunn Wållgren (*Rut Köhler*), Anita Björk (*Frida Grandé*), Stig Olin (*Ragnar Ekberg*), Olof Winnerstrand (*Mr. Grandé, Manager*), Marianne Löfgren (*Charlotte*), Georg Funkquist (*Victor*), Åke Grönberg (*Sam Svensson*),

Linnea Hillberg (*Mrs. Grandé*), Calle Reinholdz, Sif Ruud, Ella Lindblom, Artur Rolén, Victor Andersson, Björn Montin. 102 mins. For Svensk Filmindustri.

PLOT: Martin Grandé is a student at Stockholm University in the mid-Forties. He is married and has a child. He happens to meet the attractive Rut Köhler, falls desperately in love with her, and leaves his family. Rut's mother has a lover, Victor, who seduced Rut when she was twelve years old. Martin and Rut make love and quarrel, part and come together again. But finally Rut tells him that she is leaving him forever. After an attempted suicide—saved by his friend Ragnar Ekberg—Martin returns to his family. His attempt to break away from his bourgeois surroundings has failed. All this is told by Ragnar Ekberg in a long flashback. To recollect is for Martin a means of regaining his mental stability.

● 129 KVINNODRÖM/JOURNEY INTO AUTUMN/DREAMS. 1955. Script and Direction: Ingmar Bergman. Photography: Hilding Bladh. Editing: Carl-Olov Skeppstedt. Music: none. Art Direction: Gittan Gustafsson. Players: Eva Dahlbeck (*Susanne*), Harriet Andersson (*Doris*), Gunnar Björnstrand (*The Consul*), Ulf Palme (*Henrik Lobelius*), Inga Landgré (*Märta Lobelius, his wife*), Sven Lindberg (*Palle*), Naima Wifstrand (*Madame Arén*), Benkt-Åke Benktsson (*Mr. Magnus*), Git Gay (*The shop assistant*), Ludde Gentzel (*Sundström, the photographer*), Kerstin Hedeby (*Marianne*), Jessie Flaws, Marianne Nielsen, Siv Ericks, Bengt Schött, Axel Düberg. 86 mins. For Sandrews (Rune Waldekranz).

PLOT: Susanne owns a fashion photography studio. Her favourite model, Doris, has just broken off her engagement to Palle, a student. When Susanne has to go to Göteborg to take a series of photo-

graphs with Doris as model, she uses the opportunity to telephone Henrik Lobelius, and asks him to meet her. Susanne has been Lobelius's mistress and she cannot forget him. During the twenty-four hours the two girls spend in Göteborg, Susanne meets Lobelius, but realises what a coward he is. His wife surprises them at the hotel and after a violent scene proves conclusively that Henrik is tied hand and foot to her. When Susanne returns home she is cured of her dreams of a great love affair. Doris also arrives back in Stockholm dejected. She has had a depressing episode with an elderly Consul who has offered her jewels and expensive clothes merely to attract her companionship. The Consul's daughter, Marianne, arrives on the scene and attacks her father's egotism. Doris, it transpires, is strikingly reminiscent of the Consul's insane wife in her youth. When Doris returns to the studio, she is glad to throw herself into Palle's arms.

● 130 KVINNORS VÄNTAN/ WAITING WOMEN/SECRETS OF WOMEN. 1952. Script and Direction: Ingmar Bergman. Photography: Gunnar Fischer. Editing: Oscar Rosander. Music: Erik Nordgren. Art Direction: Nils Svenwall. Players: Anita Björk (*Rakel*), Maj-Britt Nilsson (*Märta*), Eva Dahlbeck (*Karin*), Gunnar Björnstrand (*Fredrik Lobelius*), Birger Malmsten (*Martin Lobelius*), Jarl Kulle (*Kaj*), Karl-Arne Holmsten (*Eugen Lobelius*), Gerd Andersson (*Maj*), Björn Bjelvenstam (*Henrik*), Aino Taube (*Anita*), Håkan Westergren (*Paul*), Kjell Nordensköld, Carl Ström, Märta Arbiin. 105 mins. For Svensk Filmindustri.

PLOT: Four women married to four brothers are spending a holiday in the Stockholm archipelago while they wait for their husbands to return from a business trip. On the last evening, before the men's train is due to arrive from Stockholm, three of them recall episodes from their past life. Rakel tells of an affair with a

lover from childhood days that led to her husband's threatening to commit suicide in the garden shed. Märta recounts her student days in Paris, her romance with a Bohemian artist, Martin, and the details of a pre-marital confinement. Karin, the oldest of the three women, describes a farcical incident after a party, when she and her husband Fredrik were trapped in a lift. The fourth woman in the party declines to tell a story, and the fifth and youngest, Maj, elopes with her boy friend just as the men return at dusk.

● 131 KÄRE JOHN/DEAR JOHN. 1964. Script and Direction: Lars Magnus Lindgren, from the novel by Olle Länsberg. Photography: Rune Ericson. Editing:

Lennart Wallén. Music: Bengt-Arne Wallin. Art Direction: Jan Boleslaw. Players: Jarl Kulle (*John*), Christina Schollin (*Anita*), Helena Nilsson (*Helena*), Morgan Andersson (*Raymond*), Synnöve Liljebäck (*Dagny*), Erik Hell (*Lindgren*), Emy Storm (*Mrs. Lindgren*), Håkan Serner (*Erwin*), Hans Wigren (*Elon*). 111 mins. For Sandrews.

PLOT: John, the skipper of the cargo vessel *Elsa,* comes ashore near Malmö so that his ship can revictual. He meets Anna, a waitress in a café who has an illegitimate daughter, Helena. John asks her out for the evening, but Anita suggests the following day when she may be able to get a baby-sitter for Helena. Early next morning he sees her again while swimming, and he accompanies her and Helena to Malmö for a day trip. On an impulse he takes them to Copenhagen. At the end of a happy day, they have supper together in the cottage while her brother is at a party. Both are anxious not to hurt, or be hurt, emotionally, but eventually they do make love. In the morning, as John prepares to sail, he learns that Anita has left the village for her holidays. But after only a moment's hesitation, he telephones her and proposes marriage.

● 132 KÄRLEKENS BRÖD/THE BREAD OF LOVE. 1953. Script: Wolodja Semitjov, from a novel by Peder Sjögren. Direction: Arne Mattsson. Photography: Sven Thermaenius. Music: Sven Sköld. Players: Folke Sundquist (*The Prisoner*), Sissi Kaiser (*Lunnaja*), Georg Rydeberg (*Ledin*), Nils Hallberg (*Tom*), Lennart Lindberg (*The Narrator*), Erik Hell (*The Scout*), Dagny Lind (*The Mother*), Yngve Nordvall (*Orthodox Priest*). For Nordisk Tonefilm.

PLOT: A young soldier comes to tell an old woman of the death of her son in the Russo-Finnish war. He is afraid to tell her how the man died. . . . A group of Finnish soldiers is pinned down in a casemate in the forest. The snow is dense and blots out the paths through the minefields. Two of the men in the camp, Tom and the narrator, are out on patrol one

Folke Sundquist in **THE BREAD OF LOVE** *(with Sissi Kaiser)*

night when they encounter a strange Russian soldier, alone and singing to the moon. They leave him, but the Scout finds him and brings him back to the casemate. The Russian prisoner tells the narrator that he has been separated from his wife on their wedding day, and that he and his beloved had promised to speak to each other through the moon. One night, singing is heard in the enemy camp, followed by firing. When it has stopped, the scout goes into the forest, where he finds the woman who had been singing. He rapes and kills her. When he returns to the casemate, he tells the others. The Russian soldier recognises his own wife in the description, and when for a few moments he is alone with the scout, he stabs him and escapes through the minefield. The Finnish soldiers follow his tracks, and reach their own lines safely.

● 133 KÄRLEK OCH JOURNALISTIK/LOVE AND JOURNALISM. 1916. Script: Harriet Bloch. Direction: Mauritz Stiller. Photography: Gustaf Boge. Art Direction: Axel Esbensen. Players: Jenny Tschernichin-Larsson (*The Clergyman's wife*), Richard Lund (*Her son, Erik Blomée*), Stina Berg (*Old servant*), Karin Molander (*Herta Weye*), Gucken Cederborg (*Rosika Amunds*). 834 metres. For Svenska Bio.

PLOT: The famous explorer Erik Blomée returns from an Antarctic expedition. He wants to keep his arrival a secret, but rumours reach the newspapers. Miss Herta Weye, an enterprising journalist, applies for a position as domestic help to Erik's mother. She studies Erik's collections and gets material for an article. When she tries to borrow portraits to illustrate her piece, she is surprised by the old servant. At first Erik cannot believe that she has deceived them, but then he notices her at a restaurant and learns that she is indeed a journalist. However, Herta

has fallen in love with Erik and tears up her "interview." At that very moment, he enters to reproach her, but instead they embrace. The newspaper loses its best reporter, but Erik's mother gets her maid back—as a daughter-in-law.

● 134 KÄRLEK 65/LOVE 65. 1965. Script, Direction, and Editing: Bo Widerberg. Photography: Jan Lindeström. Music: Bill Evans, with extracts from Vivaldi. Players: Keve Hjelm (*The Film Director, Keve*), Ann-Marie Gyllenspetz (*His wife*), Evabritt Strandberg (*Evabritt*), Ben Carruthers (*Himself*), Inger Taube (*Inger*), Björn Gustafsson (*The lecturer*), Kent Andersson, Nina Widerberg, Agneta Ekmanner, Thommy Berggren (*Players in Keve's film*). 95 mins. For Europa Film.

PLOT: Keve is a film director who finds it more and more difficult to conceive, and realise, his ideas on film. He is married with a little daughter, who is having trouble with her eyesight. One day he brings home Inger, a model with whom he has just shot a commercial, and they all go out on to the hills above the sea and fly kites for fun and relaxation. Keve wanders off, and happens to look in at a lecture in the local hall. He meets the lecturer's wife, Evabritt, and they are immediately attracted to each other. Later, Keve meets her again, and this time he seduces her in her apartment. He confides in her all the difficulties of his profession. Then Ben Carruthers arrives in Sweden to play a role in Keve's new feature. Keve greets him rudely, and Ben is offended, although he strikes up a rapport with Ann-Marie and Inger. After an alfresco party in the evening, Ann-Marie is depressed, and Keve finds her tearing up his old love letters. They have an argument, but both of them realise that they are at fault, and that they must concentrate on bringing up their child in a harmonious home. Temporarily, at least, Keve is revived.

Victor Sjöström (at right, with Tore Svennberg) in THE PHANTOM CARRIAGE

● 135 KÖRKARLEN/THE PHAN-
TOM CARRIAGE/THY SOUL
SHALL BEAR WITNESS. 1921. Script
and Direction: Victor Sjöström, from the
novel by Selma Lagerlöf. Photography: J.
Julius. Art Direction: Alexander Bakó
and Axel Esbensen. Players: Victor Sjö-
ström (*David Holm*), Hilda Borgström
(*His wife*), Tore Svennberg (*Georg*),
Astrid Holm (*Sister Edith*), Concordia
Selander (*Her mother*), Lisa Lundholm
(*Sister Maria*), and Tor Weijden, Einar
Axelsson, Olof Aas, Nils Aréhn, Simon
Lindstrand, Nils Elffors, Algot Gunnars-
son, Hildur Lithman, John Ekman. 60
mins. For Svenska Bio.

PLOT: It is New Year's Eve. Edith,
a Salvation Army nurse who is dying from
consumption, sends out a friend to look
for the drunkard David Holm. Mrs. Holm
lives in poverty with her two children and
needs help. Edith wants to make David return home. Meanwhile David is drinking
at the cemetery. During a drunken brawl
he is knocked to the ground, apparently
dead. But, according to legend, the man
who dies on the stroke of midnight on New
Year's Eve will have to drive the phantom
carriage the following year. Georg, a
former drinking companion of David's,
comes with the carriage to fetch him.

David's downfall is told in a long flashback. Tempted by Georg, he takes to drink
and goes to prison. Then he tries to reform, but when he finds that his wife has
left him he is bitter and vindictive.

83

David is not dead, but recovers and hurries home, just in time to prevent his wife from killing the children and committing suicide.

● 136 LAGERLÖF, SELMA (1858-1940). B: Mårbacka (in Värmland). Author. Studied as a teacher but left this profession after the success of "The Saga of Gösta Berling" in 1891. Her lyrical and impulsive style came from a remarkable imagination, which used material from her native province, Värmland, in several novels. The greatest of Swedish storytellers. She seldom seemed satisfied with the many film versions of her work. Films from her books: *A Girl from the Marsh Croft* 17; *The Sons of Ingmar* (Pts I and II), based on "Jerusalem Pt I," *Sir Arne's Treasure, The Downy Girl*, based on a story in "Osynliga länkar" 19; *Karin Daughter of Ingmar*, based on "Jerusalem Pt II" 20; *The Phantom Carriage/Thy Soul Shall Bear Witness* 21; *Gunnar Hede's Saga*, based on "En herrgårdssägen" 23; *The Saga of Gösta Berling* 24; *The*

Ingmar Inheritance, based on "Jerusalem Pt I" 25; *To the Orient,* based on "Jerusalem Pt II" 26; *Charlotte Löwensköld* 30; *The Downy Girl* (re-make) 41; *The Emperor of Portugal* 44; *A Girl from the Marsh Croft* (re-make) 47; *Sir Arne's Treasure* (re-make) 54; *The Phantom Carriage* (re-make) 58; *The Wonderful Adventures of Nils* 62.

● 137 LANDGRÉ, INGA (1927-). B: Stockholm. Actress. 1943: given contract at Svensk Filmindustri by Victor Sjöström (q.v.). 1949-59: married to Nils Poppe (q.v.). Several stage appearances. Also novelist and short story writer. A light comedienne in Poppe's films, and then directed imaginatively by Bergman (q.v.) as a lonely and rather bitter figure in *Journey into Autumn/Dreams, The Seventh Seal,* and *So Close to Life/Brink of Life.* Films: *The Word, The Rose of Thistle Island, Money, Crisis, The Balloon, When the Door Was Closed, If Dew Falls Rain Follows, Wedding Night, Maj from Malö, Navvies, The Roar of Hammar Rapids, Private Bom, Eve, Dangerous Spring, While the City Sleeps, The Quartet that Split Up, Bom the Customs-Officer, Flying-Bomb, Dance My Doll, Stupid Bom, Murder My Little Friend, Journey into Autumn/Dreams, It's Never Too Late, The Seventh Seal, A Dreamer's Walk, Encounters at Dusk, So Close to Life/Brink of Life, Playing on the Rainbow, We on Väddö, Yes He Has Been with Me, Loving Couples, Stimulantia,* (Sjöman episode), *Hugo and Josefin, The Corridor.*

● 138 LEK PÅ REGNBÅGEN / PLAYING ON THE RAINBOW. 1958. Script: Vilgot Sjöman. Direction: Lars-Eric Kjellgren. Photography: Gunnar Fischer. Editing: Oscar Rosander. Music: Erik Nordgren. Art Direction: P. A. Lundgren. Players: Mai Zetterling (*Vanja*), Alf Kjellin (*Björn*), Birger

Malmsten (*Hasse*), Gunlög Hagberg (*Barbro*), Isa Quensel (*Björn's mother*), Claes Thelander (*Hannes*), Else-Marie Brandt (*Blonde*), Inga Landgré (*Redhead*), Gunnar Sjöberg (*District Attorney*), Lars Egge (*Judge*). 92 mins. For Svensk Filmindustri.

PLOT: Björn is a thirty-year-old law student at Stockholm University. He meets Vanja, a social welfare officer, and they fall in love. They live together and accept the idea of free love. Björn is too mindful of his parents' unhappy marriage to be tied down by promises or commitments. Vanja is eager to settle down in the long term, and so she leaves Björn, who consoles himself and his pride by having affairs with other girls. Vanja meanwhile becomes involved with Hasse, a weak man she had once helped and been attached to. Later Hasse steals from her and he is sentenced to prison. Björn, realising his need for Vanja, asks her to marry him. But it is too late, and Vanja takes up the offer of a scholarship in America.

● 139 LINDBERG, PER (1890-1944). B: Stockholm. Director. Underestimated man of the theatre and cinema who studied under Max Reinhardt and produced many important plays during the Twenties and Thirties. Also worked in radio. His films were few but they reflected their time with accuracy and penetration. Also wrote some key books on the arts. Films: *Anna-Klara and Her Brothers, The Norrtull Gang 23; The Old Man Is Coming, Rejoice While You Are Young* (both also co-scripted) 39; *Steel, Night in June, His Grace's Will* 40; *Talk of the Town, In Paradise* (both also co-scripted) 41.

● 140 LINDBLOM, GUNNEL (1931-). B: Göteborg. Actress. 1950: trained at Göteborg Municipal Theatre, and between 1954 and 1959 acted brilliantly at Malmö. Among her best known stage parts are Marguerite in *Urfaust*

and Miss Julie in the BBC production of Strindberg's play. Her film roles emphasise her quiet, slumbrous appeal. Since *The Silence* she has played in several foreign films. Films: *Love, The Girl in the Rain, The Song of the Scarlet Flower* (56), *The Seventh Seal, Wild Strawberries, Gunpowder and Love, The Virgin Spring, Good Friends and Faithful Neighbours, Winter Light, The Silence, My Love Is a Rose, You Must Be Crazy Darling!, Loving Couples, Hunger* (in Denmark), *Woman of Darkness, The Vicious Circle, The Girls, The Father.*

● 141 LINDFORS, VIVECA (1920-). B: Uppsala. Actress. 1938-41: trained at Royal Dramatic Theatre, Stockholm. 1947: to Hollywood. Brunette star best known for her playing outside Sweden. Her interpretation of Freya, the sculptress in Joseph Losey's *The Damned* (61), was outstanding. Swedish films: *The Spinning Family, In Paradise, Suppose I Were to Marry the Clergyman, Tomorrow's Melody, The Yellow Ward, Anna Lans, The Brothers' Woman, Appas-*

85

sionata, I Am Fire and Air, Black Roses, The Serious Game, Marie in the Windmill, In Death's Waiting Room, The Wind Is My Lover.

● 142   LINDGREN, GÖRAN (1927-). B: Stockholm. Producer, and now head of Sandrews (q.v.). His energetic and broad-minded approach to production has allowed directors like Sjöman, Cornell, and Gamlin (all q.v.) to work in freedom. He has also encouraged foreign directors to work in Sweden, among them Jacques Doniol-Valcroze and Peter Watkins. Films: *Dear John, Loving Couples, The Ball Room, Calle P, The Vine Bridge, Adventure Starts Here, My Sister My Love, Night Games, Hunger* (co-prod. with Denmark and Norway), *Rooftree, Hugs and Kisses, I Am Curious—Yellow, I Am Curious—Blue, Hugo and Josefin, People Meet* (co-prod. with Denmark), *The Bathers, A Question of Rape* (co-prod. with France), *The Girls, The Black*

Palm Trees, Like Night and Day, Eriksson, The Bookseller Who Gave Up Bathing, The Gladiators, Duet for Cannibals, The Pig Hunt, Production 337.

● 143   LINDGREN, LARS MAGNUS (1922-   ). B: Västerås. Director, at his peak in *Dear John,* which was highly successful abroad as well as in Sweden. Made some 300 advertising films at Sandrews. Shorts include: *Pyret Applies for a Job, A Coin Is a Coin, Love and Statistics.* Features: *A Dreamer's Walk* 57; *Do You Believe in Angels?* 61; *Hide and Seek* 63; *Dear John* 64; *The Sadist* 66; *The Black Palm Trees* 68.

● 144   LINDSTRÖM, BIBI (1904-). B: Arbrå. Set designer. Has been an art director since the early Thirties. Since 1963: working for Swedish TV. Also some stage work. Her interiors for *Miss Julie, Sawdust and Tinsel/The Naked Night,* and *The People of Hemsö* represent her talent at its best. She has

86

some 135 credits. Main films: *Saturday Evenings, The Women around Larsson, Raggen—That's Me, Our Boy, The Quartet that Split Up* (co. Max Linder), *The Two of Us, The Man Everybody Wants To Murder, Like a Thief in the Night, Her Melody* (co. Linder), *Our Gang, We Housemaids, People of Roslagen, Can You Come Doctor?, Men-of-War, Women in Prison, A Matter of Life and Death, I Killed, Kajan Goes to Sea, Your Relatives Are Best, I Am Fire and Air, Prince Gustaf, Three Sons Went to the Air Force, The Rose of Thistle Island, In the Beautiful Province of Roslagen, The Children from Frostmo Mountain, Good Morning Bill, In Death's Waiting Room, Love and Downhill Skiing, Women in a Waiting Room, I Love You You Vixen, Hotell Kåkbrinken, Maria, Neglected by His Wife, Maj from Malö, Blomqvist the Master Detective, The People of Simlången Valley, The Poetry of Ådalen, The Evening of the Fair* (co. Lundgren), *Little Märta Returns, On These Shoulders, The Banquet, The Girl from the Gallery, Spring at Sjösala, The Realm of Man, The Maid from Jungfrusund, Fun with Boccaccio, Stora Hopare Lane and Heaven, Destination Rio, Girl with Hyacinths, The Teacher's First Child, Knockout at the "Breakfast Club," Jack of Hearts, Mrs. Andersson's Charlie* (50), *When Bengt and Anders Swapped Wives, The White Cat, My Name Is Puck, Miss Julie, Once upon a Time a Sailor, One Summer of Happiness, A Dull Clang, Because of My Hot Youth, Up with the Green Lift, Unmarried Mothers, Ursula—the Girl from the Forest Depths, The Shadow, Barabbas, The Road to Klockrike, Sawdust and Tinsel/The Naked Night, Karin Månsdotter, Salka Valka, Love Chastised, The People of Hemsö* (55), *A Little Place of One's Own, Little Fridolf and I, Tarps Elin, As You Make Your Bed . . ., Little Fridolf Becomes a Grandfather, No Tomorrow, So Close to Life/Brink of Life, The Phantom Carriage* (58), *Model in Red, Rider in Blue, May I Borrow Your Wife?, Summer and Sinners, Wedding Day, The Judge, Good Friends and Faithful Neighbours, When Darkness Falls, Mother of Pearl, Two Living and One Dead, The Wonderful Adventures of Nils, Siska, The Dress, Persona, The Bookseller Who Gave Up Bathing.*

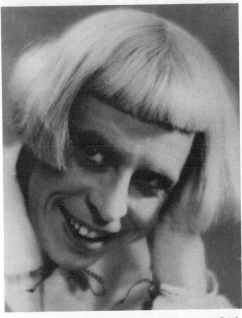

● 145 LINDSTRÖM, RUNE (1916-
). B: Västanfors. Actor and scriptwriter. Has written four plays (including *The Road to Heaven,* completed while he was studying at Uppsala). Art director for the ballet. Book illustrator. Often works for radio and TV. His first part, Mats Ersson, remains his finest achievement as an actor. Films as scriptwriter: *The Road to Heaven* (co. Sjöberg; also acted), *The Word, The Emperor of Portugal, Johansson and Vestman, It's My Model, The Clergyman from the Wilds, Aunt Green Aunt Brown and Aunt Lilac* (also dir.), *Navvies* (co.), *I Am with You* (co.; also acted), *Life Begins Now* (co.), *Where the Winds*

Lead, *Dangerous Spring, Vagabond Black-smiths* (songs only), *Woman in White* (co.), *The Realm of Man* (co.), *Stora Hopare Lane and Heaven* (co.), *Skipper in Stormy Weather* (co.), *Because of My Hot Youth* (co.), *Love* (co.), *Enchanted Walk, Victory in Darkness* (co.), *Salka Valka, The Men in Darkness* (co.), *Rasmus and the Tramp* (songs with Astrid Lindgren), *The People of Hemsö* (55), *The Song of the Scarlet Flower* (56), *The Witch* (co-prod. with France; acted only), *The Clergyman from Uddarbo, The Phantom Carriage* (58), *Hand Me a Count* (co.), *Fridolf's Dangerous Age* (co.), *A Lion in Town* (co.). Acted only: *My Sister My Love, Night Games, Woman of Darkness, What a Beautiful Day, Shame, Waltz of Sex, Teddy Bear.*

● 146 LUND, RICHARD (1885-1960). B: Göteborg. Actor. 1904: stage *début.* Extensive stage and screen acting career. The first "great lover" of the Swedish silent cinema (e.g. as Sir Archie in *Sir Arne's Treasure*), but composed

and restrained in his romantic roles. Films: *A Secret Marriage, Smiles and Tears, Lady Marion's Summer Flirtation, The Voice of Blood, On the Fateful Roads of Life, Ingeborg Holm, Life's Conflicts, The Modern Suffragette, The Clergyman, Love Stronger than Hate, People of the Border, Because of Her Love, Do Not Judge, Stormy Petrel, A Good Girl Should Solve Her Own Problems, Hearts that Meet, The Strike, The Playmates, It Was in May, His Wife's Past, To Each His Calling, His Father's Crime, The Avenger, The Governor's Daughters, Sea Vultures, His Wedding Night, At the Moment of Trial, The Lucky Brooch, Love and Journalism, The Struggle for His Heart, The Ballet Primadonna, The Architect of One's Own Fortune, Who Fired?, The Jungle Queen's Jewel, The Living Mummy, Sir Arne's Treasure, The Monastery of Sendomir, The Executioner, Family Traditions, The Girls from Åre, Carolina Rediviva, The Surrounded House, Life in the Country, A Million Dollars, Uncle Frans, False Svensson, Voice of the Heart, What Do Men Know?, Under False Colours, Walpurgis Night, Conscientious Adolf, Johan Ulfstjerna, He She and the Money, The "Paradise" Boarding House, A Cold in the Head, Adolf Armstrong, John Ericsson—the Victor at Hampton Roads, A Rich Man's Son, With the People for the Country, Great Friends and Faithful Neighbours, Nothing but the Truth, Rejoice while You Are Young, The Little WRAC of the Veteran Reserves, Whalers, Steel, Night in June, Kiss Her, A Big Hug, We Are All Errand Boys, The Gentleman Gangster, A Schoolmistress on the Spree, Sextuplets, Life on a Perch, The Knockout Clergyman, Katrina, There Burned a Flame, Frenzy/Torment.*

● 147 LUNDGREN, P. A. (1911-). B: Västra Harg (Östergötland). Set designer. Army service, followed by a spell in advertising and commercial art. A familiar name on Bergman (q.v.)

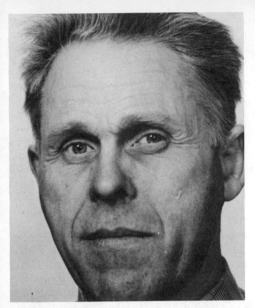

credits, Lundgren brings an impeccable sense of period to his designs (especially in *Smiles of a Summer Night* and *The Seventh Seal*—both q.v.). Films: *A Day Shall Dawn, His Excellency* (co. Åkermark), *My People Are Not Yours, We Need Each Other, The Girl and the Devil, The Clergyman from the Wilds, It Rains on Our Love/Man with an Umbrella, When Meadows Bloom, Life in the Depths of the Forest, A Ship Bound for India, Music in Darkness/Night Is My Future, The Evening of the Fair* (co. Lindström), *Lars Hård, Foreign Harbour, The Roar of Hammar Rapids, The Street, Vagabond Blacksmiths, Prison/The Devil's Wanton, The Devil and the Man from Småland, The Son of the Sea, Tall Lasse from Delsbo, Pippi Long Stocking, Bohus Battalion, Loffe Becomes a Policeman, When Love Came to the Village, The Land of Rye, Motor Cavaliers, Ghost on a Holiday, Stronger than the Law, Rolling Sea, Poker, When Lilacs Blossom, Kalle Karlsson from Jularbo, Summer with Monika* (co. Svenwall), *Hidden in the Fog, No Man's Woman, Unmarried, A Lesson in Love, Sir Arne's Treasure* (54, co. Garmland), *The Pawn Shop, Wild Birds, Violence, The Shining Light from Lund, Smiles of a Summer Night, The Seventh Heaven, Ratataa, The Song of the Scarlet Flower* (56), *The Seventh Seal, The Rusk, With the Halo Askew, Lights at Night, A Summer Place Is Wanted, A Square Peg in a Round Hole, The Great Amateur* (co. Gamlin), *Playing on the Rainbow* (co. Gustafsson), *The Jazz Boy, The Face/The Magician, Miss Chic, Crime in Paradise, Only a Waiter, Beautiful Susan and the Old Men, Good Heavens!, The Virgin Spring, The Decimals of Love, Face of Fire* (co-prod. with U.S.A.), *The Devil's Eye, On a Bench in the Park, Carnival, The Job, Through a Glass Darkly, Pleasure Garden, The Brig "Three Lilies," Just Once More, The Mistress, Winter Light, The Dream of Happiness, The Silence, 491, Now about These Women, Swedish Portraits, The Marriage Wrestler, Just Like Friends, Nightmare, The Island, The Serpent, Woman of Darkness, Stimulantia* (Molander episode), *The Red Mantle* (in Denmark), *The Vicious Circle, People Meet, Shame, An-Magritt* (in Norway), *A Passion, The Emigrants* and *Unto a Good Land.*

● 148 LÖFGREN, MARIANNE (1910-1957). B: Stockholm. Actress. Stage work during the Thirties. Reliable, forthright supporting actress in a vast number of films from 1930 to 1956. *The Dangerous Game, What Do Men Know?, The Song of the Scarlet Flower* (34), *On the Sunny Side, A Lady Becomes a Maid, The Great Love, With the People for the Country, Mr. Karlsson Mate and His Sweethearts, The Old Man Is Coming, One Single Night, Nothing But the Truth, The Little WRAC of the Veteran Reserves, Charmers at Sea, My Little Brother and I, Night in June, A Big Hug, The Little Shrew of the Veteran Reserves, The Gentle-*

man Gangster, Fransson the Terrible, A Poor Millionaire, Only a Woman, Talk of the Town, A Singing Lesson, Scanian Guerilla, Elvira Madigan (43); The Ingegerd Bremssen Case, Sailor in a Dresscoat, Nothing Will Be Forgotten, Jacob's Ladder, Woman Takes Command, Women in Prison, As You Like Me, Mr. Collin's Adventures, King's Street, Life is There to Be Lived, Kajan Goes to Sea, I Killed, Darling I Surrender, The Halta Lotta Tavern, Little Napoleon, She Thought It Was Him, Dangerous Roads, The Awakening of Youth, A Girl for Me, His Official Fiancée, I Am Fire and Air, And All These Women, The Emperor of Portugal, The Holy Lie, Watch Out for Spies!, Stop! Think of Something Else, Wandering with the Moon, The Suffering and Happiness of Motherhood, Hunted, The New Affairs of Pettersson and Bendel, The Rose of Thistle Island, Good

Morning Bill, Åsa-Hanna, The Gay Party, It's My Model, Bad Eggs, A Lovely Young Lady, Crisis, When the Door Was Closed, The Balloon, Dynamite, A Father Wanted, The Most Beautiful Thing on Earth, The Sixth Commandment, Two Women, Woman without a Face, Life at Forsbyholm, On These Shoulders, A Swedish Tiger, Miss Sunbeam, Gentlemen of the Navy, Woman in White, Prison/The Devil's Wanton, The Street, Boman Gets Crazy, Girl with Hyacinths, Knockout at the "Breakfast Club," The Quartet that Split Up, The Kiss on the Cruise, A Gentleman Maybe, My Name Is Puck, Divorced, Bom the Customs-Officer, A Fiancée for Hire, Defiance, The Time of Desire, Salka Valka, Simon the Sinner, Hoppsan!, The Merry Boys of the Fleet, Matrimonial Announcement, Love Chastised, Little Fridolf and I, Private Entrance, Children of the Night (56).

● 149 LÖWENADLER, HOLGER (1904-   ). B: Jönköping. Actor. 1923-27: trained at Royal Dramatic Theatre, Stockholm. Since then has appeared in a wide variety of roles on stage, screen and TV. One of the true professionals of the Swedish cinema, an imposing and boisterous figure in films like *The Road to Heaven* and *A Ship Bound for India*. Films: *Love and Dynamite, Karl Fredrik Reigns, Simon from Backabo, The Women around Larsson, Flirtation in the Archipelago, Poor Millionaires, Urchins in no. 57, Breakers, A Cold in the Head, A Girl Comes to Town, Happy Vestköping, You Free Old Country, They Staked Their Lives, Flowering Time, Song of the Wilds, The Gentleman Gangster, Little Shrew of the Veteran Reserves, Jacob's Ladder, The Road to Heaven, Lack of Evidence, Night in the Harbour, The Big Crash, The Word,*

The Royal Hunt, The Emperor of Portugal, A Woman for Men, Journey Out, Iris and the Lieutenant, Johansson and Vestman, A Ship Bound for India, On These Shoulders, Woman in White, Jack of Hearts, Divorced, Dangerous Curves, Barabbas, The Girl from Backafall, A Man in the Kitchen, In Smoke and Dancing, Married Life (57), *The Pawn Shop, Love Chastised, Private Entrance, The Rusk, Tarps Elin, With the Halo Askew, A Guest in One's Own Home, The Clergyman from Uddarbo, A Thief in the Bedroom, The Judge, Three Wishes, The Summer Night Is Sweet, Here Is Your Life, Thirty Times Your Money, I Am Curious—Yellow.*

• 150 MAGNUSSON, CHARLES (1878-1948). B: Göteborg. Cameraman, cinema owner, producer, director, and scriptwriter. From 1909: production manager of Svenska Bio and later of Svensk Filmindustri (1919-1928). The man behind the "golden age" of Swedish silent cinema. Gave directors like Sjöström and Stiller their chance to work in films. One of his major *coups* was to obtain the rights to all Selma Lagerlöf's (q.v.) work. Films as director (also scripted except for*). *The Waltz of the Poker, The Pirate, Fisherman's Waltz from Bohuslän, When I Was a Prince of Arcadia, The Night March in St. Erik's Lane, Memories from the Boston Club* 09; *Orpheus in the Underworld, Faderullan ur Göteborgssystemet i Grönköping, Pick Me Up, Going to the "Maxim," Entry Song from the Dollar Princess* 10; *Sailor's Dance*, The Talisman* 11; *The Vagabond's Galoshes, The Green Necklace* 12. Films as scriptwriter only: *The People of Värmland, The Tales of Ensign Steel, The Iron-Carrier, The Adventures of Two Swedish Emigrants in America* (co.), *The Death Ride under the Big Top, The Black Masks* (co. Stiller), *A Secret Marriage, Smiles and Tears, The Red Tower* (co. Stiller and others). Magnusson can also be considered as "producer" of virtually all films from Svenska Bio.

• 151 MALMSTEN, BIRGER (1920-). B: Gräsö. Actor. At first studied

acting in various theatres. During the Sixties has played in comparatively few films, devoting his time instead to the stage and TV. The axiomatic figure of Bergman's early period, the rebellious, handsome *jeune premier* of *Music in Darkness/Night Is My Future, A Ship Bound for India, Prison/The Devil's Wanton, Thirst/Three Strange Loves,* and *Summer Interlude/Illicit Interlude.* Films: *We Need Each Other, Frenzy/Torment, Count the Happy Moments Only, The Serious Game, It Rains on Our Love/ Man with an Umbrella, When Meadows Bloom, A Ship Bound for India, Crime in the Sun, Dangerous Spring, Music in Darkness/Night Is My Future, The Banquet, Eva, The Intimate Restaurant, Prison/The Devil's Wanton, Thirst/Three Strange Loves, To Joy, The Rose of the Regiment, Summer Interlude/Illicit Interlude, Waiting Women/Secrets of Women, Ursula—the Girl from the Forest Depths, No Man's Woman, All the Joy of the Earth, The Time of Desire, Gabrielle, In Smoke and Dancing, The Unicorn, The People from the Depths of the Forest, Clouds over Hellesta, As You Make Your Bed, Encounters at Dusk, Lights at Night, Playing on the Rainbow, Laila, The Gold-Diggers, The Man in the Middle, The Silence, As the Naked Wind from the Sea, Carmilla.*

• 152 MARMSTEDT, LORENS (1908-1966). B: Stockholm. Producer and director. 1927: film critic. 1938-59: production chief at Terra Film, which he founded. Married to Gio Petré (q.v.). An imaginative and courageous producer, known for his support of Hasse Ekman and Ingmar Bergman (both q.v.). Films (as producer unless stated otherwise): *A Stolen Waltz* (dir. 32), *The Love Express* (dir. 32), *A Poet Maybe* (dir. and co-script 33), *The Atlantic Adventure* (dir. and co-script 34), *Eve Goes on Board* (dir. and co-prod. 34), *Pettersson—Sweden, The Marriage Game, The King Is Coming, The Girls of Uppåkra* (co-dir. Alice Eklund 36), *The Two of Us, Her Little Majesty, A Crime, With You in My Arms, Life Goes On, First Division, Flames in the Dark, Luck Arrives, General von Döbeln, Changing Trains, Women in Prison, The Sixth Shot, Sonja, Narcosis, His Excellency, We Need Each Other, The Girl and the Devil, Crime and Punishment* (45), *In Death's Waiting Room* (co. Hasse Ekman), *It Rains on Our Love/Man with an Umbrella, Supper for Two, A Ship Bound for India, Crime in the Sun, Music in Darkness/Night Is My Future, Prison/The Devil's Wanton, The Wind Is My Lover, Fire Bird, The Yellow Squadron, Hoppsan!* (co. Jörgensen), *Gorilla, Stage Entrance* (co. Jörgensen), *Count on Trouble* (co. Jörgensen), *A Lion in the Town, Summer and Sinners, Two Living and One Dead* (co.), *The Doll, Adam and Eve* (co.), *Wedding—Swedish Style, The Cats, Nightmare, Woman of Darkness.*

• 153 MATTSSON, ARNE (1919-). B: Uppsala. Director, also editor. At first assistant to Lindberg (q.v.). An

• 154 MITT HEM ÄR COPACABANA/MY HOME IS COPACABANA. 1965. Script: Arne Sucksdorff, Joâo Bethencourt, and Flávio Migliaccio. Direction, Photography, and Editing: Arne Sucksdorff. Music: Radames Gnatelli, Luciano Perrone, Luis Antonio. Commentary spoken by: Allan Edwall. Players: Leila Santos de Sousa (*Lici*), Cosme de Santos (*Jorghino*), António Carlos de Lima (*Rico*), Josáfa de Silva Santos (*Paulinho*), Hermania, Goncalves, Dirce Migliaccio, Joâo Lucas, Flávio Migliaccio, Alvaro Perez, Andrey Salvador, António Sampio. 88 mins. For Svensk Filmindustri.

PLOT: The film revolves around four children, Lici, Jorghino, Rico, and Paulinho, who struggle cheerfully for survival in the slum area of Copacabana, on the hillside overlooking Rio de Janeiro. Jorghino, looking for a means of making money, coats the tail of his kite with powdered glass. This enables him to cut down other kites on the beach and to sell them to passers-by. But during the children's excursion to the beach, their makeshift home has been occupied by bandits, and so the four youngsters spend an uncomfortable night on the sands. They grow more desperate, and proceed from begging in the bars and restaurants to stealing, in the company of some older and more experienced delinquents. Another night is spent on the beach. The children cannot sleep and they watch a black magic celebration.

action film-maker who has worked at nearly every major Swedish company since the war and has earned himself the title of "the Swedish Hitchcock." His handling of suspense is efficient, and in his middle period (1951-55) he was pictorially imaginative; but now he is hampered by poor scripts and an excess of horror effects. Mattsson co-scripted*. Films: *The Regiment of Halland* (short) 42; *And All These Women* 44; *Marie in the Windmill, Sussie, You Who Are about to Enter* 45; *Bad Eggs, Peggy on a Spree* 46; *A Father Wanted, A Guest Came*, Navvies** 47; *Dangerous Spring* 48; *Woman in White* 49; *When Love Came to the Village, The Saucepan Journey, The Kiss on the Cruise** 50; *Rolling Sea, One Summer of Happiness* 51; *A Dull Clang, Because of My Hot Youth* 52; *The Bread of Love* 53; *Storm over Tjurö, Enchanted Walk, Salka Valka* 54; *Men in Darkness, The People of Hemsö* 55; *A Little Place of One's Own, Girl in a Dress-coat* 56; *Spring of Life* (in Argentina), *No Tomorrow* 57; *Lady in Black, The Phantom*

One of the Brazilian boys in MY HOME IS COPACABANA

In the morning, Rico complains of tooth-ache. Jorghino takes out the tooth with a pair of pliers, but the film ends with Rico's returning to Caxambou, the approved school from which he had run away in the first place.

• 155 MOLANDER, GUSTAF (1888-   ). B: Helsinki. Director and script-writer. Trained at Royal Dramatic Theatre, Stockholm, then acted in Helsinki (1909-11), and in Stockholm from 1913 to 1926. Since 1923: at Svensk Filmindustri as director. Scripted many of his own films*. Versatile, resourceful director whose career spanned Swedish cinema from its "Golden Age" to the newest generation who collaborated with him on *Stimulantia*. Married (1) to Karin Molander (q.v.). Films as director: *King of Boda** 20; *Thomas Graal's Ward**, *The Amateur Film* 22; *33.333** 24; *Constable Paulus's Easter Bomb**, *The Ingmar Inheritance* (co.*) 25; *To the Orient* (co.*), *She the Only One* 26; *His English Wife, Sealed Lips* 27; *Women of Paris, Sin* 28; *Triumph of the Heart* 29; *Charlotte Löwensköld, Frida's Songs* 30; *One Night* 31; *Black Roses, Love and Deficit, We Go Through the Kitchen* (co.*) 32; *Dear Relatives* (co.*) 33; *A Quiet Affair, My Aunt's Millions, Bachelor Father** 34; *Swedenhielms, Under False Colours* 35; *The Honeymoon Trip, On the Sunny Side, Intermezzo* (co.*), *The Family Secret* 36; *Sara Learns Manners* 37; *Dollar*

• 156 MOLANDER, KARIN (1890-
). B: Vårdinge. Actress. 1921-25
and 1930-36: engaged at Royal Dramatic
Theatre, Stockholm. Married to Gustaf
Molander (q.v.) 1910-18; and to Lars
Hanson (q.v.) 1922-65. Her insouciance
and calculated charm made her a natural
choice for many of Stiller's best roles.
Films: *Half-breed, The Red Tower,
Hearts that Meet, Madame de Thèbes,
The Avenger, Her Royal Highness, Love
and Journalism, The Fight for His Heart,
Mrs. B's Lapse, Who Fired?, Thomas
Graal's Best Film, A Girl from the Marsh
Croft, The Living Mummy, Thomas
Graal's First Child, The Substitute, Syn-
növe Solbakken, The Bomb, The Fishing
Village, Erotikon, Gabrielle.*

(co.*), *A Woman's Face, One Single
Night* 38; *Variety Is the Spice of Life,
Emilie Högqvist* (co.*) 39; *One but a
Lion* 40; *Bright Prospects* (co.*), *Tonight
or Never, The Fight Goes On* (co.*) 41;
Jacob's Ladder, Ride Tonight! (co.*) 42;
Darling I Surrender, The Word (co.*),
There Burned a Flame 43; *The Invisible
Wall, The Emperor of Portugal* (co.*)
44; *Mandragora* (co.*) 45; *It's My
Model* 46; *Woman without a Face*
(co.*) 47; *Life Begins Now, Eva*
(co.*) 48; *Love Will Conquer* (co.*) 49;
The Quartet that Split Up (co.*) 50;
Fiancée For Hire, Divorced 51; *Defiance,
Love* (co.*) 52; *Unmarried* (co.*) 53;
Sir Arne's Treasure (re-make, co.*) 54;
The Unicorn (co.*) 55; *The Song of the
Scarlet Flower* (re-make) 56; *Stimulantia*
(one episode, co.*) shot in 65 released in
67. Films as scriptwriter: *Miller's Docu-
ment* (co.), *Terje Vigen, Thomas Graal's
Best Film* (co.), *Thomas Graal's First
Child* (co.), *Gunnar Hede's Saga* (co),
*Pirates on Lake Mälar, Uncle Blue's New
Boat.*

• 157 MOLANDER, OLOF (1892-
1966). B: Helsinki. Director. Brother of
Gustaf Molander (q.v.). 1934-38: Head
of Royal Dramatic Theatre, Stockholm.
Chief Director there from 1947. A specialist in Strindberg (q.v.) productions.

Both as a stage and screen director he showed a keen psychological understanding of his material. Much admired by Bergman (q.v.). Films: *Thomas Graal's Ward* (acted), *33.333* (acted), *The Lady of the Camellias* (dir. and script, 25), *Married Life* (26, dir.), *Only a Dancing Girl* (dir. and script, 27), *The Old Man Is Coming* (acted), *A Big Hug* (acted), *General von Döbeln* (dir. and co-script, 42), *Women in Prison* (dir. 43), *I Killed* (dir. 43), *Appassionata* (dir. and script, 44), *Between Us Thieves* (dir. and co-script, 45), *Wandering with the Moon* (acted), *Mandragora* (acted), *Johansson and Vestman* (dir., 46), *We Three Are Making Our Début* (co-script with Grevenius, q.v.).

• 158 MYRBERG, PER (1933-   ). B: Stockholm. Actor. 1955-57: trained at Royal Dramatic Theatre, Stockholm, where he has frequently appeared since. Also singer. Has worked in TV. Since 1968: Municipal Theatre of Stockholm. Youthful leading man at his most effective in truculent or moody roles. Films: *The People of Värmland, The Judge, Pleasure Garden, The Mistress, Adam and Eve, The Cats, The Island, The Myth, Made in Sweden.*

• 159 NATTVARDSGÄSTERNA/ WINTER LIGHT. 1963. Script and Direction: Ingmar Bergman. Photography: Sven Nykvist. Editing: Ulla Ryghe. Music: none. Art Direction: P. A. Lundgren. Players: Ingrid Thulin (*Märta Lundberg*), Gunnar Björnstrand (*Tomas Ericsson*), Max von Sydow (*Jonas Persson*), Gunnel Lindblom (*Karin Persson*), Allan Edwall (*Algot Frövik*), Kolbjörn Knudsen (*Knut Aronsson*), Olof Thunberg (*Fredrik Blom*), Else Ebbesen (*Old woman*), Eddie Axberg. 80 mins. For Svensk Filmindustri.

PLOT: A village pastor, Thomas Ericsson, celebrates Communion with a few parishioners, including Märta Lundberg, a school teacher who has been his mistress since his wife died five years before. After the service, a local fisherman, Jonas Persson, approaches Ericsson with his wife. He tells him, or rather his wife tells him, that he is living in fear of the Chinese, who he feels will use atomic weapons without compunction. Tomas tries to cheer his spirits, but he can only talk about his own doubts and inadequacies. A short time later, after he has read a letter given him by Märta in which she appeals to his love, Tomas learns that Jonas has committed suicide. He goes to the roadside where the body is lying and then sets about breaking the news to Karin Persson. A climactic row with Märta in the school classroom leaves him feeling depressed, but chastened. He goes to another church in his parish for evensong, and begins the service even though there is only one person present—Märta.

• 160 NILSSON, MAJ-BRITT (1924-
). B: Stockholm. Actress. 1944-47:
trained at Royal Dramatic Theatre, Stock-
holm. The quiet and sensitive heroine of
Bergman's early period. Now working
mainly in the theatre. Has appeared in
German films. Films: *Our Gang, Journey
Out, It's My Model, Maria, The Street,
The Girl from the Gallery, Spring at
Sjösala, To Joy, Summer Interlude/Illicit
Interlude, Waiting Women/Secrets of
Women, Because of My Hot Youth, We
Three Are Making Our Début, Wild
Birds, A Little Place of One's Own, Pri-
vate Entrance, The Girl in a Dress-coat,
A Girl for the Summer, The Jazz Boy,
Trust Me Darling.*

• 161 NORDGREN, ERIK (1913-
). Composer. Studied at the Musical
Academy of Stockholm. The most prolific

and versatile composer of film scores in Sweden. Much of his work has been for Bergman (q.v.)*. Scores for shorts include: *Going Ashore, Indian Village, Johan Ekberg, The Butterfly and the Flame*. Features: *Crime and Punishment, Woman without a Face, Life Begins Now, Eva, Thirst/Three Strange Loves*, Love Will Conquer, This Can't Happen Here*, Summer Interlude/Illicit Interlude*, Divorced, Defiance, Waiting Women/Secrets of Women*, Summer with Monika*, Hidden in the Fog, Unmarried, Dance My Doll, Gabrielle* (co. Theselius), *Violence, Smiles of a Summer Night*, Private Entrance, Ratataa* (co. Povel Ramel), *Last Pair Out, The Seventh Seal*, Wild Strawberries*, A Square Peg in a Round Hole, Playing on the Rainbow, The Jazz Boy* (arr. only), *The Face/The Magician*, Crime in Paradise, The Virgin Spring*, Decimals of Love, Face of Fire, On a Bench in a Park* (co. Theselius), *Carnival* (orchestration), *Two Living and One Dead, Pleasure Garden, Now about These Women*, The Dress, Well Well Well*

(co.), *4 x 4* (Troell episode), *Here Is Your Life, Who Saw Him Die?* (sound effects).

• 162 NYKVIST, SVEN (1922-   ). B: Moheda. Director of photography. 1941: joins Sandrews. Has also worked in West Germany and Africa. Bergman's regular collaborator*, and one of the top lighting cameraman in Europe, particularly skilful at using filters and in achieving a translucent clarity in his images. 1943: assistant on *In the Darkest Corner of Småland*. Films: *Good Morning Bill* (co. Hilding Bladh and Göran Strindberg), *13 Chairs, Salt Water Spray and Tough Old Boys, Maj from Malö, Lazy Lena and Blue-Eyed Per, Spring at Sjösala, Tall Lasse from Delsbo, Devil and the Man from Småland* (co. Carl Edlund), *Bohus Battalion, Loffe Becomes a Policeman* (co. Strindberg), *The Land of Rye, Review at the Södran Theatre* (co.), *When Lilacs Blossom, Under the Southern Cross* (also scripted and co-dir. with Olof Bergström, doc.), *Barabbas* (co. Strindberg), *The Road to Klockrike, Sawdust and Tinsel**

(co. Hilding Bladh), *Storm over Tjurö, Karin Månsdotter, Salka Valka, Gentle Thief of Love, The Last Form, Blue Sea, Darling at Sea* (co. Strindberg), *Laughing in the Sunshine, The Brave Soldier Jönsson, Girl in a Dress-coat, Gorilla* (also co-dir.), *Children of the Night* (56), *A Dreamer's Walk, A Guest in One's Own Home, Synnöve Solbakken, Lady in Black, Laila, May I Borrow Your Wife?, The Virgin Spring*, The Judge, Trust Me Darling, Through a Glass Darkly*, Winter Light*, The Silence*, Prince Hat below Ground, Now about These Women*, The Dress, Loving Couples, To Love, The Vine Bridge* (also dir. 65), *Persona*, Hour of the Wolf*, Roseanna, The Sinning Urge/Burnt Child, Shame*, The Rite** (for TV), *An-Magritt* (in Norway), *A Passion**.

● 163 NYMAN, LENA (1944-   ). B: Actress. Entered dramatic school at six. Child star in *Dangerous Promise*. Also TV work. 1964: trained at Royal Dramatic Theatre, Stockholm. Blonde, chubby personality made famous by her part in

I Am Curious. Films: *Dangerous Promise, Music on Board, Rasmus and the Tramp, Yes He Has Been with Me, 491, I Am Curious—Yellow, I Am Curious—Blue, The Father*.

● 164 NÄRA LIVET/SO CLOSE TO LIFE/BRINK OF LIFE. 1958. Script: Ulla Isaksson, from her short story "Det vänliga, värdiga." Direction: Ingmar Bergman. Photography: Max Wilén. Editing: Carl-Olov Skeppstedt. Music: none. Art Direction: Bibi Lindström. Players: Ingrid Thulin (*Cecilia Ellius*), Bibi Andersson (*Hjördis*), Eva Dahlbeck (*Stina Andersson*), Barbro Hiort af Ornäs (*Sister Brita*), Max von Sydow (*Harry Andersson*), Erland Josephson (*Anders Ellius*), Gunnar Sjöberg (*Medical Director*), Ann-Marie Gyllenspetz (*Welfare Officer*), Inga Landgré (*Greta Ellius*), Margaretha Krook (*Dr. Larsson*), Lars Lind (*Dr. Thylenius*), Sissi Kaiser (*Sister Marit*), Monica Ekberg, Gun Jönsson, Maud Elfsiö, Inga Gill, Gunnar Nielsen, Kristina Adolphson. 83 mins. For Nordisk Tonefilm.

PLOT: A young woman, Cecilia Ellius, is brought into the emergency ward of a maternity hospital after she has started bleeding only three months into her pregnancy. She has a miscarriage, and is brought into Room E, where two other expectant mothers, Stina and Hjördis, are already installed. Stina is strong and healthy, but her baby is overdue. Hjördis is expecting an illegitimate child and has tried to abort. When Cecilia regains consciousness, she talks openly with her husband, who obviously did not want the child to be born. Hjördis tries to speak to her boy friend, but he is rude and abrupt on the telephone. She also resists the advice of the Welfare Officer, who tries to comfort her. As night falls, Stina's labour begins. Something goes wrong, and after a protracted fight, the baby is born

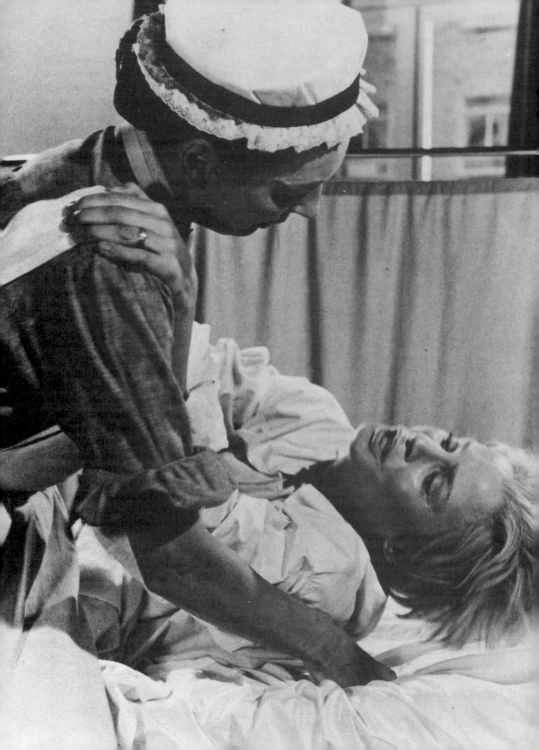

dead. In the morning, Hjördis is told she can leave the hospital; she rings up her parents, confesses everything, and decides that she now wants the child. Cecilia is visited by her sister-in-law, a lonely woman who implores her to discuss matters with her husband so that their quarrel can be forgotten. Cecilia promises. As Hjördis leaves, Stina is asleep after her tragic loss.

● 165 OLE DOLE DOFF/WHO SAW HIM DIE?/EENY MEENY MINY MOE. 1968. Script: Clas Engström, Bengt Forslund, and Jan Troell, from the novel "Ön sjunker" by Engström.

Direction, Photography and Editing: Jan Troell. Music: Erik Nordgren. Art Direction: none. Players: Per Oscarsson (*Mårtensson*), Kerstin Tidelius (*Gunvor*), Ann-Marie Gyllenspetz (*Ann-Marie*), Bengt Ekerot (*Eriksson*), Harriet Forssell (*Mrs. Berg*), Per Sjöstrand (*Headmaster*), Georg Oddner (*Georg*), Catharina Edfeldt (*Jane*), Bo Malmqvist (*Bengt*). 110 mins. For Svensk Filmindustri (Bengt Forslund).

PLOT: Mårtensson is a school teacher in the Sorgenfriskolan in Malmö. He is bitterly conscious of his failure to communicate with his class. Jane and Bengt are persistent trouble-makers, and Mårtensson finds himself resorting to panic

Opposite: Ingrid Thulin (at right, with Barbro Hiort af Ornäs) in SO CLOSE TO LIFE.
Above: Per Oscarsson with the children in WHO SAW HIM DIE?

measures in an effort to control the children. His wife, Gunvor, despises him and cannot understand his difficulties. Only Ann-Marie, another teacher, offers any kind of sympathy. On a free day, he strolls round the town and by chance meets an old friend who is now a successful fashion photographer, and he sees his own failure in an even gloomier perspective. His wife leaves him. The children become cruel in their behaviour towards Mårtensson. One day a pupil is run over by a lorry in the play area, and Mårtensson is supervising at the time. Shortly afterwards, during a swimming excursion, the boys in the water duck him repeatedly until he expires . .

● 166 OLIN, STIG (1920-   ). B: Stockholm. Actor and director. Trained in the theatre. The irascible, unpredictable hero of Bergman's earliest films. Later a director of modest comedies, and head of the entertainment section of Swedish Radio since 1962. Also singer and composer of popular songs. Directed* some of the films in which he appeared. Films: *Bright Prospects, Tonight or Never, The Fight Goes On, Poor Ferdinand, The Knockout Clergyman, Anna Lans, The Word, Frenzy/Torment, Between Us Thieves, Three Sons Went to the Air Force, Two People* (silhouette role only), *Crisis, Johansson and Vestman, Bad Eggs, The Balloon, Jens Månsson in America, Woman without a Face, Each Goes His Own Way, Port of Call, Eva, Dangerous Spring, Prison/The Devil's Wanton, The Girl from the Gallery, To Joy, This Can't Happen Here, The Quartet that Split Up, Summer Interlude/Illicit Interlude, Divorced, Class Mates, Barabbas, In Major and Showers* (*and co-script only, 53), *The Journey to You* (*and co-script, co-score, 53), *The Yellow Squadron* (*and co-script, 54), *Gentle Thief of Love, Murder My Little Friend* (*and script, 55), *Hoppsan!* (*only, 55), *Swing It Miss!* (*and script only, 56), *Stage Entrance, Rasmus, Pontus and Fool* 56; *A Guest in One's Own Home* (*and script only, 57), *You Are My Adventure* (*and script, co-score, 58), *Overlord of the Navy* (*only, 58), *Swinging at the Castle* (co-script only).

● 167 ORDET/THE WORD. 1943. Script: Rune Lindström, from the play by Kaj Munk. Direction: Gustaf Molander. Photography: Åke Dahlquist. Editing: Oscar Rosander. Music: Sven Sköld. Art Direction: Arne Åkermark. Players: Victor Sjöström (*Knut Borg Sr.*), Holger Löwenadler (*Knut, his eldest son*), Rune Lindström (*Johannes, his second son*), Stig Olin (*Anders, his youngest son*), Wanda Rothgardt (*Inger*), Gunn Wållgren (*Kristina*), Inga Landgré (*Ester*), Ludde Gentzel (*Tailor-Peter, the preacher*), Torsten Hillberg (*Dr. Bergman*), Olle Hilding (*Brandelius, a curate*), Gun-Britt Holmstedt (*Anna*), Lillemor Holmstedt (*Little Inger*), Emmy Raymond-Albin (*Maria from Myrbo*), Helga Brofeldt (*Emma*), Anders Frithiof (*The vicar*), Gabriel Alw (*The verger*), Agne Swedbäck, Erik Forslund (*Funera-*

guests), Nils Jacobson, Gunnar Ekwall (*Workmen*), John Elfström (*Worker in café*). 108 mins. For Svensk Filmindustri.

PLOT: Knut Borg is a widowed farmer who is a vigorous believer in the Old Testament. He rules his farm and his sons with an iron hand. His eldest son Knut is often rebellious. Knut's wife Inger acts as mistress of the farm. The next son, Johannes, has studied theology, but when his *fiancée* is killed in an accident, he becomes a brooding, Christ-like figure. The youngest son, Anders, is in love with Ester, the daughter of the preacher "Tailor-Peter." This love is rejected, as the fathers are bitter enemies.

Inger dies during childbirth, and then Tailor-Peter relents and offers Ester as a mistress to replace Inger. On the day of the funeral Johannes orders Inger to wake up. Only a small child can share his firm belief. But the miracle happens, and when Inger rises from her coffin Johannes's mental health is restored.

and Eve, You Must Be Crazy Darling!, My Sister My Love, Here Is Your Life, The Myth, Hunger, Who Saw Him Die?, Dr. Glas (in Denmark), Waltz of Sex, An-Magritt (in Norway), It's Up to You (also co-scripted), The Emigrants and Unto a Good Land.

• 168 OSCARSSON, PER (1927-). B: Stockholm. Actor. 1944-47: trained at Royal Dramatic Theatre, Stockholm. 1953: Göteborg Municipal Theatre. 1966: winner of Best Actor award at Cannes for role in *Hunger*. Also preacher and lecturer, as well as playwright. Tall, lean, and sensitive player who has become increasingly skilled at portraying the anguished outsider, although he has a comic flair too. Appeared briefly in Anthony Mann's *A Dandy in Aspic* (68). Has also worked in Spain, and for American TV. Films: *The Serious Game, Youth in Danger, Kristin Takes Command, Most Beautiful Thing on Earth, Son of the Sea, The Street, Destination Rio, Living at "The Hope," Meeting Life, Defiance, We Three Are Making Our Début, Barabbas, Karin Månsdotter, Wild Birds, No One Is Crazier than I Am, The Summer Night Is Sweet, Ticket to Paradise, The Doll, Yes He Has Been with Me, Adam*

• 169 PALME, ULF (1920-). B: Stockholm. Actor. 1942-45: trained at Royal Dramatic Theatre, Stockholm. Directs stage productions there now. His screen parts are usually short and terse, building an image of middle-aged restraint and discontent. His Jean in *Miss Julie* (q.v.) is probably his finest role. Films: *Black Roses, The Serious Game, Nightly Encounter, If Dew Falls Rain Follows, A Soldier's Duties, Crime in the Sun, On These Shoulders, Only a Mother, The Realm of Man, Girl with Hyacinths, While the City Sleeps, This Can't Happen Here, Miss Julie, Rolling Sea, Barabbas, Young Man Seeks Company, Sir Arne's Treasure* (54), *God and the Gipsyman, Karin Månsdotter, Journey into Autumn/Dreams, Wild Birds, The Witch, Tarps*

103

Elin, Woman in a Leopardskin, The Judge, Hide and Seek, Thirty Times Your Money, Here Is Your Life, Rooftree, The Girls, Dr. Glas (in Denmark), *The Corridor.*

● 170 PASSGÅRD, LARS (1941-). B: Borås. Actor. 1958-60; trained at Municipal Theatre, Malmö. 1962-66: TV appearances. Has filmed in Italy and Norway. In spring 1969 he was a remarkable Hamlet on stage in Ålborg in Denmark. Passgård made a startling film *début* as the vulnerable young Minus in *Through a Glass Darkly.* Other films: *The Pram, Wedding—Swedish Style, The Hunt, The Serpent, The Fateful Bell, The Princess.*

● 171 PAWLO, TOIVO (1917-). B: London. Actor. 1936-39: trained at Royal Dramatic Theatre, Stockholm. Since 1960: engaged at the Municipal Theatre, Stockholm. Various other theatres. Also TV work. A versatile and experienced actor with a very personal style, notably as the pompous Chief of Police in *The*

Portraits: Ulf Palme (above left), Lars Passgård (above right), and Toivo Pawlo (below)

Face/The Magician. Films: *Anna Lans, Young Blood, A Day Shall Dawn, The Girl and the Devil, Crime and Punishment, Stora Hopare Lane and Heaven, Count Svensson, Barabbas, No One Is Crazier than I Am, Blue Sky, Where Windmills Run, The Face/The Magician, Blackjackets, A Lion in Town, The Die Is Cast, Do You Believe in Angels?, One Zero Too Many, Hide and Seek, Dream of Happiness, The Yellow Car, Loving Couples, The Ball Room, Made in Sweden.*

• 172 PENGAR/MONEY. 1946. Script: Nils Poppe and Rolf Botvid. Direction: Nils Poppe. Technical Adviser: Lars-Eric Kjellgren. Photography: Martin Bodin. Editing: Oscar Rosander. Music: Sune Waldimir. Art Direction: Nils Svenwall. Players: Nils Poppe (*Harry Orvar Larsson*), Inga Landgré (*Maria*), Sigge Fürst (*Sigge Savage*), Calle Reinholdz (*Kalle "Feeble-Minded"*), Hilding Rolin (*Hilding "Ill-Tempered"*), Birger Åsander (*Birger "Fierce"*), Gustaf Färingborg (*Gustav "Mean"*), Alexander Baumgarten (*Helge "Resentful"*), Elof Ahrle (*The Philosopher*), Ragnar Widestedt (*Maria's father*), Carl-Hugo Calander (*Bertil Waller*), Olav Riégo (*Mr. Ernwall, lawyer*), Ulla Norgren (*Waitress in café*), Arne Lindblad (*Café owner*), Julia Caesar, Gabriel Alw, Åke Engfeldt (*Party Guests*), Erik Hell (*The stoker*). 97 mins. For Fribergs Filmbyrå.

PLOT: Harry Orvar Larsson, a vagabond, spends his life roaming the countryside with his friend, the Philosopher. But one day Orvar decides to take a job. He becomes an assistant to six brothers, rough lumberjacks, who make fun of him cruelly. Their food is cooked by an attractive young girl, Maria, who is a millionaire's daughter, tired of her previous life of luxury. Orvar has inherited a huge legacy without realising it, and now the six brothers become obsequious. But contrary to expectation

Orvar becomes a tyrant and humiliates the giant lumberjacks. After they have tricked him into writing a will to their benefit, their behaviour changes and they try to kill him. Orvar escapes, only to be outwitted by his old friend, the Philosopher. Destitute, he works for the Mint, burning old banknotes, but he cannot smuggle any of these out for his personal use. In an ironic twist even his own banknote is burnt by mistake. When he comes out into the street, he finds that Maria has left him.

• 173 PERSONA. 1966. Script and Direction: Ingmar Bergman. Photography: Sven Nykvist. Editing: Ulla Ryghe. Music: Lars Johan Werle. Art Direction: Bibi Lindström. Players: Liv Ullmann (*Elisabet Vogler*), Bibi Andersson (*Nurse Alma*), Margaretha Krook (*Woman Doctor*), Gunnar Björnstrand (*Mr. Vogler*), Jörgen Lindström (*The Boy*). 81 mins. For Svensk Filmindustri.

PLOT: Elisabet Vogler is a famous actress. In the middle of a performance of Electra, she falls silent. Even prolonged treatment at a psychiatric clinic fails to make her speak. The doctor in charge suggests to her nurse, Alma, that she should spend some time in isolation on the coast with their patient. Faced by the obstinate yet also sympathetic silence of Elisabet, Alma begins to tell her more than she should. Impressed by the physical resemblance between the two of them, she even identifies herself, subconsciously, with the actress. But the friendship is disturbed when Alma discovers from an unsealed letter to the doctor that the actress is observing her coolly and amusedly. Alma now becomes almost hysterical, trying to project her own feelings of guilt and anguish on to Elisabet, urging her wildly to speak. Back at the clinic, Alma breaks down after a final outburst. . . .

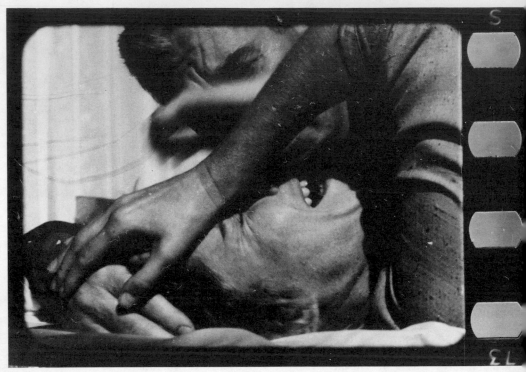

Bibi Andersson and Gunnar Björnstrand in PERSONA

• 174 PERSSON, EDVARD (1888-1957). B: Malmö. Actor. 1905: first appearance on stage. Probably the greatest box-office star in Swedish film history. A genial giant of a clown, playing with sentimental charm and songs on his Scanian traits, and enjoying his heyday in the Thirties and early Forties. Films (sometimes as director† and scriptwriter*): *The Students of Tröstehult*†* (also prod.), *The Old Manor*† 25; *Millionaire for a Day*†* 26; *Quick as Lightning, What Woman Wants*†* (also prod.) 27; *On the Cruise with the "Lightning"*†* (also prod.) 27; *The Hatter's Ball*†* 28; *Sten Stensson Stéen from Eslöv, Two Hearts and a Boat, The Ramshackles of Söder, Augusta's Little Slip, Saturday Evenings,* *The Dangerous Game*, Secret Agent Svensson, The Girls from the Old Town, The Women around Larsson, Near Relations, Larsson in His Second Marriage*, South of the Main Road, Our Boy, Ola Gods Are Still Alive, Baldevin's Wedding The Small Towns of Skanör-Falsterbo Kalle på Spången, Shy Anton, A Sailor on a Horse, Sunny Mr. Solberg, Scanian Guerilla, Sunshine over Klara, Life in the Country, The Station Master at Lyckås, At the Beginning of the Century The Gay Tailor*, 13 Chairs, The Bells of the Old Town, Jens Månsson in America, Each Heart Has Its Story, The Gay Parade* (compilation film), *House Number 17, Sven Tusan, Pimpernel Svensson Count Svensson, The Girl from Backafall*

A Night at Glimminge Castle, Blue Sky, Where Windmills Run.

• 175 PETRÉ, GIO (1937-   ).
Blonde, sensitive actress who began at the Terserus Theatre School and then trained at the Royal Dramatic Theatre, Stockholm. Has also worked in TV. Films: *Merry Boys of the Fleet, Gorilla, Stage Entrance, Wild Strawberries, Model in Red, Rider in Blue, The Die Is Cast, Summer and Sinners, Mother of Pearl, Lady in White, The Doll, Adam and Eve, Loving Couples, The Cats, I Need a Woman, Roseanna, The Vicious Circle, I—A Woman II* (in Denmark), *Waltz of Sex, The Swedish Fanny Hill, Teddy Bear, As the Naked Wind from the Sea.*

• 176 POPPE, NILS (1908-   ). B: Malmö. Actor and director. A comedian whose reputation after the war extended well beyond Sweden. A small, ingenuous, wide-eyed Chaplin of his time. But his finest performance was probably as Jof in *The Seventh Seal* (q.v.), a melancholy role demanding something more than mere knockabout charm. Films as actor (sometimes also co-scripted* and directed†): *Send No. 7 Home, Adolf as a Fireman, Ghost for Sale, The Melody from the Old Town, Brave Boys in Uniform, Like*

a Thief in the Night, The Merry-Go-Round in Full Swing, Our Boys in Uniform, Three Gay Fools, Three Funny Rascals, Professor Poppe's Crazy Eccentricities, Ghosts! Ghosts!, The Actor*, Sten Stensson Comes to Town, Bluejackets*, Money†* 46, The Balloon†* 46, Poor Little Sven*, Don't Give Up*, Private Bom*, The Count from the Lane*, Pappa Bom*, Bom the Customs-Officer*, Flying Bomb*, Dance My Doll*, Stupid Bom†* 53, The Pawn Shop, The Shining Light from Lund, The Rusk, The Seventh Seal, Overlord of the Navy*, A Lion in Town, Only a Waiter*, The Devil's Eye, Sten Stensson Comes Back*.

• 177 PRAWITZ, ELSA (1932-   ). B: Stockholm. Actress and scriptwriter. 1950-54: trained at Royal Dramatic Theatre, Stockholm. 1968: Municipal Theatre, Uppsala. 1956-66: married to Arne Mattsson (q.v.), in whose films her sexy appearance has often been successfully used. Films: Divorced, The Road to Klockrike,

Enchanted Walk, Men in Darkness, Hoppsan!, Seven Beautiful Girls, Children of the Night (56), The Girl in a Dress-coat, The Brave Soldier Jönsson, Model in Red, May I Borrow Your Wife, Summer and Sinners, When Darkness Falls, The Summer Night Is Sweet, The Doll, Yes He Has Been With Me (also script), Hide-and-seek, Three Days as a Vagabond, Morianna, The Piano Lesson (short), The Sadist, Woman of Darkness, The Murderer—an Ordinary Person, The Vicious Circle (also script), I—a Marquis (in Denmark), Teddy Bear (co-script).

• 178 PUSS OCH KRAM/HUGS AND KISSES. 1967. Script and Direction: Jonas Cornell. Photography: Lars Swanberg. Editing: Ingemar Ejve. Music: Bengt Ernryd. Art Direction: Walter Hirsch. Players: Sven-Bertil Taube (Max), Agneta Ekmanner (Eva), Håkan Serner (John), Lena Granhagen (Kickan), Rolf Larsson (Photographer), Ingrid Boström, Carl Johann Rönn, Peter Cornell. 94 mins. For Sandrews.

PLOT: John is thrown out by his mistress. He is a struggling writer, and now he seeks the hospitality of an old school friend, Max. He is allowed to stay with Max and his wife Eva provided that he takes on all domestic duties. This leads to friction between Max and Eva, and there is an open quarrel when John tries to bring a new girl friend, Kickan, into the flat. Both Max and Eva try one last trick, but it misfires and Max finds himself "displaced" by John in the marital bed.

• 179 QUENSEL, ISA (1905-   ). B: Göteborg. Actress. Originally opera singer. 1935-56: mainly theatre work. Since 1956: also teaching at the opera school. Her film appearances have been rather rare but very effective. A specialist in understanding, somewhat disillusioned women. Films: We Must Have Love, The

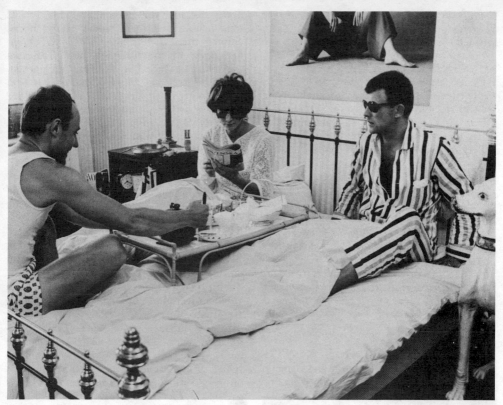

Agneta Ekmanner and Sven-Bertil Taube in HUGS AND KISSES (with Håkan Serner at left)

Love Express, Gay Musicians, Housemaids, Pettersson and Bendel, Love and Dynamite, False Greta, A Hotel Adventure, Raggen—that's Me, My Mother-in-law—the Dancer, The Girls of Uppåkra, A Girl Comes to Town, Happy Vestköping, Wanted, Marianne, Unmarried, The Chief from Göinge, The Unicorn, Clouds over Hellesta, The Manors around the Lake, A Guest in One's Own Home, Seventeen Years Old, Lady in Black, The Koster Waltz, Playing on the Rainbow, The Phantom Carriage (58), Laila, Do You Believe in Angels?, Two Living and One Dead, Mother of Pearl, Parlour Games, To Love, Wedding—Swedish Style, Loving Couples, The Cats, Woman of Darkness.

• 180 RHUDIN, FRIDOLF (1895-1935). B: Munkfors. Actor. A sophisticated comedian of the late silent period and early Thirties. Sometimes referred to as the Swedish Buster Keaton. Also singer. Films (many of which were directed by Gustaf Edgren*): *People of Värmland* (as extra only), *The Young Lady of Björneborg*, *People of Närke*, *Girl from Paradise, The People of Simlången Valley, For the Home and the Girl, Mr. Karlsson Mate and His Sweethearts*, *She He and Andersson*, *The Incendiary, The Ghost Baron, The Tragicomic Barber* (in Denmark), *Black Rudolf*, *False Svensson*, *Gentlemen in Uniform, The False Millionaire, Ship Ahoy!*, *The Boys on Storholmen, The Gay Musicians,*

Fridolf in the Lion's Cage, Secret Agent Svensson, Simon from Backabo (also scripted)*.

• 181 RIEDEL, GEORG (1934-   ). B: Czechoslovakia. Composer. 1938: comes to Sweden. Studied at the Stockholm Conservatoire, but primarily an autodidact. 1953: first professional assignment. Has often worked for Swedish Radio. His TV ballet *Riedaiglia* has been widely noted. Some music for the theatre. Films: *The Face of War, Prince Hat below Ground, Wild West Story* (co. Wiman and Brandt), *491, Wedding—Swedish Style, The Marriage Wrestler, The Ball Room, Nightmare, The Serpent, Night Games* (co. Jan Johansson), *Woman of Darkness, I Need a Woman, The Murderer—an Ordinary Person, Roseanna, The Sinning Urge/Burnt Child, Black on White* (in Finland), *Waltz of Sex, The Swedish Fanny Hill, Me and You* (co-prod. with Denmark).

• 182 ROOSLING, GÖSTA (1903-   ). B: Värmdö. Director and director of photography. His fine camerawork re-

flects his love of nature and his lyrical tendencies. Has made some sixty shorts, among them *Christmas Morn* 37, *Confirmation* 38, *Brownie* 41, and *Examination* 41. Features as director of photography: *The Road to Heaven, The Word, The Emperor of Portugal, A Woman for Men, Wandering with the Moon, Crisis, Iris and the Lieutenant, Poor Little Sven, The Banquet, Dangerous Spring.*

• 183 ROSANDER, OSCAR (1901-   ). B: Eksjö. Editor. 1928: university degree in languages. Then teacher and film translator. 1929: interpreter on Asquith's *A Cottage on Dartmoor*. 1935-61: film editor at Svensk Filmindustri. 1951-52: senior film editor for the United Nations in New York. Teacher of film editing in Swedish TV. The leading editor of his generation, if not of all Swedish cinema, Rosander has worked on a dozen Bergman films* and has also helped other directors outside Sweden (e.g. Fons Rademakers, whose *Village on the River* he cut). Films (not necessarily a complete list): *The Honeymoon Trip* (as actor only!), *Sara Learns Manners, Oh What a Night, The Old Man Is Coming, Rejoice while You Are Young, The Little WRAC of the Veteran Reserves* (also assist. dir.), *Whalers, Fellow Cadets* (also acted), *Steel, My Little Brother and I, Night in June, His Grace's Will, A Schoolmistress on the Spree, The Fight Goes On, Sextuplets, Jacob's Ladder, Life on a Perch, Hearts of Lieutenants, Ride Tonight!, The Road to Heaven, It's My Music, The Knockout Clergyman, Night in the Harbour, My Husband's Getting Married Today, His Majesty's Rival, The Word, The Royal Hunt, Frenzy/Torment, The Emperor of Portugal, Between Us Thieves, Wandering with the Moon, Mandragora, Blue-jackets, Jolanta—the Elusive Sow, The Journey Out, Money, Crisis*, The Balloon, It's My Model, Poor Little Sven, A Soldier's Duties, Woman without a Face, A Guest Is*

Coming, Port of Call*, Unto the Gates of Hell, Private Bom, Eva, The Count from the Lane, Woman in White, Thirst/ Three Strange Loves*, Only a Mother, Dangerous Spring, To Joy*, While the City Sleeps, The Quartet that Split Up, The Beef and the Banana, Bom the Customs-Officer, Skipper in Stormy Weather, Summer Interlude/Illicit Interlude*, Divorced, Meeting Life, Say It with Flowers, Blondie the Beef and the Banana, Defiance, Waiting Women/Secrets of Women*, Unmarried, In Smoke and Dancing, Victory in Darkness, A Lesson in Love*, Gabrielle, Sir Arne's Treasure (54), The Pawn Shop, Violence, Smiles of a Summer Night*, Private Entrance, The Seventh Heaven, Last Pair Out, The Song of the Scarlet Flower (56), The Rusk, With the Halo Askew, Lights at Night, A Summer Place Is Wanted, Wild Strawberries*, A Square Peg in a Round Hole, Playing on the Rainbow, The Jazz Boy, The Face/ The Magician*, Only a Waiter, Beautiful Susan and the Old Men, The Virgin Spring*, The Devil's Eye*, On a Bench in a Park, Carnival, Two Living and One Dead.

• 184 RYDEBERG, GEORG (1907-). B: Göteborg. Actor. 1929-31: trained at Royal Dramatic Theatre, Stockholm. Then acted with several Swedish theatre companies. Since 1957: attached to RDT. Tall, imposing player, with a stern avuncular manner that can be turned to comic ends. Particularly impressive as Lindhorst, the "birdman" in Hour of the Wolf (q.v.). Films: Nights in the Djurgård, Dear Relatives, Love and Dynamite, False Greta, The Girl from the Department Store, Under Notice to Leave, Alfred loved by the Girls, Walpurgis Night, A Cold in the Head, Adolf Armstrong, Dollar, A Woman's Face, Emilie Högqvist, Steel, In Paradise, A Schoolmistress on a Spree, Suppose I Were to Marry the Clergyman, Home from Babylon, Dangerous Roads, The Ingegerd Bremssen Case,

Doktor Glas (42), Changing Trains, As You Like Me, My Husband Is Getting Married Today, Gentleman with a Briefcase, That Girl Is a Discovery, Appassionata, Narcosis, Two People, Passion, You Who Are About to Enter, Harald Handfaste, Two Women, Life Begins Now, The Fire Bird, Up With the Green Lift, Because of My Hot Youth, The Shadow, Hidden in the Fog, The Bread of Love, Storm over Tjurö, Bomb of Laughter, Hoppsan!, The Last Form, The People of Hemsö (55), No One Is Crazier than I Am, Ratataa, Girl in a Dress-coat (56), Lights at Night, The Last Night, Seventeen Years Old, The Rusk, A Dreamer's Walk, Little Fridolf Becomes a Grandfather, The Clergyman from Uddarbo, Fridolf's Dangerous Age, The Judge, Swedish Portraits, The Ball Room, Hour of the Wolf, People Meet (co-prod. in Denmark), Waltz of Sex, The Father (69).

• 185 RYGHE, ULLA (1924-). Editor. Her sophisticated cutting of Bergman's trilogy and then of Persona (q.v.)

brought Miss Ryghe to the forefront of Swedish film editors. Before moving to Canada she was a teacher at the Swedish Film Institute Film School. Films: *Through a Glass Darkly, Garden of Eden, Siska, Winter Light, The Silence, Now about These Women, The Dress, Nightmare, Persona, Stimulantia* (Abramson, Bergman, Arnbom, Alfredson/Danielsson, Molander episodes), *Hour of the Wolf, Shame*.

• 186 SALKA VALKA. 1954. Script: Rune Lindström, from the novel by Halldór Laxness. Direction: Arne Mattsson. Photography: Sven Nykvist. Music: Sven Sköld. Art Direction: Bibi Lindström. Players: Birgitta Pettersson (*Salka Valka as a child*), Gunnel Broström (*Salka Valka*), Margaretha Krook (*Sigurlina, her mother*), Folke Sundquist (*Arnaldur*), Erik Strandmark (*Steintor*), Rune Carlsten (*Bogesen*). For Nordisk Tonefilm.

PLOT: Salka Valka arrives with her mother Sigurlina at a poor Icelandic fishing village. The community is dominated by Bogensen, the shop-keeper, who handles all financial transactions. Everybody works for him and everybody owes him money. Sigurlina is despised but finds a refuge with the Salvation Army. Salka Valka learns what poverty means in this barren, windswept landscape. The dreamer Arnaldur teaches her to read and gives her an idea of poetry and beauty. Her childhood comes to a brutal end when she is raped by Sigurlina's drunken *fiancé,* Steintor.

Ten years later Salka Valka is a mature woman, but she is as cynical and hard as life has taught her to be. She leads the opposition against Bogesen, but a strike fails. Her love for Arnaldur makes her weak and affects her reforming zeal. Finally Arnaldur takes the opportunity of leaving the village and emigrates to America.

• 187 SANDREW, ANDERS (1885-1957). B: Vendel. Producer. Real name: Andersson. The grocer who, with his shrewd business sense, became a legend in the Swedish film world, a stout millionaire who rode a bicycle to work. He rented his first cinema in 1926, and after ten years he was the owner of sixteen cinemas. 1937: founded AB Sandrew-biograferna. Sandrew co-operated with Schamyl Bauman (q.v.) in early years. The first of his own productions was *Can You Come Doctor?* in 1942. He made a wise move in engaging Rune Waldekranz (q.v.) as a producer and giving him a free hand. He was also a keen theatre man, and Sandrews today run four stage theatres in Stockholm. At his death, "Pappa" Sandrew was estimated to be worth some fifteen million Swedish crowns (about $2½ million), and most of the money was put into the Anders Sandrew Foundation, which promotes and aids the work of writers, actors, and young people generally. Sandrew Film & Teater AB now owns approximately fifty cinemas throughout Sweden, and production is in the hands of Göran Lindgren (q.v.).

Christina Schollin with Jarl Kulle in Lindgren's DEAR JOHN

● 188 SCHOLLIN, CHRISTINA (1937-). B: Stockholm. Actress. 1958-61: trained at Royal Dramatic Theatre, Stockholm. 1959: stage *début*. Has worked in TV and in sound broadcasting as well as on the stage. Probably the most popular Swedish actress of the Sixties within her own country. Blonde, sexy, sincere parts, not always in the best of films. *Swing It, Miss!, Black-jackets, Thief in the Bedroom, Decimals of Love, Wedding Day, Do You Believe in Angels?, Ticket to Paradise, The Wonderful Adventures of Nils, Wedding—Swedish Style, Dear John, The Serpent, Woman of Darkness, I Need a Woman, Love Thy Neighbour* (in Denmark), *The Slipper, Her Very Royal Highness* (in Norway).

● SEASTROM, VICTOR *see* SJÖSTRÖM, VICTOR.

● 189 SJÖBERG, ALF (1903-). B: Stockholm. Director. 1923-25: trained at Royal Dramatic Theatre, Stockholm. 1925-27: stage actor. 1930: Head Director at Royal Dramatic Theatre. Acted in *The Poetry of Ådalen* (28). The most respected theatre producer of his generation, Sjöberg has brought to his output of films a polished expertise and a flair for adaptation. He usually collaborates on his scripts. Films: *The Strongest* 29; *They Staked Their Lives, Flowering Time* 40; *Home from Babylon* 41; *The Road to Heaven* 42; *The Royal Hunt, Frenzy/ Torment* 44; *Journey Out* 45; *Iris and*

the Lieutenant 46; *Only a Mother* 49; *Miss Julie* 51; *Barabbas* 53; *Karin Månsdotter* 54; *Wild Birds* 55; *Last Pair Out* 56; *The Judge* 60; *The Island* shot in 64 released in 66; *The Father* 69.

• 190 SJÖBERG, GUNNAR (1909-). B: Stockholm. Actor. 1931-34: trained at Royal Dramatic Theatre, Stockholm. Since 1965: engaged at Municipal Theatre of Stockholm. Has spoken the commentary for several films by Arne Sucksdorff (q.v.). At first military roles, then more general character acting, most familiar from Bergman films like *Wild Strawberries* (as Alman) and *So Close to Life/Brink of Life* (as the doctor). Films: *Mr. Karlsson Mate and His Sweethearts, A Woman's Face, Variety Is the Spice of Life, Rejoice while You are Young, Whalers, Steel, Night in June, A Big Hug, The Gentleman Gangster, The Little Shrew of the Veteran Reserves, Göransson's Boy, First Division, Scanian Guerilla, The Ingegerd Bremssen Case, General von Döbeln, Ride Tonight!, The*

Road to Heaven, Lack of Evidence, Men-of-War, The Knockout Clergyman, Women in Prison, Elvira Madigan (43), *A Matter of Life and Death, I Killed, The Brothers' Woman, His Excellency, The Holy Lie, Prince Gustaf, Black Roses, The Children from Frostmo Mountain, The Rose of Thistle Island, The Serious Game, Youth in Danger, Sin, Backyard, Sabotage, Memory of Love, The Shadow, Victory in Darkness, Sir Arne's Treasure* (54), *The Merry Shoemaker, The Seventh Heaven, Ratataa, Lights at Night, Synnöve Solbakken* (57), *Wild Strawberries, A Square Peg in a Round Hole, So Close to Life/Brink of Life, Playing on the Rainbow, The Die Is Cast, The Devil's Eye, Do You Believe in Angels?, Hälleback Manor, Mother of Pearl, Hide and Seek.*

• 191 SJÖBERG, TORE (1915-). B: Stockholm. Producer. At first in charge of Swedish Film Department at the U.S. Embassy in Stockholm. 1945: buys Nordisk Tonefilm (Stockholm) and Folkbiografer. 1947; sells these companies and

launches Minerva Film. His wartime work is an important background to Sjöberg's interest in documentary, and these war films represent his most solid achievement, Recently he has produced screen versions of novels by Stig Dagerman (q.v.) and Artur Lundkvist. Films: *The People of Simlången Valley, The Unlucky Fellow of the Block, To Kill a Child* (short), *Games at Night* (short), *Mein Kampf, Secrets of the Nazi War Criminals, The Battle of Stalingrad, The Face of War, Adam and Eve* (co), *Wedding—Swedish Style, The Serpent, I Need a Woman, Roseanna, The Sinning Urge/Burnt Child, Waltz of Sex, The Swedish Fanny Hill.*

● 192   SJÖBLOM, ULLA (1927-   ). B: Stockholm. Actress. 1950-53: trained at Royal Dramatic Theatre, Stockholm. 1951: screen *début* in publicity film. Since 1959: TV work. This witty actress is seen all too rarely in the cinema, although her lusty "Olivia" in *Here Is Your Life* is the performance of her career. Films: *House of Women, The Journey to You,*

God and the Gipsyman, Karin Månsdotter, Young Man Seeks Company, Sir Arne's Treasure (54), *Simon the Sinner, Wild Birds, The People of Hemsö* (55), *Sleep Well, My Hot Desire, The Way via Skå, The Face/The Magician, The Sadist, Here Is Your Life, The Bookseller Who Gave Up Bathing.*

● 193   SJÖMAN, VILGOT (1924-   ). B: Stockholm. Director and script-writer. Novelist (*The Senior Master*), diarist (*L136: Diary with Ingmar Bergman* and *I Was Curious*), and essayist (*Hollywood*). Vigorous, committed director who integrates sex and violence into his studies of contemporary youth. Close friend of Bergman (q.v.), acted in *Shame,* and was his assist. dir. on *Winter Light.* Wrote his first play at age of seventeen. Films: *Defiance* (script only), *Playing on the Rainbow* (script only), *Siska* (script only, co. Ulla Isaksson), *The Mistress* (also scripted) 62; *491, The Dress* 64; *My Sister My Love* (also scripted) 65; *Stimulantia* (one episode) shot in 65

released in 67; *I Am Curious—Yellow* (also scripted) 67; *I Am Curious—Blue* (also scripted), *Journey with Father* (short) **68**; *Production 337—You're Lying!* (also scripted) 69-70.

● 194 SJÖSTRÖM, VICTOR (1879-1960). B: Silbodal (Värmland). Actor and director. 1896: makes *début* in theatre after being brought up in New York. 1898: stage manager of the Swedish theatre in Helsinki. 1912: joins Svenska Bio. Acting *début* in Stiller's *The Black Masks.* A great and prolific pioneer of the Swedish cinema, at his most impressive when adapting the novels of Selma Lagerlöf (q.v.), or passing social comment (*Ingeborg Holm, Our Daily Bread*). 1943-49: "Artistic director" at Svensk Filmindustri. 1923-30: Hollywood, where he was known as Seastrom. Final role, as Professor Isak Borg in *Wild Strawberries,* brought his name to the notice of a new generation. Starred in many of his own films†. Also scripted or co-scripted* several of them. Films as director: *The Gardener*†, *A Secret Marriage, A Summer Tale* (unreleased) 12; *The Marriage Bureau**, *Smiles and Tears, The Voice of Blood*†, *Lady Marion's Summer Flirtation*†, *Ingeborg Holm**, *The Clergyman* 13; *Love Stronger than Hate, Half-Breed, The Miracle, Do Not Judge, A Good Girl Should Solve Her Own Problems**, *Children of the Street, Daughter of the High Mountain*†*, *Hearts that Meet* 14; *The Strike**†, *One out of Many**, *Expiated Guilt**, *Keep to Your Trade**, *Judas Money, The Governor's Daughters**, *Sea Vultures, It Was in May** 15; *At the Moment of Trial*†*, *Ships that Meet, She Was Victorious*†*, *Thérèse** 16; *The Kiss of Death*†*, *Terje Vigen*†, *A Girl from the Marsh Croft** 17; *The Outlaw and His Wife*†* 18; *The Sons of Ingmar* (Pts I and II)†*, *His Grace's Will* 19; *The Monastery of Sendomir**, *Karin Daughter of Ingmar*†*, *The Executioner*†

Victor Sjöström in youth and age

Liv Ullmann and Max von Sydow in SHAME (with Karl-Axel Forsberg at right)

20; *The Phantom Carriage/Thy Soul Shall Bear Witness*† 21; *Love's Crucible*, Fire on Board/The Hell Ship*†, *The Surrounded House*†* 22; *Markurells i Wadköping*† 30 (Sjöström also directed a German version of this film the same year entitled *Väter und Söhne*). Films in Hollywood: *Name the Man* 23; *He Who Gets Slapped* 24; *Confessions of a Queen* 25; *Tower of Lies, The Scarlet Letter* 26; *The Divine Woman* 27; *The Wind, Masks of the Devil* 28; *A Lady to Love* 30. In England: *Under the Red Robe* 37. Films as actor only: *The Black Masks, In the Spring of Life, The Vampire, When Love Kills, The Child, Life's Conflicts, Because of Her Love, Thomas Graal's Best Film, Thomas Graal's First Child,*

Walpurgis Night, John Ericsson—the Victor at Hampton Roads, The Old Man Is Coming, Towards New Times, The Fight Goes On, There Burned a Flame, The Word, The Emperor of Portugal, Navvies, I Am with You, Dangerous Spring, To Joy, The Quartet that Split Up, Dull Clang, Love, Men in Darkness, Wild Strawberries.

• 195 SKAMMEN/SHAME, 1968. Script and Direction: Ingmar Bergman. Photography: Sven Nykvist. Editing: Ulla Ryghe. Music: none. Art Direction: P. A. Lundgren. Players: Max von Sydow (*Jan Rosenberg*), Liv Ullmann (*Eva Rosenberg*), Gunnar Björnstrand (*Jacobi*),

Sigge Fürst (*Filip*), Birgitta Valberg (*Mrs. Jacobi*), Hans Alfredson (*Lobelius*), Ingvar Kjellson (*Oswald*), Frank Sundström (*Interrogator*), Ulf Johanson (*Doctor*), Frej Lindqvist (*The Stooping Man*), Rune Lindström (*Elderly man*), Willy Peters (*Officer*), Bengt Eklund (*Guard*), Åke Jörnfalk (*The Condemned Man*), Vilgot Sjöman (*Interviewer*), Lars Amble (*Another officer*), Björn Thambert (*Johan*), Karl-Axel Forsberg (*Secretary*), Gösta Prüzelius (*Rector*), Brita Öberg (*Lady in school-house*), Agda Helin (*Lady in shop*), Ellika Mann (*Female Warder*), Barbro Hiort af Ornäs (*Woman on boat*), Monica Lindberg, Gregor Dahlman, Nils Whiten, Per Berglund, Stig Lindberg, Jan Bergman, Nils Fogeby, Brian Wikström, Börje Lundh, Georg Skarstedt, Lilian Carlsson, Eivor Kullberg, K. A. Bergman. 103 mins. For Svensk Filmindustri.

PLOT: 1971. There is a civil war sweeping across the Baltic lands. Eva and Jan are musicians who have withdrawn to a remote island where they eke out a living by growing and selling fruit. The island is invaded. A guerilla movement arises, involving many civilians. Jan's old friend, Jacobi, proves to be a quisling. He arrests Jan and Eva, but soon releases them. He comes to their cottage and tries to make some kind of meaningful contact with them. While Jan is asleep Jacobi and Eva make love together. When Jan discovers this, he steals Jacobi's savings. Jacobi cannot buy himself out of trouble, and Jan becomes his unwilling executioner. Jan and Eva flee with their scanty possessions. They purchase a place on board a rowing boat. But food and water run out. The boat is left to drift for ever in the vast sea.

● 196 SKEPPSTEDT, CARL-OLOV (1922-   ). Editor, who has worked for most of the Swedish production companies. Main films: *The Poetry of Ådalen, The Devil and the Man from Småland, Pippi Long-Stocking, Fun with Boccaccio, The Land of Rye, Ghost on Holiday, When Lilacs Blossom, Kalle Karlsson from Jularbo, Unmarried Mothers, Ursula—the Girl from the Forest Depths, Sawdust and Tinsel/The Naked Night, Dance My Doll, Storm over Tjurö, The Yellow Squadron, Taxi 13, Blocked Rails, Journey into Autumn/Dreams, A Girl for the Summer, Children of the Night* (56), *Girl in a Dress-coat, Clouds over Hellesta, Mother Takes a Holiday, Little Fridolf and I, So Close to Life/Brink of Life, The Phantom Carriage* (58), *Susanne, Ringside* (doc.), *Wedding Day, Good Friends and Faithful Neighbours, Mother of Pearl, The Wonderful Adventures of Nils, Yes He Has Been with Me, The Yellow Car, Adam and Eve, Parlour Games, My Love Is a Rose, Swedish Portraits, The Marriage Wrestler, Just like Friends, To Go Ashore, Well Well Well, The Island, Woman of Darkness, Stimulantia*, (Sjöman episode), *The Bookseller Who Gave Up Bathing, Duet for Cannibals.*

● 197 SMULTRONSTÄLLET/WILD STRAWBERRIES. 1957. Script and Direction: Ingmar Bergman. Photography: Gunnar Fischer. Editing: Oscar Rosander. Music: Erik Nordgren. Art Direction: Gittan Gustafsson. Players: Victor Sjöström (*Professor Isak Borg*), Ingrid Thulin (*Marianne, his daughter-in-law*), Bibi Andersson (*Sara*), Gunnar Björnstrand (*Evald, Isak's son*), Folke Sundquist (*Anders*), Björn Bjelvenstam (*Viktor*), Naima Wifstrand (*Isak's mother*), Gunnar Sjöberg (*Alman*), Gunnel Broström (*Mrs. Alman*), Jullan Kindahl (*Agda, the housekeeper*), Gertrud Fridh (*Isak's wife*), Åke Fridell (*Her lover*), Max von Sydow (*Åkerman*), Sif Ruud (*Aunt*), Yngve Nordwall (*Uncle Aron*), Per Sjöstrand (*Sigfrid*), Gio Petré (*Sigbritt*), Gunnel Lindblom (*Charlotta*), Maud

Hansson (*Angelica*), Anne-Marie Wiman (*Mrs. Åkerman*), Eva Norée (*Anna*), Lena Bergman, Monica Ehrling (*Twins*), Per Skogsberg (*Hagbart*), Göran Lundquist (*Benjamin*), Professor Sigge Wulff (*Rector, Lund University*), Gunnar Olsson (*Bishop*), Josef Norman (*Professor Tiger*). 95 mins. For Svensk Filmindustri.

PLOT: Professor Isak Borg, seventy-eight years of age, is called from his home in Stockholm to the university town of Lund to receive an honorary Doctorate for his services to science. He travels with his daughter-in-law, Marianne, who feels resentful towards him because his son—her husband—displays all the egotistical traits of the old man, and does not wish to have children. *En route,* Borg gives a lift to Alman and his wife after an accident, and Alman later returns to interrogate the Professor during one of the many dreams that haunt him during the journey. They also encounter three young hikers, Sara, Anders, and Viktor, and take them in the car to Lund. During a visit to his family's former summer house, a break for lunch beside a lake, and in the car afterwards, Isak is assailed by nightmares in which he is made aware of his faults. He re-lives old sufferings and moments of error. But after the ceremony at Lund, he finds that Sara and her friends really hold him in great affection, and he seems able to relax and look forward to sleep, at peace with his conscience.

Bibi Andersson and Victor Sjöström in WILD STRAWBERRIES

• 198 SOLDAT BOM/PRIVATE BOM. 1948. Script: Per Schytte (Adolf Schütz and Paul Baudisch) and Nils Poppe. Direction: Lars-Eric Kjellgren. Photography: Gunnar Fischer. Editing: Oscar Rosander. Music: Kai Gullmar and Sune Waldimir. Art Direction: Nils Svenwall. Players: Nils Poppe (*Fabian Bom*), Inga Landgré (*Agnes*), Douglas Håge (*Major Killman*), Gunnel Wadner (*Gabriella*), Åke Jensen (*Lt. Allan Forsberg*), Ludde Juberg (*Zakarias*), Julia Caesar (*Carolina Hård*), Gunnar Björnstrand (*Sgt. Berglund*), Gösta Cederlund (*The Colonel*), Karl-Erik Flens (*The Corporal*), Birger Åsander (*The Gaoler*), Nils Hallberg (*Joker Kalle*), Rune Andreasson (*Little Brother*), Anders Andelius (*Red Riding Hood*), Rune Ottosson (*The Student*), George Adelly (*Fiffikus*), Naima Wifstrand (*Head Nurse*), Margareta Weivers (*Reception Nurse*), Nils Jacobsson (*Military Surgeon*), Wiktor Andersson (*Engine-driver*), Karl-Axel Elving (*Recruit on the road*), Rolf Bergström (*Sad man*). 89 mins. For Fribergs Filmbyrå and Komiska Teatern.

PLOT: Fabian Bom is an extremely conscientious station-master. The trains have never been so much as a tenth of a second late at his station. Never has the heart been allowed to prevail over the watch. One day he finds a young girl, Agnes, in his waiting room. She is a somewhat Bohemian character who has escaped from a boarding school run by Bom's strict aunt. To please the beautiful "Plumplum" Bom enlists. He takes the hardships of army life as a joke. The military spirit appeals to his sense of punctuality. However, Bom's army career is far from successful, and he is subjected to hard punishment drill; but nothing can break his spirit. Finally "Plum-plum" falls for a Lieutenant, and for the first time Bom yields to his feelings when he becomes aware of his love for Agnes.

• 199 SOMMAREN MED MONIKA/SUMMER WITH MONIKA/MONIKA. 1953. Script: Ingmar Bergman and P. A. Fogelström from an idea, synopsis, and novel by the latter. Direction: Ingmar Bergman. Photography: Gunnar Fischer. Editing: Tage Holmberg, Gösta Lewin. Music: Erik Nordgren. Art Direction: P. A. Lundgren, Nils Svenwall. Players: Harriet Andersson (*Monika*), Lars Ekborg (*Harry*), John Harryson (*Lelle*), Georg Skarstedt (*Harry's father*), Dagmar Ebbesen (*Harry's aunt*), Åke Fridell (*Monika's father*), Naemi Briese (*Monika's mother*), Åke Grönberg, Sigge Fürst, Gösta Prüzelius, Arthur Fischer, Torsten Lilliecrona, Bengt Eklund, Gustaf Färingborg, Ivar Wahlgren, Renée Björling, Catrin Westerlund, Harry Ahlin. 97 mins. For Svensk Filmindustri.

PLOT: Harry is a young errand boy in a crockery warehouse. When by chance he meets Monika, a wild, erotic girl working in a neighbouring grocer's shop, he is immediately infatuated. Monika has a quarrel with her father and decides to "borrow" a motor boat for a holiday with Harry in the archipelago outside Stockholm. Towards the end of an idyllic period on a remote island, Monika announces that she is pregnant. Harry agrees to do the proper thing and marry her. They move into a shabby flat, and Monika is soon disgruntled with the unglamorous tasks of motherhood. Harry returns from a business trip to find that she has been sleeping with another man in his absence. There is a row, and Monika flounces out of the flat. Harry is left alone with the baby, not knowing what the future may bring.

• 200 SOMMARLEK/SUMMER INTERLUDE / ILLICIT INTERLUDE. 1951. Script: Ingmar Bergman and Herbert Grevenius, from an original script by Bergman. Direction: Ingmar Bergman.

Harriet Andersson in SUMMER WITH MONIKA

Photography: Gunnar Fischer. Editing: Oscar Rosander. Music: Erik Nordgren. Art Direction: Nils Svenwall. Players: Maj-Britt Nilsson (*Marie*), Birger Malmsten (*Henrik*), Alf Kjellin (*David*), Annalisa Ericson (*Kaj*), Georg Funkquist (*Uncle Erland*), Stig Olin (*Ballet-master*), Renée Björling (*Aunt Elisabeth*), Mimi ´Pollak (*Little woman in black*), John Botvid (*Karl*), Gunnar Olsson (*Vicar*), Douglas Håge, Julia Caesar, Carl Ström, Torsten Lilliecrona, Marianne Schüler, Ernst Brunman, Olav Riego, Fylgia Zadig, Sten Mattsson, Carl Axel Elfving, Gösta Ström. 96 mins. For Svensk Filmindustri.

PLOT: Marie is a ballerina attached to the Opera in Stockholm. During a summer vacation in the Archipelago, she falls in love with Henrik. But their happiness is clouded by the jealousy of Marie's uncle Erland, who was once infatuated with her (Marie's) mother and now lives in bitterness with his wife, Elisabeth. Henrik's gardienne is also a depressing figure. She is dying from cancer. Then, just as autumn creeps in and the time comes to return to Stockholm, Henrik is killed in a diving accident on the shore. Marie is overcome by grief. A journalist, David, tries to comfort her, but it is not until uncle Erland sends her the diary that she kept during that idyllic summer that she can pluck up the courage to visit the island again and purge herself of her memories. This "journey to the past" allows her to move forward with David to a new independence.

- 201 SOMMARNATTENS LEENDE/SMILES OF A SUMMER NIGHT. 1955. Script and Direction: Ingmar Bergman. Photography: Gunnar Fischer. Editing: Oscar Rosander. Music: Erik Nordgren. Art Direction: P. A. Lundgren. Players: Ulla Jacobsson (*Anne Egerman*), Gunnar Björnstrand (*Fredrik Egerman*), Eva Dahlbeck (*Desirée Armfeldt*), Margit Carlquist (*Charlotte Malcolm*), Harriet Andersson (*Petra*), Jarl Kulle (*Count Malcolm*), Åke Fridell (*Frid*), Björn Bjelvenstam (*Henrik Egerman*), Naima Wifstrand (*Old Mrs. Armfeldt*), Jullan Kindahl (*The Cook*), Gull Natorp (*Malla, Desirée's maid*), Bibi Andersson, Birgitta Valberg (*Actresses*). 104 mins. For Svensk Filmindustri.

PLOT: Fredrik Egerman, a prosperous lawyer, attends the theatre with his young wife, Anne, and later goes backstage to arrange a rendezvous with his former mistress, Desirée Armfeldt. Desirée's lover of the moment is Count Malcolm, who is affronted by the presence of Egerman. The two encounter each other again when Desirée's old mother holds a weekend party at her manor in Skåne. Henrik, Egerman's son by an earlier marriage, is studying

Gunnar Björnstrand, Eva Dahlbeck, and Jarl Kulle in SMILES OF A SUMMER NIGHT

theology, but he is constantly being ogled by Petra, the maid. In fact, during the interlude at Mrs. Armfeldt's, Henrik finds himself drawn to Anne, who has been neglected by Egerman; Petra rolls in the hay with Frid, the groom; and Egerman is seduced by the Count's wife, Charlotte, with the result that he has to fight a duel by Russian roulette with his rival. But the gun has a blank cartridge filled with soot, and Egerman, though humiliated, survives to impress and regain the affections of Desirée.

● 202 STATENS BIOGRAFBYRÅ. The official name for the Swedish Board of Film Censors. Sweden was the first country in the world to introduce state film censorship (1911). The films submitted are divided into four categories: 1. Universal exhibition. 2. Exhibition to all over the age of eleven. 3. Exhibition to all over the age of fifteen. 4. Banned. It could be said that, compared to international practice, Swedish film censors are tolerant towards sex but hard on violence and sadism. Up to January 1, 1969, exactly 107,606 films (features, shorts, newsreels, publicity films etc.) had been submitted. Present head: Erik Skoglund.

● 203 STILLER, MAURITZ (1883-1928). B: Helsinki. Director, actor, and scriptwriter. Emigrated to Sweden at age of twenty-seven. 1925: leaves for Hollywood with Garbo (q.v.). 1912: joins Svenska Bio. With Sjöström (q.v.) the greatest Swedish director of the silent period, equally at home with comedy and drama. Films as director (sometimes acted*, or scripted†): *Mother and Daughter*†*, *The Black Masks*†, *The Tyrannical Fiancé** 12; *The Vampire*†, *When Love Kills*†, *The Child*, *When the Alarm Bell Rings*, *The Modern Suffragette*†, *On the Fateful Roads of Life*†, *The Unknown Woman*†, *The Model*†, *Life's Conflicts* 13; *The Brothers*†, *When Mother-in-law*

Reigns†*, *People of the Border*, *Because of Her Love*, *The Chamberlain*, *Stormy Petrel*, *The Shot*, *The Red Tower*† 14; *When Artists Love*, *The Playmates*†, *His Wife's Past*, *The Dagger* (banned by censors), *Ace of Thieves*, *Madame de Thèbes* 15; *The Avenger*, *The Mine-Pilot*, *His Wedding Night*, *The Lucky Brooch*, *Love and Journalism*, *The Wings*†, *The Fight for His Heart*†, *The Ballet Primadonna* 16; *Thomas Graal's Best Film*†, *Alexander the Great*† 17; *Thomas Graal's First Child*† 18; *Song of the Scarlet Flower*†, *Sir Arne's Treasure*† 19; *Fishing Village/The Vengeance of Jacob Vindås*, *Erotikon*† 20; *Johan*†, *The Exiles*† 21; *Gunnar Hede's Saga*† 23; *The Saga of Gösta Berling*† 24. Films in Hollywood: *Hotel Imperial*, *The Temptress* (completed by Fred Niblo) 26; *The Woman on Trial*, *The Street of Sin* (co. Josef von Sternberg) 27. Stiller also scripted *The Gardener*, and acted in *In the Spring of Life*.

● 204 STRANDBERG, EVABRITT (1943-   ). B: Stockholm. Actress. 1962: private drama school. 1965-67:

trained at Royal Dramatic Theatre, Stockholm. Later on stage in Göteborg and Norrköping. Also TV work. This grave, sensual young actress is a kind of Swedish Monica Vitti, and made a striking *début* as the mistress in *Love 65.* Features: *Love 65, The Myth, Masculin/Féminin* (co-prod with France), *I Love You Love.*

● 205 STRANDMARK, ERIK (1919-63). B: Torsåker. Actor. 1938-41: trained at Royal Dramatic Theatre, Stockholm. 1945-47: merchant navy. Much theatre and TV work. A controlled and yet elaborate style allowing ample room for his personal temperament to show through. A splendid Carlsson in *The People of Hemsö.* Early and untimely death in an accident. Films: *The Invisible Wall, We Need Each Other, The Royal Rabble, Rolling Sea, U-boat 39, Love, Unmarried Mothers, Barabbas, The Road to Klockrike, Sawdust and Tinsel/The Naked Night, Hidden in the Fog, Possessed by Speed, Victory in Darkness, Karin Månsdotter, Salka Valka, Wild Birds, No One Is Crazier than I Am, The*

People of Hemsö (55), *Kulla-Gulla, Children of the Night* (56), *The Tough Game, Girl in a Dress-coat, Little Fridolf and I, Stage Entrance, The Seventh Seal, The Way via Skå, Tarps Elin, Encounters at Dusk, Lights at Night, The Master Detective Leads a Dangerous Life, The Clergyman from Uddarbo, Nothin' but Blondes, Woman in a Leopardskin, We on Väddö, Beautiful Susan and the Old Men* (also dir. and co-script), *No Time to Kill.*

● 206 STRINDBERG, AUGUST (1849-1912). B: Stockholm. Author. This giant of Swedish literature, apart from being a master both of realism and expressionism in modern drama, exerted a strong influence on Swedish film-makers (notably Bergman, q.v.). His third wife, Harriet Bosse, was a famous Norwegian actress who also appeared in films later. Strindberg was interested in cinema and was perfectly happy for screen versions to be made of his work. Films from his books: *The Father, Miss Julie* 12; *The People of Hemsö* 19; *For High Ends,*

based on a short story 21; *Married Life* 26; *Sin,* based on a play "Brott och brott" 28; *The People of Hemsö* (re-make) 44; *Miss Julie* (re-make) 51; *Karin Månsdotter,* based on a play "Erik XIV" 54; *The People of Hemsö* (re-make) 55; *Married Life* (which also told the story of "A Doll's House") 57; *The Father* (re-make) 69.

● 207 STRINDBERG, GÖRAN (1917-   ). B: Stockholm. Director of photography. 1937-42: assistant at Europa Film. 1942-58: director of photography at Sandrews and Terra Film. 1954-61: works abroad. Now instructor at the Swedish Film Institute Film School. The leading lighting cameraman of the Forties, with some magnificent work to his credit in *Miss Julie* (q.v.). Films: *Men-of-War, Changing Trains, A Springtime Tune, I Killed, Kajan Goes to Sea, We Need Each Other* (co.), *My People Are Not Yours, Little Saint, Prince Gustaf, Crime and Punishment, Good Morning Bill* (co. Nykvist and Bladh), *The Rose of Thistle Island, The Clergyman from the Wilds,*

Desire, It Rains on Our Love/Man with an Umbrella (co. Bladh), *The Song about Stockholm, Maria, A Ship Bound for India, Neglected by His Wife* (co. Bladh), *The People of Simlången Valley, Music in Darkness/Night Is My Future, On These Shoulders, Prison/The Devil's Wanton, Vagabond Blacksmiths* (co. Carl Edlund), *The Girl from the Gallery, The Realm of Man, Stora Hopare Lane and Heaven, Girl with Hyacinths, The White Cat, Knockout at the "Breakfast Club," Loffe Becomes a Policeman* (co. Nykvist), *Miss Julie* (51), *One Summer of Happiness, Revue at the Södran Theatre* (co), *Ghost on Holiday, House of Folly, Rolling Sea, The Fire Bird, Barabbas* (co. Nykvist), *Stupid Bom, Journey to You, Dancing on Roses, Yellow Squadron* (co. B. Westfeldt), *Two Rascals* (co. Bladh), *Darling at Sea* (co. Nykvist), *Stage Entrance, Mother Takes a Holiday, The Koster Waltz.*

● 208 SUCKSDORFF, ARNE (1917-   ). B: Stockholm. Director of documentaries. Since 1951: freelance producer.

All Sucksdorff's films reflect his deep love of nature, and especially of central Sweden, although he has gone to the Far East (*The Flute and the Arrow*) and South America (*My Home Is Copacabana*) for material. He studied under Rudolf Klein-Rogge in Berlin. Shorts: *An August Rhapsody* 39; *Your Own Land* 40; *A Summer Tale* 41; *The Wind from the West, Reindeer Time* 43; *The Gull* 44; *Dawn, Shadows across the Snow* 45; *People of the City/Rhythm of a City, Dream Valley* 47; *Moving On/ The Open Road, A Divided World* 48; *Going Ashore, The Living Stream* 50; *Indian Village, The Wind and the River* (last two in India) 51. Features (also scripted): *The Great Adventure* 53; *The Flute and the Arrow* 57; *The Boy in the Tree* 61; *My Home Is Copacabana* 66.

● 209 SUNDQUIST, FOLKE (1925-
). B: Falun. Trained at Göteborg and Malmö Municipal Theatres. Actor who made his reputation with *One Summer of Happiness* and has not had any really outstanding parts in the past few

years. Films: *One Summer of Happiness, Because of My Hot Youth, The Bread of Love, Enchanted Walk, Salka Valka, Love Chastised, A Little Place of One's Own, Girl in a Dress-coat, The Spring of Life, Wild Strawberries, The Summer Night Is Sweet, The Vine Bridge, Hour of the Wolf, Teddy Bear.*

● 210 SUNDSTRÖM, FRANK (1912-
). B: Stockholm. Actor. 1931-34: trained at Royal Dramatic Theatre, Stockholm. 1945-51: in U.S.A. Since 1965: Head of the Municipal Theatre of Stockholm. Most of his time has been devoted to the stage, but his few screen appearances confirm him as an intelligent and sober actor. Films: *People of Hälsingland, Young Hearts, A Gentleman Maybe, 33.333, Bombi Bitt and I, Father and Son* (released 40—see Gösta Ekman entry), *Home from Babylon, Katrina, The Royal Hunt, Your Relatives Are Best, The Last Form, The People of Värmland* (57), *No Time to Kill, 491, Loving Couples, Just like Friends, Shame.*

● 211 SVEDLUND, DORIS (1926-
). B: Stockholm. Actress. 1944-47: trained at Royal Dramatic Theatre, Stockholm. 1947-61: engaged at same theatre. Then in Göteborg. TV work. Blonde, unobtrusive star of *Prison/The Devil's Wanton* and other characteristic Forties films, although most of her appearances were after 1950. Films: *When Meadows Bloom, Vagabond Blacksmiths, Prison/The Devil's Wanton, Bohus Battalion, The White Cat, Divorced, Meeting Life, Blondie the Beef and the Banana, Love, God and the Gipsyman, The "Lunchbreak" Café, Paradise, Violence, Clouds over Hellesta, Encounters at Dusk.*

● 212 SVENSKA FILMINSTITUT-ET/THE SWEDISH FILM INSTITUTE. This was founded on July 1, 1963 in an attempt to reorganise the Swedish film industry, to ensure a continuous and a continuing pattern of production, and to reward creative work. The entertainment tax was abolished, and 10% of every cinema ticket was passed to the Institute (giving it an estimated annual income of about 12 million Kr. or $2,350,000). This is divided into various percentage groups: to cover general support to Swedish feature films in proportion to their income from box-office receipts; to quality awards (about 18%) for Swedish features; to similar awards for Swedish shorts (about 2%); to a "Guarantee Fund" which guarantees loans of up to 25% of a Swedish film's production costs and waives these if the picture fails to break even; to public relations and promotion (about 5%); to distribute compensation for winners of quality awards that have not recovered their budget; and to various cultural activities (30%), including the financing of the Film School, the film archive, film societies, and film scholarship.

The master mind behind the new scheme was Harry Schein's. The 1963 reform was unique in film history, and other countries, such as Denmark and Yugoslavia, have evolved similar systems since. The most important aspect of Svenska Filminstitutet is that it acts as an insurance against loss for producers of quality films that cannot necessarily draw a large audience.

● 213 SVENSK FILMINDUSTRI. The foremost Swedish production company for over fifty years. It developed from the Handelsbolaget Kristianstads Biografteater, which started screening films in September 1905 in southern Sweden. Charles Magnusson (q.v.) became managing director in 1909—the company then being known as Svenska Bio. He moved to Stockholm in 1911, building a set of studios at Lidingö (although these were destroyed in the Forties). In 1919 he took over AB Skandia, his chief rival, and the new concern was christened Svensk Filmindustri (December 27, 1919).

In 1928, Magnusson retired. Two later heads of the company have been Carl Anders Dymling and Kenne Fant (both q.v.). Most of the great Swedish directors have worked at SF, beginning with Victor Sjöström and Mauritz Stiller in the silent period and continuing in later years with Alf Sjöberg and Ingmar Bergman (all q.v.). Actresses like Greta Garbo and Ingrid Bergman (both q.v.) also began at SF.

During the past ten years, more than fifty films have been completed at SF, whose studios are now at a new site in Stocksund. The organisation owns 113 cinemas, more than any other company in Sweden.

● 214 SVENWALL, NILS (1918-). Set designer who has also worked in TV. Films: *My Husband Is Getting Married Today, Night in the Harbour, The Clock at Rönneberga, The Emperor of Portugal* (co. Åkermark), *A Woman for Men, Two People, His Majesty Will Have To Wait* (co. Åkermark), *Nothing but Old Nobility* (co. Åkermark), *The Journey Out* (co. Åkermark), *Money, Kristin Takes Command, The Balloon* (co. Åkermark), *The Art of Love, A Father Wanted, A Girl from the Marsh Croft* (47), *Woman without a Face* (co. Åkermark), *Navvies, Don't Give Up, I Am with You, Life at Forsbyholm, A Swedish Tiger, Life Begins Now, Port of Call, Unto the Gates of Hell, Private Bom, Eva, Gentlemen of the Navy, Dangerous Spring, The Count from the Lane, Woman in White, Thirst/Three Strange Loves, Only a Mother, Swedish Horseman, Love Will Conquer, Pappa Bom, To Joy, While the City Sleeps, This Can't Happen Here, Backyard, The Kiss on the Cruise, The Quartet that Split Up, The Beef and the Banana, Fiancée for Hire, Bom the Customs-officer, Skipper in Stormy Weather, Summer Interlude/ Illicit Interlude, Divorced, Meeting Life, Say It with Flowers, Blondie the Beef* and the Banana, Defiance, Waiting Women/Secrets of Women, Summer with Monika (co. Lundgren), We Three Are Making Our Début, In Smoke and Dancing (co. Gamlin), Victory in Darkness, Gabrielle.

• 215 SYDOW, MAX VON (1929-). B: Lund. Actor. Real name: Carl Adolf von Sydow. Son of university professor. 1948-51: trained at Royal Dramatic Theatre, Stockholm. Has performed on stage in Hälsingborg, Malmö, Norrköping, and Stockholm. 1962: goes to Hollywood to play Christ in The Greatest Story Ever Told. Later plays in The Reward, Hawaii, and The Quiller Memorandum. One of Bergman's favourite actors, Sydow has scored in many Swedish films through his tall, powerful presence and his deep voiced delivery. At his most authoritative in historical works like The Seventh Seal and The Virgin Spring (both q.v.) Films: Only a Mother, Miss Julie, No Man's Woman, The Right to Love, The Seventh Seal, Wild Strawberries, The Clergyman

from Uddarbo, So Close to Life/Brink of Life, The Face/The Magician, Female Spy 503, The Virgin Spring, Wedding Day, Through a Glass Darkly, Winter Light, The Mistress, The Wonderful Adventures of Nils, 4 x 4 (Troell episode), Here Is Your Life, Hour of the Wolf, The Black Palm Trees, Shame, Made in Sweden, The Emigrants and Unto a Good Land, A Passion.

• 216 SYSKONBÄDD 1782/MY SISTER MY LOVE. 1966. Script and Direction: Vilgot Sjöman. Photography: Lars Björne. Editing: Lennart Wallén. Music: none. Art Direction: P. A. Lundgren. Players: Bibi Andersson (Charlotte), Per Oscarsson (Jakob), Jarl Kulle (Alsmeden), Gunnar Björnstrand (Schwartz), Tina Hedström (Ebba Livin), Berta Hall (Mrs. Küller), Åke Lindström (Her son), Rune Lindström (Pastor Storck), Sonya Hedenbratt (His wife), Gudrun Östby (Dress-maker), Lena Hansson, Leif Hedberg, Lasse Pöysti. 96 mins. For Sandrews.

PLOT: Jakob, a young nobleman, returns from Paris after spending five years abroad, and finds that his sister, Charlotte, intends to marry Baron Alsmeden. When he learns of the plans for the wedding, he becomes violently jealous. His feelings correspond to Charlotte's when she sees him courting Ebba Livin. Brother and sister gradually realise that they are in love with each other, and they spend a night together. But Charlotte's efforts to persuade Jakob to run away with her, and to convince Alsmeden that she is pregnant by another man, all fail. In the end, it is the jealous Ebba who becomes aware of the true situation, and in a fit of hysteria she shoots Charlotte. The baby is delivered from the dead girl's womb by an old cowwoman from the estate. It survives.

Opposite: Bibi Andersson and Jarl Kulle in MY SISTER MY LOVE

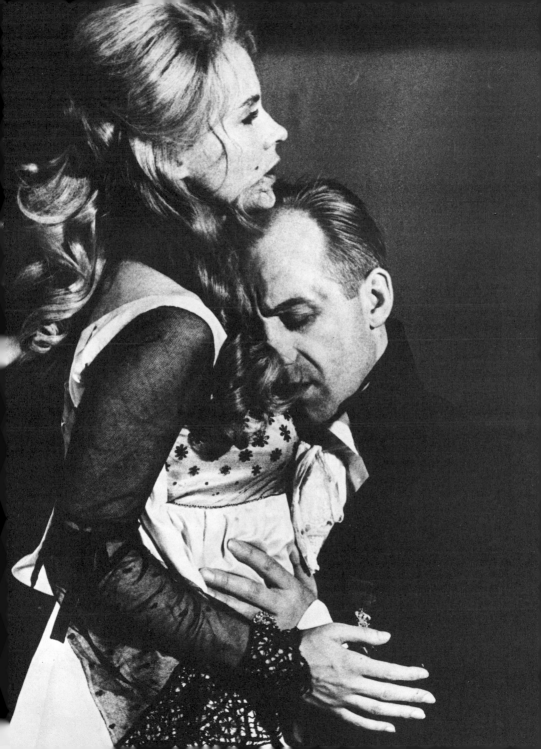

• 217 SÅSOM I EN SPEGEL/
THROUGH A GLASS DARKLY.
1961. Script and Direction: Ingmar
Bergman. Photography: Sven Nykvist.
Editing: Ulla Ryghe. Music: J. S. Bach,
Suite No. 2 in D Minor for Violincello.
Art Direction: P. A. Lundgren. Players:
Harriet Andersson (*Karin*), Gunnar
Björnstrand (*David*), Max von Sydow
(*Martin*), Lars Passgård (*Minus*). 91
mins. For Svensk Filmindustri.

PLOT: Karin, recently released from a
mental hospital, is recuperating on a lonely
island in the Baltic with her husband,
Martin, a doctor; her father, David, a
writer; and her seventeen-year-old brother,
Minus. David has just returned from
Switzerland and upsets his family by suggesting that he will soon be leaving again
on a lecture tour. Minus is in the awkward
stage of puberty, and feels neglected by
his father. Karin imagines that she can
hear strange voices in an upstairs room
in their cottage, and when she reads in
her father's diary that he is spying on her
illness, using it as material for his writings,
she rejects the real world and enters her
own private world of visions and voices.
During a storm she shelters with Minus
in a wreck on the shore, and seduces him.
When David and Martin return from a
trip to the mainland, Karin is in a severe
state of schizophrenia, and has to be trans-
ferred to hospital. David is left alone with
his son and tries to explain his concept of
love. Minus is delighted. His father has

Harriet Andersson and Lars Passgård in THROUGH A GLASS DARKLY

come into contact with him at last.

● 218 TAUBE, MATHIAS (1876-1934). B: Lindesberg. Actor. Studied outside Sweden as a painter, but soon turned to the theatre. 1912-1921: Intimate Theatre, Stockholm. Also worked for radio. A very serious character actor with great natural style. Films: *Ships that Meet, Thérèse, The Gold Spider, Johan, For High Ends, The Girl from Paradise, The People of Simlången Valley, The Ingmar Inheritance, She He and Andersson, The Poetry of Ådalen* (28), *The Land of Rye, The Voice of the Heart, Tomorrow for a Woman, A Night of Love on Öresund, The People of Värmland, We Go through the Kitchen, Under Notice to Leave.*

● 219 TAUBE, SVEN-BERTIL (1934-   ). B: Stockholm. Actor. 1958-61: trained at Royal Dramatic Theatre, Stockholm, and later engaged there. Son of Evert Taube, one of the most popular masters of the *chanson* in Sweden. Taube is a singer himself. In films he is the handsome, well-dressed hero whose *forte* is

occasionally deadpan comedy. Films: *Spring at Sjösala, To Love* (Taube dubbed Cybulski's part), *The Dream Boy, Just Like Friends, With Gunilla, The Island, Stimulantia* (Donner episode), *Hugs and Kisses, Summer of the Lion/ Vibration* (also co-scored), *Hot Snow, Me and You* (in Denmark).

● 220 TEJE, TORA (1893-   ). B: Stockholm. Actress. 1908-11: trained at Royal Dramatic Theatre, Stockholm. Much stage work, especially at the RDT. *The* actress of her generation in the Swedish theatre. Very intense screen playing. Films: *The Monastery of Sendomir, Karin Daughter of Ingmar, Erotikon, Family Traditions, Witchcraft through the Ages, The Norrtull Gang, 33.333, The Lady of the Camellias, Married Life* (26), *The Old Man Is Coming.*

● 221 TENGROTH, BIRGIT (1915-   ). B: Stockholm. Actress. 1926-31: trained as a ballerina. Refused by the Royal Dramatic Theatre, Stockholm, she

131

became a child star and during the Thirties matured into an actress of considerable power and presence. She has published nine books, one of which, a collection of stories, was the basis of Bergman's *Thirst/Three Strange Loves*. Films: *Sin* (28), *His Greatest Match, The Boys on Storholmen, Boman's Boy, Marriageable Daughters, What Do Men Know?, The Atlantic Adventure, The Song of the Scarlet Flower* (34), *Bachelor Father, Alfred Loved by the Girls, Ebberöds Bank, The King Is Coming, It Pays to Advertise, Johan Ulfstjerna, The Family Secret, Oh What a Night, A Rich Man's Son, The Sugar Bowl, Dollar, The Old Man Is Coming, Rejoice while You Are Young, Between Us Barons, Like a Thief in the Night, Heroes of the West Coast, An Able Man, How To Chastise a Husband, One Man Too Many, Jacob's Ladder, People of Roslagen, Can You Come Doctor?, Lack of Evidence, Katrina, A Matter of Life and Death, Night in the Harbour, Sonja, The Forest Is Our Inheritance, A Woman for Men, On Dangerous Roads, The Clergyman from the Wilds, Dynamite, A Soldier's Duties, Sin* (48), *Thirst/Three Strange Loves, Girl with Hyacinths.*

• 222 TERJE VIGEN/A MAN THERE WAS. 1917. Script: Gustaf Molander, based on the poem by Henrik Ibsen. Direction: Victor Sjöström. Photography: J. Julius. Art Direction: Jens Wang. Players: Victor Sjöström (*Terje*), Bergliot Husberg (*Terje's wife*), August Falk (*English captain*), Edith Erastoff (*English Lady*). 1,129 metres. For Svenska Bio.

PLOT: During the Napoleonic Wars, a fisherman named Terje pierces the English blockade and brings back provisions from Denmark for his family. But after a protracted chase, he is captured by an English frigate, and flung into prison. When the war is over he is released, and Terje returns to his village only to find that his wife and baby son have died of starvation. He retreats in misery to a remote island. Then, during a storm, he has to rescue the crew of a small boat, and discovers that he has saved the life of the English captain who captured him so long ago. His first impulse is to let him drown; but when he catches sight of the baby in the arms of the captain's wife, he relents.

• 223 THOMAS GRAALS BÄSTA BARN/THOMAS GRAAL'S FIRST CHILD. 1918. Script: Gustaf Molander and Mauritz Stiller (under the pseudonym Harald B. Harald). Direction: Mauritz Stiller. Photography: Henrik Jaenzon. Art Direction: Axel Esbensen. Players: Victor Sjöström (*Thomas Graal*), Karin Molander (*Bessie Douglas*), Jenny Tschernichin-Larsson (*Her mother*), Torsten Winge (*A Passer-by*), Josef Fischer (*Douglas*), Axel Nilsson (*The valet*), Edvin Adolphson. 1,737 metres. For Svenska Bio.

PLOT: Thomas is going to marry Bessie and the church is full of people. Only Thomas himself is missing. He is late because he has lost his collar stud, but finally he arrives and handles the situation.

Soon afterwards, Mrs. Graal is going to have a baby. She fills the house with classical sculpture—to make her child beautiful! After the birth she is very keen on hygiene. Thomas is not allowed to kiss either her or the child. She dresses reasonably but hardly attractively. Thomas is furious and writes a short story about the way a man wants a woman to dress: coquettishly, with silk stockings, high-heeled shoes, and a corset. Then he says, "Don't look at my desk. There's something you mustn't see." When he comes home, he finds that Bessie is transformed. Of course she could not resist reading the story.

• 224 THOMAS GRAALS BÄSTA FILM/THOMAS GRAAL'S BEST FILM. 1917. Script: Gustaf Molander and Mauritz Stiller (under the pseudonym of

Harald B. Harald). Direction: Mauritz Stiller. Photography: Henrik Jaenzon. Art Direction: Axel Esbensen. Players: Albin Lavén (*Douglas, Landowner*), Jenny Tschernichin-Larsson (*His wife*), Karin Molander (*Bessie, their daughter*), Victor Sjöström (*Thomas Graal, a writer*), Thyra Leijman, Axel Nilsson, Adolf Blomstedt, William Larsson. 1,794 metres. For Svenska Bio.

PLOT: Thomas Graal, a writer, is working on a film script, but his inspiration is lacking. Both the manager of the Union Film Company and the great director are waiting eagerly for the scenario. Thomas meets a young girl, Bessie, and hires her as a typist. When he tries to kiss her, she gets angry and runs away. Suddenly Thomas is inspired and writes a new script entitled "The Little Adventuress," based on Bessie's "true life" story about poverty and a drunken father. But in fact Bessie is a very rich girl and she runs away from her home yet again. Pursued by her father, she happens to meet a man who is about to attack a young girl. Bessie starts horse-whipping him only to find that she is in the middle of a film production. Thus she is reunited with Thomas, who wants her to be the heroine of his new film.

Son of the Sea, Love Will Conquer, Jack of Hearts, When Love Came to the Village, Living at the "Hope," Meeting Life, Kalle Karlsson from Jularbo, A Night in the Archipelago, The Chief from Göinge, Two Rascals, In Smoke and Dancing, Hoppsan!, The Dance Hall, Never in Your Life, Wild Strawberries, So Close to Life/ Brink of Life, The Face/The Magician, The Judge, Winter Light, The Silence, La Guerre est Finie, Night Games, Hour of the Wolf, The Bathers, The Rite (for TV). Also starred in and directed *Devotion* (short) 65.

- 225 THULIN, INGRID (1929-). B: Sollefteå (northern Sweden). Actress. Studied ballet at Norrköping Theatre. 1948-50: trained at Royal Dramatic Theatre, Stockholm. 1954: first contact with Bergman (q.v.). Has worked in foreign films increasingly in recent years (*Foreign Intrigue, The Four Horsemen of the Apocalypse, Agostino, Sekstet, Return from the Ashes, Adelaide, The Damned* etc.). Married to Harry Schein (founder of the Swedish Film Institute), this cool blonde actress has appeared best in Bergman's films and in Resnais's *La Guerre est Finie*, a Franco-Swedish co-production. Films: *Where the Winds Lead,*

- 226 TIDBLAD, INGA (1901-). B: Stockholm. Actress. 1919-22: trained at Royal Dramatic Theatre, Stockholm. 1932-63 engaged at same theatre. Primarily a versatile stage actress, she has made relatively few films, but her brilliant technique makes her roles in such different films as *The Royal Hunt* and *Mother of Pearl* among the most memorable in Swedish cinema. Films: *Andersson, Pettersson and Lundström, Pirates on Lake Mälar, The Norrtull Gang, The Counts of Svansta, Man of Destiny, Uncle Frans, Black Rudolf, For Her Sake, The General, Longing for the Sea, People of Hälsingland, She or Nobody, The Song of the Scarlet Flower* (34), *Jansson's Temptation, Intermezzo, Flames in the Dark, There Burned a Flame, The Invisible Wall, Royal Hunt, Mandragora, Divorced, House of Women, Gabrielle, The Unicorn, Mother of Pearl.*

● 227 TILL GLÄDJE/TO JOY. 1950. Script and Direction: Ingmar Bergman. Photography: Gunnar Fischer. Editing: Oscar Rosander. Music: Mendelssohn, Mozart, Smetana, and Beethoven. Art Direction: Nils Svenwall. Players: Maj-Britt Nilsson (*Märta*), Stig Olin (*Stig*), Victor Sjöström (*Sönderby*), Birger Malmsten (*Marcel*), John Ekman (*Mikael Bro*), Margit Carlquist (*Nelly Bro*), Sif Ruud (*Stina*), Rune Stylander (*Persson*), Erland Josephson (*Bertil*), Georg Skarstedt (*Anker*), Berit Holmström (*Lisa*), Björn Montin (*Lasse*), Carin Swenson, Svea Holm, Svea Holst, Agda Helin, Maud Hyttenberg. 9,148 ft. For Svensk Filmindustri.

PLOT: At the start of the new orchestral season in Hälsingborg, the veteran conductor Sönderby welcomes two newcomers—Stig and Märta, both violinists. Both have met before without coming into close contact. Now they see each other more often and soon they decide to get married. The first crisis in their relationship comes when Stig tries to give a solo performance with the orchestra, despite his immaturity. Sönderby tries to dissuade him, but Stig insists. It is a ghastly experience and Stig's pride is wounded by Märta's quiet and dispassionate reaction. There is a quarrel and Stig goes for a walk in the night through Hälsingborg. He runs into a besotted actor, Mikael Bro, and goes home with him. Here he meets Nelly, Mikael's young, beautiful, and extremely voluptuous wife. Stig leaves, disgusted with this *ménage,* but some years later, after the birth of his two children, he meets Nelly again. This time he becomes her lover. Märta leaves him and takes the children with her. There is a reconciliation, followed by tragedy, when Märta and the little girl are killed by an exploding kerosine stove. Stig returns to orchestra rehearsal, and as he listens to Sönderby's rendering of Beethoven's Ninth Symphony, and sees his son watching by the door, he realises that he must continue to live and not lose hope.

● 228 TROELL, JAN (1931-   ). B: Malmö. Director and cameraman. Troell, born in Scania, in southern Sweden, is a former school teacher whose patience, perception, and perfectionism have combined to bring him to the front of European directors. Already his films have won several international awards. Dir. of phot. on all his own films and: *The Boy and the Kite, The Pram, Summer Train.* Shorts: *The Boat, New Year's Eve on the Scanian Plains* 61; *The Return, The Old Mill* 62; *Trakom, Johan Ekberg* 64; *Portrait of Åsa, Stopover in the Marshland* (part of *4 x 4*) 65. Features (all co-scripted by Troell): *Here Is Your Life* 66; *Who Saw Him Die?* 68; *The Emigrants* and *Unto a Good Land* 70.

● 229 TSCHERNICHIN-LARSSON, JENNY (1867-1937). B: Finland. Actress. First appeared with Mauritz Stiller (q.v.) on stage at August Palm's Intima teatern in Stockholm. Well-known silent star, brilliant at playing elderly ladies and unwelcome mothers-in-law. Her husband, William Larsson (1873-1937) was also an actor in some of her films. *The Tyrannical Fiancé, The Unknown Woman, On the Fateful Roads of Life, Life's Conflicts, The Modern Suffragette, The Clergyman, When Mother-in-law Reigns, People of the Border, The Miracle, The Chamberlain, Do Not Judge, Stormy Petrel, The Shot, A Good Girl Should Solve Her Own Problems, Children of* the Street, Hearts that Meet, Ace of Thieves, In This Way Which Is So Usual Nowadays, The Governor's Daughters, Sea Vultures, His Wedding Night, She Was Victorious, Love and Journalism, The Ballet Primadonna, The Million Inheritance, The Secret of the Inn, Thomas Graal's Best Film, A Girl from the Marsh Croft, The Outlaw and His Wife, Thomas Graal's First Child, The Sons of Ingmar (Pts I and II), The Downy Girl (19), The Monastery of Sendomir, Fishing Village, A Wild Bird, The Eyes of Love, People of Hälsingland, The Virago of the Österman Brothers, For the Home and the Girl, The Devil and the Man from Småland (27), A Stolen Waltz, Lame Lena and Cross-eyed Per.

● 230 TYSTNADEN/THE SILENCE. 1963. Script and Direction: Ingmar Bergman. Photography: Sven Nykvist. Editing: Ulla Ryghe. Music: J. S. Bach's Goldberg Variations (25th Movement). Art Direction: P. A. Lundgren. Players: Ingrid Thulin (*Ester*), Gunnel Lindblom (*Anna*), Jörgen Lindström (*Johan*), Håkan Jahnberg (*Floor waiter in hotel*), Birger Malmsten (*Waiter in café*), The Eduardini (*The Dwarfs*), Eduardo Gutierrez (*Dwarf manager*), Lissi Alandh (*Girl in Cabaret*), Leif Forstenberg (*Man in Cabaret*), Olof Widgren. 96 mins. For Svensk Filmindustri.

PLOT: Two Swedish women and a ten-year-old boy, Johan, are returning

Eddie Axberg and Max von Sydow in Troell's THE EMIGRANTS

from a holiday, and pause in a foreign city, Timoka, where the language is incomprehensible. In a hotel suite it becomes obvious that Ester and Anna are at odds with each other. Ester is an intellectual, a translator suffering from some strange lung disease that almost causes her to suffocate during her spasms. Anna is the opposite, sensual, indolent, and sexually frustrated because she finds the Lesbian relationship with her partner (or sister) ever more repugnant and meaningless. After seeing a couple copulate vigorously in a dimly-lit cabaret, she seduces the waiter from a nearby café. Later, after a quarrel, Ester is forced to watch a repetition of this love-play, and the film ends with Anna's leaving Timoka with her son

Johan while Ester sinks into a presumably fatal coma.

● 231 TÖRST/THIRST/THREE STRANGE LOVES. 1949. Script: Herbert Grevenius from a collection of short stories by Birgit Tengroth. Direction: Ingmar Bergman. Photography: Gunnar Fischer. Editing: Oscar Rosander. Music: Erik Nordgren. Art Direction: Nils Svenwall. Players: Eva Henning (*Rut*), Birger Malmsten (*Bertil*), Birgit Tengroth (*Viola*), Mimi Nelson (*Valborg*), Hasse Ekman (*Dr. Rosengren*), Bengt Eklund (*Raoul, the Captain*), Gaby Stenberg (*Astrid, his wife*), Naima Wifstrand (*Miss Henriksson, dancing instructress*), Sven-Eric Gamble (*The worker*), Gunnar

Nielsen (*The assistant*), Estrid Hesse (*A patient*), Helge Hagerman (*A pastor*), Calle Flygare (*Another pastor*), Else-Merete Heiberg, Monica Weinzierl, Herman Gried. 88 mins. For Svensk Filmindustri.

PLOT: Basle, 1946. Rut and Bertil prepare, in an atmosphere of boredom and vindictiveness, to return to Stockholm after a trip. They are married. Bertil is an art historian. Rut is a former ballet dancer, and is apparently unable to bear children on account of a clumsy abortion after an affair with a ship's captain. In a parallel story, Bertil's former wife, Viola, is seen trying to overcome her loneliness. She visits a psychiatrist, Dr. Rosengren, who tries to seduce her, and later meets another woman, Valborg (who was also a friend of Rut's when they were both learning ballet). But when Viola finds that Valborg is a Lesbian who wishes to exploit her, she breaks away and, during Midsummer's Eve, goes down to the harbour to commit suicide. Meanwhile Rut and Bertil move nearer to Stockholm, and their bickering reaches a climax when Bertil dreams that he has murdered his wife. They both realise that they cannot live in loneliness and they decide to face the future with a more sensible outlook.

• 232 TÖSEN FRÅN STORMYR-TORPET/THE GIRL FROM STORMYCROFT/A GIRL FROM THE MARSH CROFT. 1919. Script: Esther Juhlin and Victor Sjöström, from a novel by Selma Lagerlöf. Direction: Victor Sjöström. Photography: Henrik Jaenzon. Music: Fourteen piece orchestra directed by Rudolf Sahlberg. Players: Lars Hanson (*Gudmund Erlandsson*), Greta Almroth (*Helga*), Georg Blomstedt, Jenny Tschernichin-Larsson, Karin Molander, Hjalmar Selander, Concordia Selander, William Larsson, Thekla Borg, Nils Aréhn, Gösta Cederlund, Edla Rothgardt. 1,749 metres. For Svenska Bio.

PLOT: Gudmund Erlandsson, a farmer's son, goes to town, gets drunk, and is involved in a brawl. The following morning he can't remember anything, but in the newspaper his mother reads that a workman has been found murdered with a broken blade from a knife lodged in his body. Gudmund looks at his own clasp-knife and finds that the blade is missing. He tries to destroy the evidence, but his honest father notices it and denounces his son.

The girl from the Marsh Croft, Helga, is despised because she is an unmarried mother. She is a servant in Gudmund's house. When everybody thinks that Gudmund is guilty of murder and his proud *fiancée* breaks with him, Helga saves him by telling the truth. She happened to break the blade when she used the knife, but she was afraid to tell Gudmund. Now he understands that Helga is brave and honest, much better than his *fiancée*.

• 233 ULLMANN, LIV (1938-). B: Tokyo. Norwegian actress. Studied

137

acting in London, then at Rogalund Theatre, Stavanger. Noted for her brilliant interpretations on the Oslo stage. Her queenly beauty has only been glimpsed in Bergman's recent films*, where she plays the distraught and usually unglamorous wife of Max von Sydow (q.v.). Has a major role in Fred Zinnemann's *Man's Fate* (70). Films in Norway: *Fjols til Fjells, Tonny, De kalte ham skarven, Ung flukt, An-Magritt*. Films in Sweden: *Pan, Persona*, *Hour of the Wolf*, *Shame*, A Passion*, The Emigrants* and *Unto a Good Land*.

- 234 VALBERG, BIRGITTA (1916-). B: Stockholm. Actress. 1940-43: trained at Royal Dramatic Theatre, Stockholm. Also radio and TV work. Warm and motherly supporting actress, best known for her role as Töre's harassed wife in *The Virgin Spring*. Her powerful style is seen to better advantage on stage. Films: *The Fight Goes On, In Paradise, Life in the Country, Port of Call, Love Will Conquer, Divorced, Barabbas, House of Women, Taxi 13, Karin Månsdotter, Merry

Boys of the Navy, Dangerous Promise, Smiles of a Summer Night, Ratataa, The Last Night, Synnöve Solbakken, The Virgin Spring, To One's Heart's Content, The Mistress, Dream of Happiness, Swedish Portraits, Just like Friends, The Princess, Shame, Like Night and Day.

- 235 VARGTIMMEN/HOUR OF THE WOLF. 1968. Script and Direction: Ingmar Bergman. Photography: Sven Nykvist. Editing: Ulla Ryghe. Music: Lars Johan Werle, extract from Mozart's "Der Zauberflöte," and extract from an "Experiment" by J. S. Bach. Art Direction: Marik Vos-Lundh. Players: Liv Ullmann (*Alma*), Max von Sydow (*Johan Borg*), Erland Josephson (*Baron von Merkens*), Gertrud Fridh (*Corinne von Merkens*), Bertil Anderberg (*Ernst von Merkens*), Georg Rydeberg (*Lindhorst*), Ulf Johanson (*Curator Heerbrand*), Naima Wifstrand (*Old Lady*), Ingrid Thulin (*Veronica Vogler*), Lenn Hjortzberg (*Kapellmeister Kreisler*), Agda Helin (*Maid*), Mikael Rundqvist (*Boy*), Mona Seilitz. 89 mins. For Svensk Filmindustri.

PLOT: Johan Borg is a painter who lives with his wife, Alma, on a Frisian island, where they have a summer cottage. One day they are invited to his castle by Baron von Merkens, the owner of the island. At the dinner, Borg is mocked and intimidated by his hosts. In the meanwhile, Alma has discovered a diary of Johan's, in which he recalls incidents involving his former mistress, Veronica Vogler, and an apparent murder of a boy on the shore. Borg now goes steadily insane. He tries to shoot Alma with a gun given him by Heerbrand, and then storms up to the castle again. Lindhorst powders him ceremoniously, and then introduces him into a vault where Veronica lies corpse-like on a bier. She awakes, and embraces him violently, to the amusement of the other members of the castle party. Later Johan

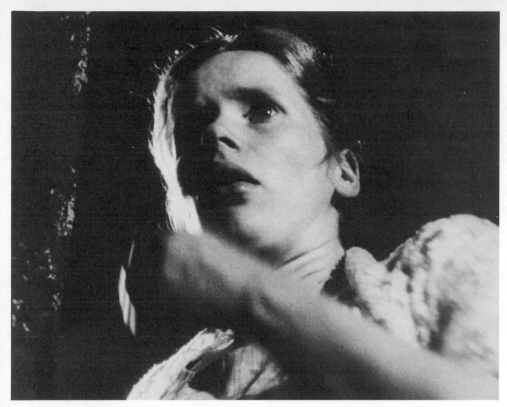

Liv Ullmann in HOUR OF THE WOLF

disappears in a swamp, and Alma, now pregnant, is left on the verge of instability herself.

- 236 WALDEKRANZ, RUNE (1911-). B: Turinge. Producer and film historian. Studied literature and Nordic languages at Uppsala university where he founded (1936) the first Student Film Society. 1942-64: producer at Sandrews. Since 1964: Principal of the Swedish Film Institute Film School. Waldekranz was responsible at Sandrews for some of the finest postwar Swedish pictures. Gave her first chance as both actress and director to Mai Zetterling (q.v.). Has written several scholarly studies of various aspects of Swedish cinema. Films as producer (or production manager): *Can You Come Doctor?* (co-script only), *Men-of-War, A Matter of Life and Death, I Killed, A Day Shall Dawn, Nothing but Old Nobility* (co-prod. and co-script), *The Rose of Thistle Island* (also co-script), *The Girls of Småland* (co-script only), *The Clergyman from the Wilds, Life in the Depths of the Forest* (co-script only), *Maj from Malö* (co-script only), *The Poetry of Ådalen, Lars Hård, Foreign Harbour, Spring at Sjösala, The Maid from Jungfrusund* (also co-script?), *Pippi Long Stocking, Miss Julie, The Land of Rye, Helen of Troy* (also co-script), *When Lilacs Blossom, U-boat 39, Kalle Karlsson from Jularbo, She Came like a Wind, Ursula—the Girl from the Forest Depths,*

Barabbas, The Road to Klockrike, Sawdust and Tinsel/The Naked Night, All the Joy of Earth, God and the Gipsyman, The "Lunchbreak" Café, Storm over Tjurö, Karin Månsdotter, Young Man Seeks Company, Journey into Autumn/ Dreams, Blue Sea, A Girl for the Summer (co-prod. with Germany), *Kulla-Gulla, Children of the Night* (56), *Swing It Miss!, Clouds over Hellesta, The Way via Skå, A Guest in One's Own Home, Synnöve Solbakken, Seventeen Years Old, Music on Board, Model in Red, Laila, Rider in Blue, May I Borrow Your Wife?, The Judge, When Darkness Falls, Swedish Floyd, The Boy in the Tree, Lady in White, One Zero Too Many, Pan, Prince Hat below Ground, A Beautiful Day, Wild West Story, To Love, Loving Couples.*

● 237 WALLÉN, LENNART (1914-1967). Editor. Son of Sigurd Wallén (q.v.). A long and distinguished career. Acted in *Queen of Pellagonia* and *Jansson's Temptation*. Films as editor: *The Nature Healer* (also assist. dir.), *A Poor Millionaire, People of Roslagen* (also assist. dir.), *Changing Trains, Women in Prison, I Killed, In the Darkest Corner of Småland, A Day Shall Dawn, Your Relatives Are Best, His Excellency, The Little Saint, I Am Fire and Air, Like Most People, Prince Gustaf, The Royal Rabble, Nothing but Old Nobility, The Rose of Thistle Island, In the Beautiful Province of Roslagen, Jarl the Widower, In Death's Waiting Room, Nightly Encounter, Women in a Waiting Room, The Clergyman from the Wilds, Salt Water Spray and Tough Old Boys, Desire, When Meadows Bloom, Hotell Kåkbrinken, When the Door Was Closed, Supper for Two, The Song about Stockholm, Maria, No Way Back, Lazy Lena and Blue-Eyed Per* (also dir. 47), *Neglected by His Wife, Maj from Malö, Music in Darkness/Night Is My Future, Each Goes*

His Own Way, The Evening of the Fair, Little Märta Returns, Lars Hård, Robinson of Roslagen, On These Shoulders, The Banquet, That Woman Drives Me Crazy, Vagabond Blacksmiths, Prison/The Devil's Wanton, The Girl from the Gallery, Spring at Sjösala, The Maid from Jungfrusund, Swedish Horseman, The Wind Is My Lover, Sampo the Little Lapp, Bohus Battalion, Stora Hopare Lane and Heaven, My Sister and I, Girl with Hyacinths, Knockout at the "Breakfast Club," Jack of Hearts, When Love Came to the Village, This Can't Happen Here, Backyard, The Kiss on the Cruise, Mrs. Andersson's Charlie, When Bengt and Anders Swapped Wives, The White Cat, Motor Cavaliers, My Name Is Puck, The Revue at the Södran Theatre, The House of Folly, Stronger than the Law, Rolling Sea, Poker, One Summer of Happiness, Helen of Troy, U-boat 39, The Fire Bird, Class Mates, One Fiancé at a Time, Bread of Love, Dolls and Balls, Wild Birds, The Right to Love, The Seventh Seal, Count on Trouble, No Tomorrow, Synnöve Solbakken (57), *Johan at Snippen Wins the Game, Woman in a Leopardskin, Model in Red, Laila, Rider in Blue, Blackjackets, A Lion in Town, The Man in the Middle, Summer and Sinners, When Darkness Falls, Do You Believe in Angels?, Swedish Floyd, The Job, Hällebäck Manor, The Brig "Three Lilies," Lady in White, The Mistress, One Zero Too Many, No Time To Kill, One Fine Day, Hide and Seek, Dream of Happiness, Prince Hat below Ground, Wild West Story, To Love, Dear John, Morianna, My Sister My Love.*

● 238 WALLÉN, SIGURD (1884-1947). B: Tierp. Actor and director. Began his career in the theatre. Specialised in folk comedy. Regular radio work. He became famous for his interpretations of Albert Engström's books about the archipelago outside Stockholm. Films as director (sometimes acted* or scripted†): *Mrs.*

Andersson's Charlie 22; *Mrs. Andersson's Charlie and His New Pranks, The Suitor from the Road*†* 23; *Lame Lena and Cross-eyed Per**, *Dan Aunt and Little Miss Söderlund, The Counts of Svansta* 24; *Her Little Majesty* 25; *A Million Dollars, Uncle Frans, Ebberöds Bank* 26; *The Queen of Pellagonia* 27; *Jansson's Temptation* †* 28; *Ville Andeson's Adventures* 29; *The Boys on Storholmen*†*, *Darlings of Fortune*†* (co. dir. Ivar Johansson) 32; *Marriageable Daughters*†*, *A Night at Smygeholm* 33; *Mrs. Andersson's Charlie, Pettersson—Sweden** 34; *The Count from Munkbro* (co-dir. Edvin Adolphson), *Ebberöds Bank*†* 35; *Conscientious Adolf, Shipwrecked Max* (co-dir. Fritz Schulz) 36; *Adolf Armstrong, The Andersson Family**, *Walking along the Main Road** 37; *Two Years in Each Form**, *With the People for the Country*†*, *Sigge Nilsson and I**, *The Nature Healer** 38; *Towards New Times** 39; *Brave Boys in Uniform*†*, *The Merry-Go-Round in Full Swing** 40; *Our Boys in Uniform, Newly Married**, *A Poor Millionaire** 41; *The People of Hemsö*†*, *God Pulls Johansson's Hair** 44; *Skipper Jansson*†*, *Jarl the Widower*†* 45. Films as actor only: *Only a Dream, The Temptations of Stockholm, The Darling of the Stockholm Ladies, The Sisters, Alexander the Great, The Sons of Ingmar* (Pts. I and II), *His Grace's Will* (19), *Frida's Songs, Motley Leaves, Red Day, Skipper Love, His Greatest Match, Black Roses, Love and Deficit, We Go through the Kitchen, Boman's Boy, Pettersson and Bendel, Karl Fredrik Reigns, Swedenhielms, Love from Music, People of Småland, Jansson's Temptation* (36), *Marvellous Karlsson, Bombi Bitt and I, Conflict, John Ericsson—the Victor at Hampton Roads, A Woman's Face, You Free Old Country, Adolf as a Fireman, Charmers at Sea, Like a Thief in the Night, Night in June, A Big Hug, A Crime, An Able Man, Life Goes On, People of Roslagen,*

It Is My Music, Women in Prison, That Girl Is a Discovery, Night in the Harbour, In the Darkest Corner of Småland, Your Relatives Are Best, Crime and Punishment, Salt Water Spray and Tough Old Boys, When Meadows Bloom.

● 239 WEISS, PETER (1916-   ). B: Berlin. Experimental film-maker. 1936-38: studied at Academy of Arts in Prague. Author and painter, as well as book illustrator. Though best known for his *avant-garde* plays, Weiss has shot a number of films in Sweden. Shorts: *Studie I, Studie II* 52; *Studie III* 53; *Studie IV* 54; *Studie V* 55; *The Studio of Dr. Faustus, Faces in the Shadows* (co. Christer Strömholm) 56; *Nothing Unusual, According to the Law* 57; *What Shall We Do Now?* 58; *Behind Uniform Facades* (in Denmark) 61. *Feature: The Mirage* (also script) 59. Weiss also co-scripted and co-edited *Paris Playgirls.*

● 240 WERLE, LARS JOHAN (19?-   ). Composer. His subtle and polyphonic scores have contributed a sense of alienation and disquiet to Bergman's recent work. Also opera composer. Films: *The Island, Persona, Hour of the Wolf.*

● 241 WERNER, GÖSTA (1908-   ). B: Östra Vemmenhög. Director of shorts and feature films. Educated at Lund University, then journalist and film translator. Also an experienced editor and scriptwriter. Has written books and articles on the cinema. Best known abroad for his shorts, *Midwinter Sacrifice* and *The Train*. Main shorts: *Early Morning* 45; *Midwinter Sacrifice* 46; *Forty Years with the King, Spring at Skansen* 47; *The Train* 48; *The Tale of Light* 49; *Spring, To Kill a Child* 52; *Journey in Sweden, A Great Swedish Industry, The Butterfly and the Flame* 54; *City Twilight* 55; *Destinies beyond the Horizon, Responsibility* 56; *The Forgotten Melody* 57; *Land*

of *Liberty* 58; *Gold and Green Woods* 59; *A Glass of Wine* 60; *Living Colour* 62; *Human Landscape, Waiting Waters* 65; *When People Meet* 66. Film as scriptwriter: *The Nature Healer*. Features: *Loffe as a Vagabond, Miss Sun-Beam* 48; *The Street* 49; *Backyard* 50; *Meeting Life* 52; *Matrimonial Announcement* 55.

- 242 WIDERBERG, BO (1930-). B: Malmö. Director. Also novelist (*Autumn Term, Kissing*—a collection of short stories, etc), and playwright. 1960: articles on cinema in *Expressen* and *BLM*. 1962: publishes polemical book, *Vision in Swedish Film*. 1961: makes short film, *The Boy and the Kite*, for TV, in collab. with Jan Troell (q.v.). The "angry young man" of modern Swedish cinema, committed to contemporary themes but scoring his biggest success to date with the period romance *Elvira Madigan*. Scripts all his own films. In 1968 Widerberg led a team of cameramen and film-makers who compiled a documentary called *The White*

Game on the occasion of the abortive tennis Davis Cup tie between Sweden and Rhodesia. Films: *The Pram, Raven's End* 63; *Love 65* 65; *Thirty Times Your Money* 66; *Elvira Madigan* 67; *The Ådalen Riots* 69; *Joe Hill* (in U.S.A.) 70.

- 243 WIDGREN, OLOF (1907-). B: Stockholm. Actor. 1928-31: trained at Royal Dramatic Theatre, Stockholm. Since 1936: engaged there. Also TV work. Subdued style but convincing psychological approach to his characters. Films: *Ulla My Ulla, A Poet Maybe, South of the Main Road, Career, Money from the Sky, Steel, Night in June, Home from Babylon, Can You Come Doctor?, The Sixth Shot, Young Blood, Gentleman with a Brief-case, A Day Shall Dawn, Count the Happy Moments Only, I Am Fire and Air, The Turnstile, The Serious Game, The Clergyman from the Wilds, Only a Mother, Barabbas, Karin Månsdotter, Love Chastised, Last Pair Out, Tarps Elin, No Tomorrow, The Silence*.

● 244 WIFSTRAND, NAIMA (1890-1968). B: Stockholm. Actress. At first singer, and after the Second World War a director at the Stockholm Opera. During the last twenty years of her life she played small but highly entertaining roles on screen, such as the mother in *Wild Strawberries* and *The Face/The Magician* (both q.v.). Also some foreign films. Films: *Madame Visits Oslo, King's Street, Watch Out for Spies, Born: a Daughter, Sten Stensson Comes to Town, Girls in the Harbour, Hotell Kåkbrinken, Handsome Augusta, I Love You You Vixen, The Long Road, Nights in the Djurgård, The Art of Love, Life in the Depths of the Forest, A Guest Came, Two Women, The Nightwatchman's Wife, People of the Simlång Valley, Music in Darkness/Night Is My Future, The Poetry of Ådalen* (48), *Lapp Blood, Private Bom, The Roar of Hammar Rapids, Miss Sun-beam, Revue at the Södran Theatre, Gentlemen of the Navy, That Woman Drives Me Crazy, Playing Truant, The Devil and the Man from Småland, Thirst/Three Strange Loves, The Wind Is My Lover, My Name Is Puck, A Fiancée for Hire, Because of My Hot Youth, Say It with Flowers, Dull Clang, Waiting Women/Secrets of Women, The Road to Klockrike, Wing-beats in the Night, Ursula—the Girl from the Forest Depths, Gentle Thief of Love, Journey into Autumn/Dreams, Smiles of a Summer Night, The Dance Hall, Paradise, Girl in a Dress-coat* (56), *My Hot*

Naima Wifstrand (centre) with Victor Sjöström and Ingrid Thulin in Bergman's WILD STRAWBERRIES.

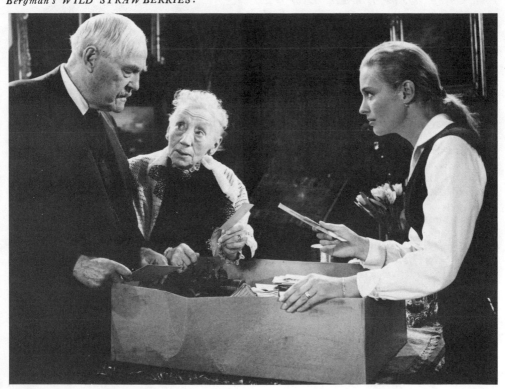

Desire, The Witch, Seventeen Years Old, Wild Strawberries, The Face/The Magician, The Judge, The Brig "Three Lilies," The Myth, Night Games, Hour of the Wolf, Waltz of Sex.

- 245 **WÅLLGREN, GUNN** (1913-
). B: Göteborg. Actress. 1934-37: trained at Royal Dramatic Theatre, Stockholm. Since 1954: appeared regularly in plays in Stockholm, and has played in several radio dramas. Was married to Erik "Hampe" Faustman (q.v.), who directed her from time to time*. Comparatively few screen appearances, although one treasures her ardent performance in *Woman without a Face*. Films: *Women in Prison, Sonja*, The Word, The Sixth Shot, The Emperor of Portugal, The Girl and the Devil*, Journey Out, Crime and Punishment*, Desire, When the Door Was Closed, Woman without a Face, Each Goes His Own Way, Unmarried, The Dress.*

- 246 **ZETTERLING, MAI** (1925-
). B: Västerås. Actress and director. Stage *début* at sixteen in a play by Pär Lagerkvist. 1942-45: trained at Royal Dramatic Theatre, Stockholm. 1946: first British film (*Frieda*), followed by contract with Rank Organisation. Film, theatre and TV work in Britain and U.S.A. until 1964, when she directed her first feature film for Sandrews. Resident in Britain. Since the mid-Forties, when she was a romantic partner for Alf Kjellin (q.v.), Miss Zetterling has been a confident and attractive actress, good at comedy. As a director, she is passionately concerned with the position of women in the contemporary world. Swedish films as actress: *Lasse-Maja, I Killed, Frenzy/Torment, Prince Gustaf, Iris and the Lieutenant, If Dew Falls Rain Follows, Music in Darkness/Night Is My Future, Life Begins Now, Married Life, Playing on*

the Rainbow, The Vine Bridge. As director: *The War Game* (short in Britain) 63; *Loving Couples* 64; *Night Games* 66; *Doctor Glas* (in Denmark), *The Girls* 68.

- 247 **ÅDALEN 31/THE ÅDALEN RIOTS.** 1969. Script and Direction: Bo Widerberg. Photography (Technicolor): Jörgen Persson. Editing: Bo Widerberg. Players: Peter Schildt (*Kjell*), Kerstin Tidelius (*His mother*), Roland Hedlund (*Harald, his father*), Stefan Feierbach (*Åke, his brother*), Martin Widerberg (*Martin, his brother*), Marie de Geer (*Anna*), Anita Björk (*Her mother*), Olof Bergström (*Her father*), Jonas Bergström (*Nisse, Kjell's friend*), Olle Björling (*The strike-breaker*), Pierre Lindstedt (*The foreman*). 115 mins. For Svensk Filmindustri.

PLOT: It is 1931. A strike has been proclaimed in the Ådalen valley in the north of Sweden. The boss of the factory decides to call in strike-breakers. The workers grow rebellious, and some three thousand of them join together to banish the strike-breakers and then to march to

One of the strike-breakers is removed in **THE ÅDALEN RIOTS**

Lunde in a sympathy movement. On the way into Lunde, the military confront the strikers. They warn them that they cannot go any further. But the marchers press on, and are fired upon indiscriminately by the soldiers. Five men are killed and many others wounded. One of the dead is Harald, whose son Kjell has become involved with Anna, the daughter of the director of the factory. While the march is under way, Anna is in Stockholm having an abortion on her mother's orders. Kjell resolves to help his mother to face the years ahead, and also to try to change the social structure in Sweden.

● 248 ÅKERMARK, ARNE (18?-1962). Set designer, at his busiest during the Thirties, when he designed about ninety features. Worked on over two hundred films, including the British *Scott of the Antarctic* (48). Main films: *Tired Teodor, One Night, The Boys on Storholmen, Karl Fredrik Reigns, Simon from Backabo, Swedenhielms, Johan Ulfstjerna, John Ericsson—the Victor at Hampton Roads, Dollar, A Woman's Face, The Old Man Is Coming, Rejoice while You Are Young, Steel, Night in June, A Big Hug, His Grace's Will* (40), *Ride Tonight!, The Road to Heaven, There Burned a Flame, Night in the Harbour, The Word, The Royal Hunt, His Excellency* (co. Lundgren), *The Invisible Wall, Frenzy/Torment, The Emperor of Portugal* (co. Svenwall), *Wandering with the Moon,*

Mandragora, The Journey Out (co. Sven-wall), *Crisis, Johansson and Vestman, The Balloon* (co. Svenwall), *Iris and the Lieutenant, A Soldier's Duties, Woman without a Face* (co. Svenwall), *Married Life* (57), *The People of Värmland, Miss April, Ticket to Paradise.*

• 249 ÄLSKANDE PAR/LOVING COUPLES. 1964. Script: Mai Zetterling and David Hughes, from the novels "Fröknarna von Pahlen" by Agnes von Krusenstjerna. Direction: Mai Zetterling. Photography: Sven Nykvist. Editing: Paul Davies. Music: Rodger Wallis. Art Direction: Jan Boleslaw. Players: Harriet Andersson (*Agda*), Gunnel Lindblom (*Adele*), Gio Petré (*Angela*), Anita Björk (*Petra*), Gunnar Björnstrand (*Jacob Lewin*), Inga Landgré (*Mrs. Lewin*), Jan Malmsjö (*Stellan*), Frank Sundström (*Ola Landborg*), Eva Dahlbeck (*Mrs. Landborg*), Heinz Hopf (*Bernhard Landborg*), Toivo Pawlo (*Mr. Macson*), Margit Carlquist (*Mrs. Macson*), Hans Strååt (*Tomas*), Jan-Erik Lindquist (*Peter*), Bengt Brunskog (*Tord*), Barbro Hiort af Ornäs (*Lilian*), Märta Dorff (*Alexandra*), Lissi Alandh (*Bess*), Åke Grönberg (*Elderly lecher in street*), Hans Sundberg, Sten Lonnert, Axel Fritz, Henrik Schildt, Berit Gustafsson, Lars Grundtman, Lennart Grundtman, Dan Landgré, Lo Dagerman, Rebecca Pawlo, Catharina Edfeldt, Anja Boman, Nancy Dalunde, Meta Velander, Claes Thelander, Börje Mellvig. 118 mins. For Sandrews (Rune Waldekranz).

PLOT: Three women are in hospital expecting babies. They are in the charge of Dr. Jacob Lewin. The film consists of their memories of the events that shaped their lives. Angela recalls being orphaned as a child, being attached to her Aunt Petra, and some contact with Lesbianism at school. Agda thinks of her childhood escapades, the highpoint of which is her

Gio Petré and Hans Strååt in
LOVING COUPLES

146

being seduced by an elderly lecher, and then of her carefree love affairs in youth. Adele had a more unhappier childhood and, after a brief affair, drifted into a marriage of convenience with the steward of the Landborg estate. At a Midsummer Eve party held by the Landborgs, all three women are together and "resolve" their destinies. In the hospital, Adele has a still-born baby; Agda gives birth while flirting with Dr. Lewin; and Angela's child, the most eagerly desired, is born after excruciating labour.

- 250 ÄLSKARINNAN/THE MISTRESS. 1962. Script and Direction: Vilgot Sjöman. Photography (AgaScope): Lars-Gunnar Björne. Editing: Lennart Wallén. Music: none. Art Direction: P. A. Lundgren. Players: Bibi Andersson (*The Girl*), Per Myrberg (*The Boy Friend*), Max von Sydow (*The Married Man*), Öllegård Wellton (*His wife*), Birgitta Valberg (*The Elderly Woman*). 77 mins. For Svensk Filmindustri.

PLOT: A young Swedish secretary falls in love with a married man, despite her already serious friendship with a dull but reliable boy. She suffers intense emotional strain during the affair, especially as her lover refuses to try for a divorce from his wife; so with considerable effort she confesses to her boy friend and gives up the association with the older man. Hoping that a change of air will help to restore her emotional equilibrium, she accepts a six-month job in Rome. But as she boards her boat train, her lover rejoins her, telling her he is still madly infatuated with her. They spend the night together in the train, and in the morning the girl decides that she must continue her journey, breaking free of both relationships and starting a new chapter in her life.

Bibi Andersson in THE MISTRESS

Ingmar Bergman and Max von Sydow on location for SHAME

Appendix

THE FOLLOWING TABLE gives the number of feature films produced in Sweden during each year from 1896 to 1968 as far as facts are known (once again the pioneering research work of Sven G. Winquist is gratefully acknowledged).

1896:	1	1927:	12	1949:	36
1897:	3	1928:	14	1950:	24
1907:	2	1929:	7	1951:	32
1908:	5	1930:	16	1952:	33
1909:	9	1931:	29	1953:	32
1910:	12	1932:	23	1954:	37
1911:	23	1933:	29	1955:	37
1912:	37	1934:	22	1956:	37
1913:	22	1935:	21	1957:	32
1914:	20	1936:	28	1958:	29
1915:	22	1937:	23	1959:	21
1916:	39	1938:	30	1960:	24
1917:	25	1939:	31	1961:	18
1918:	8	1940:	37	1962:	17
1919:	16	1941:	34	1963:	21
1920:	22	1942:	35	1964:	20
1921:	21	1943:	43	1965:	24
1922:	14	1944:	42	1966:	28
1923:	22	1945:	43	1967:	20
1924:	23	1946:	35	1968:	33
1925:	20	1947:	44		
1926:	16	1948:	37		

Bibi Andersson in Bergman's WILD STRAWBERRIES

Index

BOTH THE SWEDISH and English (or American) titles are listed in this Index, although the release date of each film appears only after its Swedish name and this only occasionally, for most dates are included in the director filmographies.

Where the director of a film is not featured in the text, his name is printed in brackets after the title in the Index. In all other instances the *first* number refers to the relevant director's biography, the next group of numbers to actors and actresses; the numbers in *italics* to technicians; and the final group to producers, scriptwriters and authors. A number followed by a capital "E" indicates that the film itself has a separate entry in the body of the book. Some rarely-used alternative titles in English are listed in the Index, but readers should refer to the Swedish original for the appropriate numbers in the text.

Where more than one film has the same title, versions are identified by the last two digits of the year, given in brackets immediately following the titles.

Titles preceded by an asterisk* are still in production at the time of writing and the information about them may be unreliable.

Films *not* indexed comprise shorts, and films made outside Scandinavia. For reasons of space, the English articles "A" and "The" have been omitted from the Index.

Where two English-language titles follow the Swedish original, the first usually refers to the British release version, and the second to the American release, e.g. Sommarlek/ *Summer Interlude/Illicit Interlude.*

IMPORTANT NOTE: the Swedish alphabet has been followed throughout the Index. Foreign readers should therefore look for titles beginning with Å, Ä, and Ö at the end of the Index. Similarly, within each letter group, titles whose second letter is å, ä, or ö will appear at the end of that particular group.

A

152

B

Opposite: Max von Sydow in Lindgren's THE BLACK PALM TREES

C

Opposite: Halldoff's THE CORRIDOR (with Per Ragnar and Bo Halldoff)

D

161

162

Dynamit/*Dynamite* (Åke Ohberg 1947) 49, 148, 221; *123*
Dynamite/Dynamit 49, 148, 221; *123*
Dårskapens hus/*House of Folly* 52; 5, 71; *207, 237*
Där fyren blinkar/*Where the Lighthouse Flashes* (Ivar Kåge 1924) 2

Där möllarna gå/*Where Windmills Run* (Bengt Järrel 1956) 171, 17
Dödskyssen/*Kiss of Death* 194; *111*
Dödsritten under cirkuskupolen/*Death-Ride under the Big Top* 122; 53; 150
Dömen icke/*Do Not Judge* 194; 3, 7, 53, 146, 229

E

Each Goes His Own Way/Var sin väg 52; 22, 24, 30, 33, 85, 118, 245; *237*
Each Heart Has Its Story/Vart hjärta har sin saga 24, 66, 174
Ebberöds Bank (26) 238; 15
Ebberöds Bank (35) 238; 113
Ebberöds Bank (47) 113; 221
Een blandt mange/*One among Many* (Astrid and Bjarne Henning-Jensen 1961 in Denmark) 68
Eeny Meeny Miny Moe/Ole dole doff
Efterlyst/*Wanted* 13; 2, 179
Egen ingång/*Private Entrance* 52; 4, 47, 72, 76, 121, 148, 149, 160; *68, 161, 183*
Eld ombord/*Fire on Board* 194; 91; *111*
Eldfågeln/*Fire Bird* 52; 64, 97, 184; *207, 237*; 152
Elsk din naeste/*Love Your Neighbour* (Egil Kolsto 1967 in Denmark) 188
Elvira Madigan (Åke Ohberg 1943) 97, 148, 190
Elvira Madigan (67) 55E; 242; 17, 35
Emilie Högquist 155; 92, 184
Emigrants/Utvandrarna 228; 9, 44, 168, 215, 233; *147*; 70
Emperor of Portugal/Kejsarn av Portugallien 155; 24, 148, 149, 194, 245; *182, 183, 214, 248*; 136, 145
En av de många/*One out of Many* 194; 3, 14
En bröllopsnatt på Stjärnehov/*Wedding Night at Stjärnehov* (Torsten Lindqvist 1934) 113

En dag skall gry/*Day Shall Dawn* 52; 2, 24, 171, 243; *147, 237*; 236
En djungelsaga/*Flute and the Arrow* 56E; 208
En dotter född/*Born: a Daughter* 30; 244
*En dröm om frihet/*Dream of Freedom* 89; 70
En drömmares vandring/*Dreamer's Walk* 143; 2, 28, 102, 126, 137, 184; *162*
En enda natt/*One Single Night* 155; 2, 19, 148
En fattig miljonär/*Poor Millionaire* 238; 118, 148; *23, 237*
En flicka för mej/*Girl for Me* (Börje Larsson 1943) 24, 29, 148
En flicka kommer till stan/*Girl Comes to Town* (Thor Brooks and Carlo Keil-Möller 1937) 118, 149, 179
En fluga gör ingen sommar/*One Swallow Doesn't Make a Summer* 52; 22, 97
En fästman i taget/*One Fiancé at a Time* 13; 2, 22, 29, 118; *23, 237*
En förtjusande fröken/*Lovely Young Lady* (Börje Larsson 1946) 30, 148
En hjulsaga/*Tale of Wheels* (direction unknown) 51
En karl i köket/*Man in the Kitchen* (Rolf Husberg 1954) 149
En kvinna ombord/*Woman on Board* (Gunnar Skoglund 1941) 2, 48, 67, 85
En kvinnas ansikte/*Woman's Face* 155; 19, 24, 98, 184, 190, 238; *248*

163

Opposite: Birger Malmsten (with Barbro Kollberg) in Bergman's IT RAINS ON OUR LOVE

F

167

Opposite: Bibi Andersson in Zetterling's THE GIRLS

G

Gabrielle 52; 22, 97, 151, 156, 226; *68, 161, 183, 214*
Galgmannen/*Mandragora* 155; 2, 24, 26, 76, 155, 157, 226; *183, 248*
Game of Truth/Sällskapslek
Gardener/Trädgårdsmästaren 194; 14, 51; *111*; 203
Gatan/*Street* 241; 31, 102, 118, 148, 160, 168; *147*
Gatans barn/*Children of the Street* 194; 14, 15, 53, 229
Gay Harry/Harry Munter 83
Gay Musicians/Muntra musikanter 179, 180
Gay Parade/Glada paraden 174
Gay Party/Det glada kalaset 49; 29, 148
Gay Tailor/Den glada skräddaren 174
General/Generalen 2, 226
General von Döbeln 157; 2, 22, 53, 97, 190; *23*; 152
Generalen / *General* (Gustaf Bergman 1931) 2, 226
Gentle Thief of Love/Den underbara lögnen 92, 166, 244; *162*
Gentleman att hyra/*Gentleman for Hire* (Ragnar Arvedson 1940) 29, 30, 65, 76, 97
Gentleman for Hire/Gentleman att hyra 29, 30, 65, 76, 97
Gentleman Gangster / Gentlemannagangstern 53, 146, 148, 149, 190
Gentleman Maybe/Kanske en gentleman 30, 113, 118, 148, 210; 2
Gentleman with a Brief-case/Herre med portfölj 49, 118, 121, 184, 243
Gentlemannagangstern/*Gentleman Gangster* (Weyler Hildebrand 1941) 53, 146, 148, 149, 190

Gentleman in Uniform/Kronans kavaljerer 43; 15, 180; *111*
Gentlemen of the Navy/Flottans kavaljerer 43; 2, 148, 244; *214*
Ghost Baron/Spökbaronen 43; 2, 180
Ghost for Sale/Spöke till salu 176
Ghost of Bragehus/Spöket på Bragehus 113
Ghost on Holiday/Spöke på semester 71, 118; *147, 196, 207*
Ghost Reporter/Spökreportern 13; 52
Ghosts! Ghosts!/ Det spökar, det spökar 76, 176
"Gift of Health" Ltd/Aktiebolaget Hälsans gåva 122; 115
Giftas/*Married Life* (26) 157; 24, 220; 206
Giftas/*Married Life* (57) 82E; 98; 2, 20, 26, 30, 65, 149, 246; *248*; 206
Giftasvuxnar döttrar / *Marriageable Daughters* 238; 48, 221; *111*
Girl and the Devil/Flickan och djävulen 67; 24, 45, 118, 171, 245; *23, 147*; 152
Girl and the Press Photographer/Pigen og pressefotografen 126
Girl Comes to Town/En flicka kommer till stan 118, 149, 179
Girl for Me/En flicka för mej 24, 29, 148
Girl for the Summer/Sommarflickan 160; *196*; 236
Girl from Backafall/Flickan från Backafall 66, 149, 174
Girl from Paradise/Flickan från paradiset 24, 180, 218
Girl from Stormyrtorpet / Tösen från Stormyrtorpet (17) 232E; 194; 3, 7, 30, 90, 156, 229; 136
Girl from the Department Store/Flickan

171

H

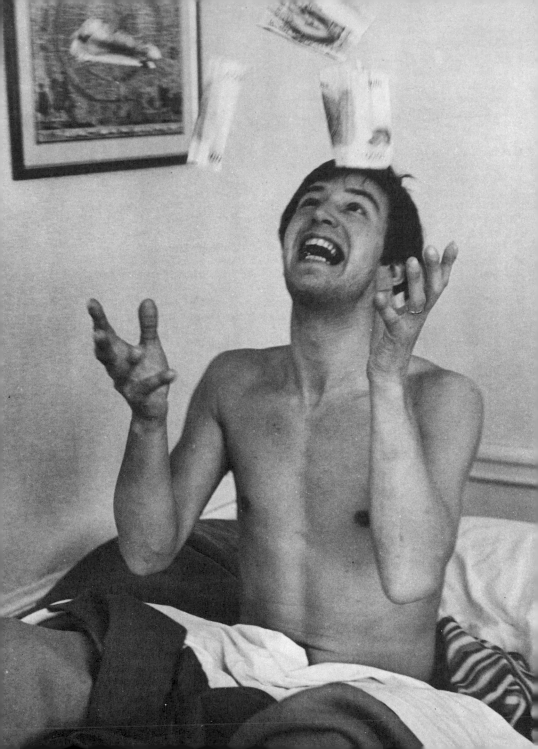

Opposite: Thommy Berggren in Widerberg's THIRTY TIMES YOUR MONEY

Lena Nyman in Sjöman's I AM CURIOUS - BLUE

I

Marie Öhman in Grede's HUGO AND JOSEFIN

J

K

185

L

Opposite: Agneta Ekmanner in Cornell's LIKE NIGHT AND DAY

M

190

191

N

O

Opposite: Fant's THE WONDERFUL ADVENTURES OF NILS *(with Sven Lundberg)*

Opposite: Folke Sundquist and Ulla Jacobsson in Mattsson's
ONE SUMMER OF HAPPINESS

P

201

Victor Sjöström (left) in his own THE PHANTOM CARRIAGE
(with Tore Svennberg)

Q

R

S

Nils Poppe (left) and Gudrun Brost (right) in Bergman's THE SEVENTH SEAL

Opposite: Liv Ullmann and Max von Sydow in Bergman's SHAME

Opposite: STIMULANTIA (with Lena Granhagen and Hans Alfredson)

T

U

V

W

Y

Å

Ä

Ö